A new view of Chaucer

A new view of Chaucer

George Williams

Duke University Press, Durham, North Carolina 1965

© 1965, Duke University Press

Library of Congress Catalogue Card number 64-8173

Printed in the United States of America
by the Seeman Printery, Inc., Durham, N.C.

Preface

The point of the following book is that at least half of Chaucer's poetry reflects his intense preoccupation with individual personalities whom he knew and actual events in which he was personally involved or with which he was immediately concerned. This statement, furthermore, is especially true of those early poems of the so-called "French" and "Italian" periods that are usually regarded as the mere exercises, derivative and artificial, of a romantic imagination. The "new view" offered here is that of a Chaucer whose writings are much less given to "peaceful, impartial spectatorship," to non-committal impersonality, to objective non-involvement than has been generally supposed.

The text used for reference and quotation is, for the most part, that of F. N. Robinson (*The Works of Geoffrey Chaucer*, Second Edition, 1957); but Robinson's punctuation has often been altered, and variant readings have occasionally been preferred.

G. W.

Contents

A new view of Chaucer

Chapter I. Introduction: Obstructions to the view

If I were a reader just picking up this book and glancing at its title, I am sure that I should say to myself: "After more than a century of active Chaucerian scholarship, with the best minds of Europe and America expressing their views in scores of books and many thousands of articles and lectures—what 'new view of Chaucer' does this writer think he can reveal? Why hasn't it, if it is worth revealing, been revealed long before now?"

The questions are reasonable, and deserve answering. The simple explanation is that Chaucerian criticism itself has often contained elements that obstruct the view. Perhaps some of these obstructing elements should be identified here.

Factual commentary] For a long time the chief obstruction was the kind of scholarship that was entirely concerned with such matters as the sources of Chaucer's poems, previous parallels to his phrases, analogues of his narratives, interpretation of his vocabulary, explication of his references, dating of his poems, establishing the canon, and so on. The value of this work is beyond estimate. But it is not the entire story. It disregards the poet himself—a human being trying to come to terms with his own heart and with the world; and it disregards the poem as poem—a "patterned organic unit" expressing and being a significant experience of the poet, and constituting a significant experience for the reader.

The New Criticism] A second obscuring element has been the type of literary criticism that has lately been dominating the scholarly and critical world. Wellek and Warren, in a little volume that has become a kind of handbook of modern criticism, express one aspect of the modern position very succinctly: "The whole idea that the 'intention of the author' is a proper subject of literary history seems quite mistaken."[1] That is to say, the "intentional fallacy"[2] must not obstruct the view of the poem itself as it appears to the critic. Or, in other words, the modern critic must concern himself more with what he himself can discover in a poem than with what the poet himself intended to put there. "The poet's appearance in his own argument is a major irrelevance."[3]   Or, more specifically, as J. A. W. Bennett, the British Chaucerian puts it, information about the personal, biographical, occasional, or historical material that may appear in Chaucer's poetry "does not illuminate" the poetry, and "gives scant opportunity, or none, for literary judgement."[4]

In this approach to poetry, the critic's chief business is discovering symbols, identifying mythic archetypes, analyzing ambiguities, comprehending semantic references, exploring the use of certain aesthetic devices, perhaps determining aesthetic values—and so on. Criticism of this sort was, of course, a much-needed antidote to the mere factual commentary of some of the early Chaucerians.   But this kind of criticism is often inadequate for full appreciation, in all perspectives, of even the poem-as-poem.   It is like a Napoleonic cavalryman stabling his horse in a Moscow cathedral, and, while deliberately ignoring the intentions of the architect who designed the cathedral, judging it in relation to his own needs and ideals as a cavalryman.   This kind of criticism has obscured the view of Chaucer that the present book tries to reveal.

Modern aesthetic standards]   Today's critic is often much exercised over such literary values as unity, subordination, balance, economy, consistency, structure, and logical design—and he assumes that Chaucer too must have been exercised over the same matters.   Hence we have any number of critical papers on "Unity in the *House of Fame*," "The Mature Form of the *Parliament of Fowls*," "The Aesthetic Design of the *Book of the Duchess*," and the like.   No one would deny that such matters are of absorbing interest to the modern reader; but the fact is that they hardly concerned the medieval artist.   His notions of artistic excellence were quite different.   One has only to glance at, say, the plan of a church like Westminster Abbey (see, for example, the large historical map in H. F. Westlake's *Westminster Abbey*, Vol. II) with its dozens of medieval additions, constructed over several centuries, sprawling in careless disarray—or one has only to examine fourteenth-century tapestries and intricately illuminated manuscripts and stained glass and thronging cathedral statuary—to be aware that crowding figures, rhythmic conglomerations, rich details, elaboration rather than economy, multiplicity rather than stark unity, variety rather than simplicity, fancy rather than realistic fact, overwhelming abundance rather than careful subordination are the ideals of the Middle Ages.   "An intricate and complex intellectual play... goes hand in hand with the gorgeous and colorful splendour of chivalrous courtliness."⁵ This does not mean that the medieval artist was deliberately self-contradictory, inconsistent, or pointless; it means only that he did not mind including in the same work matters that a modern artist or critic would find superfluous, irrelevant, or even incongruous and distracting.

In fourteenth-century English literature, *Sir Gawain and the Green Knight*, with its beautifully unified structure, stands out like a bell-tower over a wilderness of structureless medieval romances. But even the author of *Sir Gawain* duplicated this performance in no other work attributed to him. *Piers Plowman* never achieved such harmonious and concise structure, doubtless never attempted it; Gower and Lydgate and even Malory a century later missed it. The mature Chaucer himself, in works like the *Legend of Good Women*, the "Man of Law's Tale," the "Tale of Melibeus," the "Monk's Tale," and the "Parson's Tale" missed it. The cumulative and processional richness of the *Roman de la Rose*, and the wandering inchoateness of Guillaume de Machaut are more typical of medieval literature than is the formally proportioned architecture of *Sir Gawain*.

Though Chaucer did sometimes write poems economically designed and sharply chiseled, such works are usually derived straight from early Renaissance Italian poems that had felt the purifying influence of Greco-Roman example. The belief that he concerned himself invariably, or often, or even at all, with aesthetic criteria that the modern critic values is not justified. Chaucer was a medieval artist, not a modern; and to try to prove that his work fulfils the requirements of modern aesthetic systems is to misunderstand him. This does not mean, of course, that Chaucer was a lesser artist for being medieval—any more than a Gothic cathedral is poorer architecture than a glittering and functional modern skyscraper. Chaucer was only a different kind of artist; and he must be read in the light of his age's aesthetic standards, not ours. Admiring certain characteristics in the literature of our own age, "we naturally," says D. W. Robertson, Jr., "ascribe these same characteristics to Chaucer's narrative art in order to express our admiration for it. But such criteria are basically misleading when used in this way. They are inconsistent with fourteenth-century stylistic conventions."⁶ To see Chaucer clearly is to see that he was a medieval poet who constructed his poetry according to medieval, not modern, aesthetic principles.

Disregard of Chaucer's working method] A fourth obstruction to
the view of Chaucer that is being offered here is the tacit assumption
of some critics that Chaucer's poems, as we have them now, are
essentially (barring certain variant readings of scattered words and
lines) finished products—that Chaucer completed them once and for
all, approved them, and laid them aside, never to be tampered with
again—and not to be questioned or suspected by any presumptuous
modern reader. Nothing could be farther from the truth.

Miss Germaine Dempster describes Chaucer's probable working
method with the *Canterbury Tales*, as Manly saw it: "The first
draft of a Canterbury piece (tale, prologue, or link) would be
written by Chaucer on paper but quite possibly on waxed tablets;
from this draft, a copy, presumably on paper, would be made by
a hired scribe; the scribal copy would then be proofread by Chaucer;
in many cases it would, at some time or other, be used by Chaucer
for revision of his work.... In some manuscripts, omission or
misplacement of some passages within tales or links occurs under
conditions which suggest either cancellation or an addition made by
Chaucer on the originals."[7] At Chaucer's death, copies of his poems
were probably found in his house. "Those would represent work at
different stages of development. Some pieces may well have been
considered finished, but in others Manly finds indications that lines
were left incomplete on the originals, or that Chaucer had remained
uncertain as to the inclusion of some passages or the wording of
others; some pieces had been partly revised, while on others very
necessary revision had probably not begun." Moreover, "it is taken
as almost inevitable" that Chaucer passed around to his friends
"copies before he put a work in general circulation,"[8] and also that
these friends passed around copies to *their* friends, and that partial,
or even complete, copies of poems may have been made at any
point in this process of circulation, or in the process of Chaucer's
revisions. Any of these copies (even though incomplete, incorrect, or
uncorrected), as well as deliberate alterations made by others in the
copy either before or after Chaucer's death, may be ancestral to the
particular version of the poem that survived the centuries, and that
we possess.

Root has the same conception of Chaucer's method of composing
Troilus and Criseyde—with, at different times, perhaps years apart,
"the addition of new passages, the rearrangement of other passages,
the new turning of a phrase."[9] Charles A. Owen thinks that the

manuscript of *The Equatorie of Planets* (presumed to be in Chaucer's own hand) furnishes "rather startling confirmation of Professor Root's inferences.... In this manuscript are to be found the erasures, the interlineations, the tangle of rewritings and blotted lines, postulated by Professor Root, plus two extended passages which Chaucer canceled with the notation 'this canon is fals' and with some diagonal lines, both of which a careless scribe might have ignored."[10]

We have positive proof of Chaucer's penchant for revising in the two versions of the Prologue of the *Legend of Good Women*, where not merely words, phrases, and lines were recast, but whole passages were inserted, excised, or transposed. Root suggests that the Proems of Books II, III, and IV of the *Troilus* were added after the work was completed;[11] and there has long been a feeling among scholars that parts of the *Troilus* epilogue were added after the work was completed—along with, perhaps, Troilus' hymn to love and his soliloquy on fate and free will. As a matter of fact, most of Chaucer's works exhibit plain evidence of continual poetic carpentry going on —in the false counting of the "nyne and twenty" Canterbury pilgrims; the Man of Law who says he is going to tell a tale in prose, and then tells one in rhyme; the Second Nun who calls herself a "*son* of Eve"; the Knight who, while telling a tale to a group of pilgrims, speaks of *writing* it (KT, 1201); the Shipman who unmistakably refers to himself as if he were a woman; the Canon's Yeoman who addresses a group of churchmen who are not present—and so on. In the Retractions at the end of the *Canterbury Tales*, a "book of the xxv. Ladies" is mentioned, in reference, doubtless, to the *Legend of Good Women*—which, however, contains the history of only ten women. Furthermore, the Man of Law, in the Introduction to his tale, lists sixteen women whom Chaucer has memorialized— naming eight who do not appear in the *Legend*, and omitting two who do appear. The Retractions mentions "the book of the Duchesse"; but the Man of Law says of Chaucer, "In youthe he made of Ceys and Alcione"—as if this legend, now incorporated in the *Book of the Duchess*, were an entirely separate work. In the Prologue of the *Legend of Good Women* Chaucer says (G, 414) that he has translated Pope Innocent's "Wreched Engendrynge of Mankynde"; and he gratuitously inserts a section of his translation (perhaps versified from an original prose translation) into the Man of Law's Prologue, where it has no apparent relation to the Man of

Law or his tale, and uses other parts of the translation within the "Man of Law's Tale" itself. It is generally conceded that the "Knight's Tale" was written before the *Canterbury* scheme was conceived, and was subsequently adapted to and inserted into the *Canterbury* series. The same thing is true of the "Second Nun's Tale," and probably of still others in the series.

Examples such as these, showing that Chaucer was constantly busy reworking and regrouping his poems could be discussed for quite a while. Never having experienced the *fait accompli* of a printed volume, Chaucer was at liberty to keep revising his poems as long as he lived. Apparently, he took full advantage of this liberty.

His itch to revise may have been due to an artist's desire for perfection (as Root suggests); or to an attempt (obvious in the G version of the Prologue of the *Legend of Good Women*) to bring an old poem up to date; or perhaps to save labor by incorporating old material into new works (as when tales written early were incorporated, years later, into the *Canterbury Tales*). In addition, it is quite possible that Chaucer (knowing how manuscripts, in his time, tended to disappear) may have deliberately inserted into longer, more substantial works certain minor efforts of which he was proud, and which he wished to preserve—the fly embedded in amber. This may have been the case with the verses translated from the "Wreched Engendrynge" already mentioned; and it may also have been the case with the Ceyx and Alcyone story now embedded in the *Book of the Duchess*. Finally, it is not impossible that ignorant or presumptuous scribes, editors, or friends who, at Chaucer's death, possessed manuscripts of his poems, took it upon themselves to join together (in accordance with their own tastes) works or scraps of works that Chaucer himself would have kept asunder.

At any rate (and keeping in mind what was said just previously about the medieval artist's lack of concern for strict unity, balance, logical design, and the like) there seems to be abundant evidence that Chaucer was such a persistent reviser that we have a right to believe that almost any poem of his (as we have it today) may well be the end-result of a long succession of alterations, excisions, additions, transpositions, and patchings that went on as long as Chaucer lived, and may not have been finally adjusted to suit him even at the end of his life, and may even have been tampered with by others after his death. This view that any poem of Chaucer's may be, quite possibly, a poem in the making, or a poem undergoing major repairs, or a poem for which final plans had not yet taken shape even in the poet's own mind—this view is not common in recent Chaucerian criticism.

Distrust of allegory] Recent Chaucerian criticism has not been loath to discover a wealth of symbols and allegorical statements of abstract concepts in Chaucer's poetry. The older criticism was no less loath to discover personal or historical allegories in the poetry. But for various reasons (some of which will be suggested later in this chapter) the older critics never could find personal or historical allegories that were convincing to their contemporaries, or to more recent critics. The parallels suggested always seemed forced and fantastic. As a result of these past failures, modern criticism has generally adopted one of two attitudes: either that no personal or historical allegory exists, or that if it does exist it should not matter to the reader, whose interest should be entirely confined to the poem-as-poem. This latter attitude goes back to those modern misgivings about the "intentional fallacy" that have already been mentioned; and it blocks out a fully meaningful view of Chaucer's poetry.

As has often been said, Chaucer had many qualities of a novelist —including a lively and passionate interest not only in human nature at large, but also in the foibles, the virtues, the eccentricities, the absurdities of individual characters. Manly has shown that, almost of a certainty, Chaucer used real-life models for some of the individual characters who appear in the General Prologue of the *Canterbury Tales*.[12] The Host, the Sergeant of the Law, and the Shipman have been identified as real-life acquaintances of Chaucer whose names we know. The Franklin, the Merchant, the Reeve, and the Cook have been less certainly identified as adumbrations of actual persons; and the Pardoner and the Wife of Bath are so highly individualized that we can hardly help believing that they were suggested by real people whom Chaucer knew.

In going to real life for his characters, Chaucer is doing just what many (perhaps most) novelists have done—from Defoe and Fielding right on through Balzac, Flaubert, Maupassant, Dickens, Conrad, Maugham, Dreiser, Wolfe, Joyce, and a hundred others. This does not imply that the fictional character whom the novelist (or Chaucer) creates is necessarily a precise replica of the real character: Mr. Micawber is not a facsimile of Dickens' father, or Long John Silver a facsimile of Ernest Henley, or Charles Strickland a facsimile of Paul Gauguin. Maugham, who is noted for having drawn his most convincing characters from life, says somewhere: "Nothing is so unwise as to put into a work of fiction a person drawn line by line from life"; rather, the fictional character should be the result of "imagination founded on fact." We need not look in Chaucer's poetry for photographic portraits of his acquaintances; but it would be astonishing if a man so alert and responsive, as he evidently was, to the world of people thronging about him, never allowed that world to invade his writing.

Everyone admits that Chaucer used real-life figures allegorically in the *Book of the Duchess*; and many critics suspect personal allegory in the *Parliament of Fowls*, the Prologue of the *Legend of Good Women*, and perhaps the *House of Fame*. As a medieval writer, Chaucer would have been an unusual case if he had eschewed allegory, whether personal or abstract. Machaut, Deschamps, and Froissart (Chaucer's early masters) resorted again and again to personal allegory; so did Boccaccio and Dante (Chaucer's later masters); and so did, almost certainly, Chaucer's contemporaries, the authors of *Vox Clamantis, Piers Plowman, Richard the Redeless*, and many other political songs and poems of the fourteenth century. The thing was so much in the air that Chaucer could hardly have escaped it.

Confusion about Chaucer's birth year] Because much of what will be written later in this book concerning the *Parliament of Fowls* and *Troilus and Criseyde* has a close relationship to Chaucer's age, the establishment of the poet's birth year is of some importance.

Early in the nineteenth century, 1328 was widely accepted as the correct date; by the beginning of the twentieth century it was 1340 or 1341; and by the middle of the twentieth century a date close to 1345 was favored. Several considerations have caused most modern Chaucerians to adopt this last approximation.

First, there was, till quite recently, a reluctance to believe that a poem formerly regarded as so "immature" as the *Book of the Duchess* (written in 1369 or 1370) could have been the work of a great poet already about thirty years old when it was written. This reluctance resulted from an attitude already mentioned, namely, a tendency to judge Chaucer's poetry *by modern aesthetic standards,* and when any poem was found wanting, to shrug it off as "immature." It should be noted, however, that several more recent studies have tended to upgrade this poem, even by modern aesthetic standards, so that many critics now regard it as a work of sophisticated structure exhibiting considerable imagination and taste.[13] By medieval standards, it could have been an even more admirable work—nothing for which a poet nearly thirty years old at the time of writing it need have apologized.

A second reason (seriously accepted in some quarters) for dating Chaucer's birth year later than 1345 is the fact that, in 1399, he leased a house for fifty-three years at a rental of 53s. 4d. It has been argued that the coincidental figure of fifty-three, together with the fact that the poet could not possibly have hoped to live to see the expiration of his lease, suggests a humorous whimsy reflecting Chaucer's age at the time of the lease.[14] By this criterion, Chaucer was fifty-three years old in December, 1399—which would make his birth year 1346. Manly was convinced, however, that the fifty-three years of the lease represented merely the unexpired portion of an earlier lease;[15] and it has been noted that the sum of 53s. 4d. is exactly four marks—the mark being a common medium of exchange in the fourteenth century—and that its reduction to shillings and pence was probably nothing more than legalistic precision unrelated to Chaucer's age.[16]

Another reason for the choice of some year close to 1345 as the birth year is the belief that Chaucer was a page in the household of the Countess of Ulster in 1357. This belief has a certain romanticism about it that has doubtless attracted some people. It has also been pointed out that, if Chaucer had been born as early as 1340, he would have been seventeen years old in 1357, and therefore too old (by fourteenth-century standards) to have been a page—yet certain perquisites he received from the Countess were so small as to suggest that Chaucer was only a boy when he received them.

The basis for these conclusions should be more closely examined; all the facts are contained in a mutilated account book,[17] still extant, listing expenditures of the Countess' household. This account book records that a short cloak (a "paltock") was bought for Chaucer at a cost of 4s. in April or May, 1357. Scholars point out that the cost of the paltock was so small that the garment may not have been meant for a full-sized man, but for a boy. By way of contrast, a paltock bought on September 12 for one John Hynton, also of the Countess' household, cost over twice as much: 8s. 3d.

The logic of this argument deserves scrutiny. In the first place, 4s. (ca. $40 in today's money*) is not a niggardly sum to pay for a short coat. At about the same time, a tunic for the famous Philippa Pan, a damsel of the Countess' court, cost only 2s. 6d.; and later in the year a tunic and a cape for someone whose name is missing cost only 2s. Furthermore, one Thomas, who is actually designated as a page, was given a paltock costing 6s. 8d. in January, 1359. How can the difference in the prices of the two paltocks be explained—if Geoffrey too was a page? Are we to believe that he was a smaller page than Thomas? Probably not. It would seem that the very fact that Thomas was a page would imply that he had to appear often in the best company, and that therefore he would be given a more showy and expensive paltock than an ordinary employee. The difference in the two prices suggests, therefore, that Geoffrey was *not* a page. Or there may be a simpler explanation. Fourteenth-century courtiers in great households were ordinarily granted money for clothing twice a year (summer and winter). Geoffrey's paltock, given him in April or May, was doubtless meant to be a summer garment; and John Hynton's and Thomas Page's paltocks, given in September and January, were winter garments that would naturally have cost more than summer garments. But however we take it, the difference in the prices of the various paltocks does not prove that Chaucer was a page in 1357; if anything, the difference suggests that he was not a page. Thus, no case at all can be made, from the paltock, for Chaucer's being less than sixteen or seventeen years old in 1357.

It is also argued that a gift of 2s. 6d. given to Chaucer for necessities at Christmas, 1357, was very small compared with gifts to certain other members of the Countess' court. This is true; some of the courtiers received many times this sum. But not all were so fortunate. One John Schynnare received only 2s. at the time Chaucer received 2s. 6d. Later on, a gift of 2s. was made to William

* Expressing money values of one age in terms of those in another age is always frustrating and misleading. From my own investigations I should be inclined to value the fourteenth-century penny at about $1.50 in American money in the mid-1960's. But I defer to the editors of Edith Rickert's *Chaucer's World* (1948), who estimated that, in 1947, the *minimum* value of a shilling in 1376 was about the equivalent of $7.50 in the United States of 1947 (p. 175, n. 57). Adjusted to money values of the mid-1960's, the latter sum would amount to about $10.50. In order to be conservative, and also to deal in round numbers for the sake of convenience in this book, I estimate the fourteenth-century shilling at $10 in modern money.

Hunte; 2*s.* to someone else whose name is missing from the damaged manuscript; only 12*d.* to one Simon Yrichess; and only 16*d.* to the page Thomas. In other words, it looks as if Chaucer was not one of the high-paid employees of the Countess, nor yet one of the very lowest paid. Besides, if he was really a page, why was he not so designated? Thomas was twice, in the short manuscript, distinguished by the title "pagettus."

What all this means is that the Countess' household records do not prove, or even lend support, to the hypothesis that Chaucer was a page, and therefore a boy under sixteen years of age, in 1357. What the records really show is that he was a minor employee in 1357, and probably *not* a page.

Another record frequently cited as proof that Chaucer was of tender years in 1359, and therefore probably a page in 1357, is the statement in the official report of the famous Scrope-Grosvenor trial that Chaucer had, at the time of the trial in 1386, "borne arms for twenty-seven years"—that is, since 1359.[18] Since men of the fourteenth century matured early, it has been assumed that Chaucer had just turned sixteen when he started to "bear arms" in 1359.

The actual record is not in Chaucer's own words, but in those of a court reporter who merely summarized proceedings—doubtless partly from memory and partly from notes after the court had recessed for the day. The wording of the record is this: "Geffray Chaucere Esquier ... armeez p[ar] xxvii ans." Since fourteenth-century men, regardless of their age, donned weapons more or less as they pleased (*vide* Simkin in the "Reeve's Tale"), without special ceremony, the twenty-seven years referred to so precisely must designate some particular occasion in 1359 when Chaucer became officially "armeez"—an armed man, or a man-at-arms. He went as a soldier with the English army invading France in the autumn of 1359, and his subsequent testimony in the trial concerns his activities on this very campaign. Accordingly, the statement that he became "armeez" for the first time in 1359 undoubtedly means that he first took up arms in the king's wars in 1359.

Now, since the king's levies called up able-bodied men between the ages of sixteen and sixty,[19] it has been argued that Chaucer, having *first* taken up arms in 1359, must have been only sixteen that year. As a matter of fact, however, there had been no military expedition for Chaucer to join (except the Black Prince's private raid in 1356) since 1355. That is to say, he would have had no occasion to become "armeez" in the king's service before the autumn of 1359—unless he had been born before the autumn of 1339. What this part of the record shows, therefore, is that Chaucer was at least sixteen years old in the autumn of 1359—but whether just sixteen, or several years older, is not indicated. He could have been anything from sixteen to twenty.

The record of the Scrope-Grosvenor trial contains another interesting item bearing on Chaucer's birthdate. The record reads:

> Geffray Chaucere Esquier del age de xl ans & plus armeez p xxvii ans prduct pr la ptie de mons Richard Lescrop jurrez & examinez demandez si les armeez dazure ove un bende dor appteignent ou deyvent appteigner au dit mon Richard du droit & de heritage. dist q oil qar il lez ad veu estre armeez en Fraunce....

> (Geoffrey Chaucer, Esquire, of the age of forty years and more, having been armed for twenty-seven years, produced by Sir Richard Le Scrope's party, sworn and examined, [was] asked if the arms of *azure* with a bend *or* belonged, or ought to belong, to the said Sir Richard by right and by inheritance. Said yes, for he had seen them being armed in France....)

The words "del age de xl ans & plus" have kindled much scholarly debate. Does the "& plus" mean only a few months past forty, or a few years, or many years? Taken narrowly, the phrase says, in effect, that Chaucer was born in 1346. But if he was indeed born that year, he went to France as an armed soldier when he was thirteen—not an impossibility, but improbable in view of Chaucer's considerable education derived from books, not battlefields, the prosperity of a family that could have bought him out of military service, the king's own minimum-age requirement of sixteen years, and the rather large sum (£16, or $3,200) that the king contributed to ransom him from the French a few months later.

Much more significant is the fact that, in the summer of 1360, Chaucer was employed by Prince Lionel as a courier bearing the Prince's letters between France and England.[20] It seems probable to the point of certainty that a boy just turned fourteen (even if so old) would never have been chosen by a royal prince for such work in a period when a man was not officially counted a man till he was sixteen.

It seems, then, that the words "del age de xl ans & plus" do not mean that Chaucer was born in 1346. But if they cannot be thus narrowly construed, how loosely should they be understood? Several considerations may help determine the answer. First, the words are not quoted directly from Chaucer—whose actual statement begins several lines farther along. Second, the whole passage is not a verbatim transcript of evidence, but only a court reporter's words, based perhaps on something said in court (and possibly set down later, as the reporter remembered it), or perhaps on the reporter's own knowledge or belief. London was a small city in 1386, and the number of its gentry still smaller; the court reporter himself may have known enough about Chaucer to write down confidently that he was "over forty." Or Chaucer may have given a specific age, and the reporter may have recorded it only roughly, not realizing that people six hundred years later would be interested. The essential fact in the reporter's mind was not, very likely, Chaucer's age, but that he had been one of the king's men-at-arms on the campaign of 1359-60. Third, many other items in this same record prove either that the men of the fourteenth century were profoundly ignorant of their ages, or incredibly careless in remembering them, or (more probably) that the court reporter described witnesses from his own information (or misinformation) without consulting them or else without trying to be accurate concerning what he deemed unessential and troublesome details. Thus, as Moore pointed out long ago, twenty-three of the persons testifying in the Scrope-Grosvenor trial are credited with ages that are inaccurate by from three to seventeen years; fourteen others are inaccurate by from one to two years; and of one hundred and forty witnesses, no less than seventy-five are credited with ages in round numbers (thirty, forty, fifty, sixty—sometimes with and sometimes without the "et plus").[21] In a letter to the *Times Literary Supplement* in 1957 Mr. G. D. G. Hall, himself a lawyer, expressed doubts that the "xl ans & plus" in the Scrope-Grosvenor record meant very much. He pointed out that, in an almost contemporary case, a good many deponents said that their age was forty, or forty "et plus." Of these, the ages of six can be ascertained with some exactitude. Their actual ages were 49, 45-47, 51, *ca.* 56, 45, and 39-40. The reliability of such court records, Mr. Hall pointed out, depends entirely on the royal clerks who made them, "and on the interest or lack of interest they showed in establishing the precise age of deponents."[22] O. F. Emerson, investigating the whole problem in the light of actuarial statistics, concluded that Chaucer was probably about forty-five in 1386, and was therefore born in 1341, or perhaps in 1340.[23]

In short, there actually exists no evidence worth the name, in any record, that Chaucer was born in 1345, or within two years of that time. All that the records permit us to say is that Chaucer was born before 1346. But in view of the fact that he had a responsible position as Prince Lionel's courier in 1360, and that this position would certainly not have gone to a mere stripling, we must believe that Chaucer was at least twenty years old in 1360. In other words, he was born no later than 1340, or possibly early 1341, and he may have been born a little earlier than 1340.

Prejudice against John of Gaunt] One of the largest and most opaque obstructions to the view of Chaucer presented in this book is a universal scholarly prejudice against that John of Gaunt, who, as will be seen later, cut so large a figure in the life and the poetry of Chaucer. Though most modern scholarship is forced by available evidence to admit a close relationship between the two men, there has been a universal reluctance to follow up this relationship to see how it affected Chaucer's career and his poetry. There have been many understandable reasons for this reluctance:

1] Because Gaunt vigorously opposed the growth of the Church's temporal power in England, as well as the flagrant abuses (so well depicted by Chaucer) of individual churchmen, and because for a while he espoused the cause of John Wyclif—Gaunt became the victim of every possible scurrilous attack by contemporary ecclesiastical chroniclers, the historians of the day. As a result, his reputation as an "abandoned libertine" has persisted for centuries. It is little wonder that lovers of Chaucer have hesitated to link the name of the great poet too closely with that of Gaunt. This hesitancy was especially apparent among Victorian critics. The fact is that Gaunt laid himself peculiarly liable to censure by cohabiting, over a period of nearly twenty-five years, with Katharine Swynford—even though he did eventually marry her. To the Victorian mind such conduct placed Gaunt outside the pale of decency and made him no fit companion for Chaucer.

But Chaucer was not a Victorian. In an age when bastardy was considered almost normal, when every great man was expected to have mistresses, and when the quite immoral system of "courtly love" was universally accepted in theory if not in practice—Chaucer must have realized that Gaunt was no worse than others in sexual behavior, and better than most. Gaunt's brother the Black Prince had several illegitimate children, and no one thought the worse of him for it. Gaunt had a daughter by Marie de St. Hilaire before his marriage to Blanche of Lancaster; and he ever afterward made good provision for both the mother and the daughter.[24] He had four children by Katharine Swynford; and he afterward married her and went to much trouble and expense to legitimize her children. Chaucer, unlike the chroniclers and the Victorians, must have regarded such a man as a marvel of honor.

2] Gaunt consistently opposed the assumption of power by the Commons. But in the nineteenth and early twentieth centuries, English history was almost invariably written in terms of the growth of representative government. Accordingly, an enemy of the Commons, like Gaunt, was given short shrift by the historians. No lover of Chaucer would willingly have shown the poet in close association with the constitutional villain.

But Gaunt himself, whose social and political views were those of a typical medieval baron, doubtless regarded the ambitions of the Commons about as the president of some great modern corporation would regard the ambitions of labor leaders to control the organization, the policies, the administration, and the distribution processes of the corporation. Not until at least three hundred years after Gaunt did Englishmen as a whole begin to trust the Commons. To Chaucer, Gaunt's opposition to the Commons must have seemed normal and even commendable. Chaucer himself had no love for popular government.[25]

3] Gaunt was the chief target for the hatred of the peasants in the Peasants' Revolt, and of rioters at various times in London. Again, this hostility of the people toward Gaunt has not endeared him to the modern world. To be sure, Gaunt was a feudal lord, and that state itself was (in the eyes of modern democratic society) inherently evil. As the richest and most powerful, and not the least arrogant or even the least corrupt, of the feudal lords under Richard II, he symbolized to the rebellious peasants the malignity of the entire system under which they suffered. Yet Gaunt himself has left no record of cruelty or harshness toward his own peasants; he was notably lenient to his peasants after the Revolt; and on a good many occasions he contributed funds to the welfare of individual peasants. As for the Londoners who rioted against him, two points must be made: (*a*) as a young man Gaunt was undoubtedly proud,

abrupt, undiplomatic, even arrogant; and (*b*) the rioters were egged
on by certain City magnates who were jealous of their own profitable
privileges that Gaunt was trying to undermine (see next chapter).
Chaucer (who never showed any sympathy for the Peasants' Revolt,
and, as will be seen later, was not unaware of the corruption of the
City) could never have sympathized with the peasants or with the
Londoners in their enmity toward Gaunt.

4] Gaunt is accused of having run the government to suit himself, without authority from anybody, during the last years of his
father's reign. This is true. But *somebody* had to run it. The
king himself, as everyone admits, had fallen into an increasing
dotage; the Black Prince was a slowly dying invalid, who did indeed
die a year before his father; the Black Prince's son Richard was hardly more than an infant. Chaucer, who, as a king's esquire, must
have been privy to the entire situation, could not have seriously
objected to Gaunt's assumption of power during the prolonged
crisis. If it had not been Gaunt, it would have been another of the
great nobles, or one of the great churchmen, or the Parliament that
neither Gaunt nor Chaucer admired, or some clique of great merchants from the City. Gaunt was preferable to any of the alterna-
tives.

5] Gaunt is blamed (by even his biographer Armitage-Smith)
for having been inordinately ambitious to become King of Spain,
and for having spent English money on that eventually fruitless
ambition. Yet Gaunt (like everyone else) must have been acutely
conscious of the disastrous crumbling of English power on the
Continent in the 1370's and 1380's, must have longed to do something to correct the situation, and must have honestly felt that, if he
could control Spain, he and the English king could then crush the
French between them, regain the lost territories, and dominate
Europe from Gibraltar to Scotland. It was a grandiose dream; and
if Parliament had not dawdled so long before finally lending Gaunt
half-hearted assistance in his project, he might actually have brought
the thing off, and become one of England's great heroes. Observing
the situation with eyes sympathetic to Gaunt, Chaucer could not have
blamed him (as modern historians do) for his continental ambitions.

6] Gaunt has been accused of lacking military genius. Perhaps
he did. On the other hand, his Great March through France (which
modern historians consider a disaster) was regarded in his own time

as an extraordinarily brilliant military feat.[26] In a period, indeed, when England had no military leaders of consequence, Gaunt was the best available. In him alone rested all the military hope of England.

On the positive side, Gaunt's character, especially after he had outgrown his youthful impatience and haughtiness, had in it the essential elements of nobility. There is no record of his ever having betrayed a friend, or swerved in loyalty to a supporter. His continued protection of Wyclif, even after he broke with the Reformer on theological issues, and even after supporting him became unpopular and dangerous, is well known.[27] His biographer Armitage-Smith speaks of him as one who held the laws of chivalry sacred (p. 411); who had a fine "knightly modesty" (p. 412); who was notably courageous (pp. 48, 52, 412); who valued learning (pp. 413, 415); who left behind him a record, in a century that could be savage, "extraordinarily free from acts of violence and oppression" (p. 416); who sympathized with the poor and the humble (p. 418); who did many an act of kindness and of charity (p. 418); and who had a reputation for sincere and profound piety.[28]

We should not feel either surprised or outraged if we find that Chaucer regarded this man as both great and good, and felt honored by his friendship. Rather (if we try to view matters with fourteenth-century eyes) it would have been surprising and even disgraceful of Chaucer not to have esteemed such a man. Because Chaucerian scholarship has often failed to see Gaunt as Chaucer saw him, Chaucerian scholarship has often failed to see Chaucer himself clearly.

Chapter II. Chaucer and John of Gaunt

So much of the material in subsequent pages of this book concerns John of Gaunt, Duke of Lancaster, third son of Edward III, and (from 1371) titular King of Spain, that certain facts and inferences about the relationship of Gaunt and Chaucer should be examined.*

The relationship of the two has not been studied extensively since J. R. Hulbert wrote *Chaucer's Official Life* (1912). In the introduction of the book just mentioned, Hulbert cites Nicolas, Ward, Morley, Snell, and Skeat as believing that Gaunt was Chaucer's patron—and Lounsbury and Jusserand as being more cautiously committed to the same view.[1] Since Hulbert wrote, Coulton,[2] Cowling,[3] Chesterton,[4] Coghill,[5] and Kemp Malone,[6] among others, have mentioned Gaunt as Chaucer's patron. A few other writers, however, have held different opinions. Marchette Chute, for example, writes: "It used to be the custom to speak of John of Gaunt as Chaucer's patron, but this he was not. In the strict sense of the word, Chaucer never had a patron. He was a hard-working public official and fully earned the perquisites he received."[7] Hulbert's own thesis is similar. "There is no particular reason to suppose," he writes, "that he [Chaucer] had any patron";[8] he "received his offices and royal annuities from the king rather than from John of Gaunt."[9]

Hulbert's conclusion is based on three types of evidence: (*1*) that "there is no exceptional feature of his [Chaucer's] career as an esquire which points to patronage by anyone";[10] (2) that Chaucer's friends and associates were either enemies of Gaunt or not connected with Gaunt in any way; (*3*) that Chaucer's advancements came "at times when John of Gaunt's influence would have been harmful rather than beneficial, or when John of Gaunt was not in England to exercise it."[12]

* Unless otherwise noted, the information contained in this chapter is derived from the Chaucer *Life-Records* (*Publications of the Chaucer Society*, 2nd series, Nos. 12, 14, 21, 32), Sidney Armitage-Smith's *John of Gaunt*, and appropriate entries in the *DNB*. Since all these sources are arranged chronologically or alphabetically for easy reference, I have not thought it worth while to footnote every item obtained from them.

Chaucer as the "average esquire"

Attempting to prove that Chaucer was only an "average esquire,"[13] Hulbert tells a good deal about other "average esquires" serving the king contemporaneously with Chaucer. The information he gives is, in itself, sufficient to show that these young men, almost without exception, must have owed their positions at court to the influence of powerful friends or relatives. There were William and John Beauchamp, son and young relative respectively of the Earl of Warwick; John Legge, son of the Lord Mayor of London; Nicholas Careu, son of an executor of Edward III's will and guardian of the Privy Seal; Robert Ferrers, son of a baron who was one of the knights of the king's chamber; Nicholas D'Abrichecourt, nephew of a famous knight who was a favored protégé of Queen Philippa[14]—and so on. Other esquires contemporary with Chaucer had served, before coming to the king, in the households of various of the king's children, and certainly could not have advanced to employment by the king himself without favorable reports from their former employers. Many of these esquires, or their families, were closely connected, in one way or another, with John of Gaunt himself. William Beauchamp was a retainer of Gaunt's;[15] and a John Beauchamp was receiving gifts from Gaunt in 1372,[16] and was appointed by Gaunt to be a surveyor of weirs and fisheries in 1380.[17] John D'Abrichecourt (relative of Nicholas D'Abrichecourt, the esquire) was a retainer of Gaunt's;[18] George Felbrigge, another esquire, was the subject of several letters from Gaunt relieving Felbrigge ("nostre cher et bien ame George Felbrigge"[19]) of certain suits against him, and was also the recipient of a handsome gift of 26s. 7d. (about $265) from Gaunt;[20] Robert Ferrers held property from Gaunt by "knight service," and later on married Gaunt's daughter; Robert de Louth, another king's esquire, was son of a retainer of Gaunt's ("nostre cher et bien ame Robert de Louth conestable de nostre chastel de Hertford"[21]); Gilbert Talbot, another king's esquire, was son of Sir John Talbot, a veteran retainer of Gaunt's;[22] several members of the Cheyne family were king's esquires, and John Cheyne (perhaps the same John Cheyne who was an esquire) was treasurer of Gaunt's household in 1374 and 1380;[23] the king's esquire Richard Wirle was a retainer of Gaunt's;[24] a Robert Ursewyk was a king's esquire, and a Walter Ursewyk (probably father of the former) was chief keeper of several forests belonging to Gaunt.[25]

What all this means is that (if human nature was human nature in the fourteenth century) a great many of the king's "average esquires" must have owed their court positions to their connections with influential personages—including Gaunt himself. As a matter of fact, the benefits must have worked both ways—for it could not but have been advantageous to himself for some great nobleman like Gaunt to have loyal henchmen of his own surrounding the king. It seems, then, that even if Chaucer was only an "average esquire," he might well have been the protégé of some great person.

Hulbert seems to think that if Chaucer had had a powerful friend like Gaunt, Chaucer would have become a more important public figure than he actually became.* It is quite possible, however, that Gaunt, though he was fond of Chaucer, did not consider him temperamentally fitted for high public office. Furthermore, Chaucer himself may have remained an "average esquire" from choice. He may have preferred, especially as he grew older, the quiet, relatively humble, relatively secure life of poet and scholar to the dangers and responsibilities of high office, the hurly-burly of worldly competition and struggle. In his poems "Fortune," "Truth," and "The Former Age" he indicates as clearly as possible that he thinks "wrastling for this world axeth a fall," and that he values most a life of calm self-sufficiency.

Though Chaucer received various appointments from the king— especially that of controller in the customs service, which he held for twelve years—Hulbert himself notes that the king's esquires were regularly appointed to lucrative positions that they filled through deputies, the profits made by esquires through this arrangement being in lieu of salary increases drawn directly from the king's own coffers.[26] "Offices of the customs," says Hulbert, "seem to have been used regularly as sinecures for the esquires."[27]

It is possible, if not extremely likely, that Chaucer performed through deputies much of the customs work for which he was paid; for though his commission required that he keep records in his own hand and not by deputy, the same sort of commission to other controllers seems to have been regularly honored in the breaking. Indeed, several of the king's esquires held controllerships in several

* E. P. Kuhl believes that Chaucer actually was "a towering public personage." *PQ*, XXV (1948), 280.

different ports simultaneously, and could not possibly have performed their duties in person.[28] At any rate, the records remaining from Chaucer's customs service are written in a formal chancery hand that is almost certainly not Chaucer's, and he was absent from his customs duties again and again, often for months together, with no formally named deputy to replace him—until right at the end of his tenure.

Actually, the official salary of £10 ($2,000) was far from being the chief source of Chaucer's income, nor was it so large as to be irresistibly attractive. The major part of a controller's income resulted from fees and fines coming to him by virtue of his office, whether or not he performed his duties in person. In view of his many absences on official business, the large amount of poetry he wrote, and his probable frequent attendance at court, where he read his poems, it is likely that Chaucer was a controller more often in title than in actual performance of a controller's duties. By merely holding the title he was assured a cozy addition to his income, and at the same time secured for himself leisure to write.

In short, even if Chaucer was only an "average esquire," there was a good chance that he owed the position and its perquisites to the influence of some powerful personage—or at least not simply to the fact that he was a "hard-working public official."

Chaucer's friends and associates

Hulbert's second point is that Chaucer's friends and associates were either enemies of Gaunt, or unassociated with Gaunt—and that therefore Chaucer must not have been closely associated with Gaunt.

Hulbert's conclusion seems to have been based on the assumption that political parties, or factions, were well defined in the fourteenth century; that individuals could be distinguished precisely as belonging to the "king's party" or "the Black Prince's party" or "Gaunt's party"; that Chaucer had a few friends not definitely in "Gaunt's party"; and that therefore Gaunt was not Chaucer's patron. Actually, loyalties in the fourteenth century seem to have been strictly personal, and a man could be simultaneously loyal to, or friendly with, several persons who were not closely associated, or who even disliked one another.

Furthermore, it is far from certain that modern scholars really

understand the involved intrigues of English noblemen in the 1370's
and 1380's. The appalling intricacy of the situation can only be
suggested here, not analyzed. For example, the article on the Black
Prince in the *Dictionary of National Biography* has it that the
Black Prince was the chief opponent of "Lancaster and his disreputa-
ble clique of courtiers." But McKisack, writing in 1959, says that
fourteenth-century writers were "at pains to emphasize...the mutual love and admiration of the Black Prince and Gaunt."[29] And
Armitage-Smith, Gaunt's biographer, says that there is insufficient
evidence "for drawing an imaginary line of cleavage between the
Prince of Wales on the one hand and the King and the Duke of
Lancaster on the other."[30] (In any event, the Black Prince made
Gaunt the chief executor of his will.) Again, Armitage-Smith
writes that Alice Perrers, mistress of the aging Edward III, was
Gaunt's principal rival for power in the kingdom;[31] but the fact is
that, after the Good Parliament banished Alice from the king's
presence and seized her properties in 1376, Gaunt, regaining complete power in the kingdom a few months later, immediately recalled Alice to London and the king and saw that all her forfeited
properties were restored to her. Gaunt is credited with heading a
party hostile to the succession and the rule of Richard II, the Black
Prince's son; and Richard, or his favorites, plotted on more than
one occasion to have Gaunt killed. But Richard's mother, Princess
Joan, was always on the best of terms with Gaunt, and was a peace-
maker between him and her son; and even Richard, when his
favorites or his follies got him into a tight place, habitually called
on Gaunt to rescue him. Gaunt's brother Gloucester was an open
enemy of Richard; but he was friendly toward Gaunt, and on one
occasion drew his sword in the king's very presence, and offered to
slay forthwith anyone (including the king) who called Gaunt a
traitor. Gaunt's son, Henry Bolingbroke, sided with Gloucester
against Richard. But in 1389 it was Richard himself who urgently
recalled Gaunt to England to help curb Gloucester's high-handed
treatment of Richard; and it was Gaunt who then protected Gloucester against the high-handed treatment that Richard would have
liked to accord Gloucester.

Or consider the complex relationships of Gaunt, London, and
the king. During the years (1374-86) when Chaucer was controller
of customs in London, the city's economic life was normally dominated by a powerful victuallers' guild that in turn was dominated

by rich merchants (William Walworth, John Philipot, and Nicholas Brembre were the leaders) who conspired to maintain high food prices in the city, lend money to the king, and through their financial influence on the king persuade him to issue various commercial edicts profitable to themselves. It should be added that, in general, these merchant magnates opposed continental adventures of English armies such as had been the lifeblood of the Black Prince and of Edward III in his younger days.

During the last few years of Edward's reign, however, the Black Prince was an invalid too ill to have much influence on international affairs, and peace was not distasteful to the aging king. Then, in the minority years of Richard II, the Commons (capitalists, burgesses, knights of the shires, citizens) stubbornly resisted the war party of great noblemen who were attempting to raise money, by new taxations, for fresh military adventures on the Continent. John of Gaunt was of this war party.

Now in the prime of his manhood, and a true son of the Age of Chivalry, he burned to carry on the glorious military tradition of his family; and, as titular King of Spain, he burned with equal ardor to become King of Spain in fact as well as in name. But if we try to see the matter with his eyes, and remember that people seldom do anything for one reason only, we may assume that it was not personal ambition alone that fired Gaunt. Knowing that the English position in France was steadily worsening and that English lands were steadily slipping away, he must have been gravely concerned. Furthermore, he must have realized that, if Plantagenets were on the thrones of both Spain and England, France, caught between upper and nether millstones, might be brought to acknowledge again the overlordship of the English king. It was a grandiose dream. In Gaunt's eyes, no doubt, the refusal of the London merchants and the petty gentry to dream this dream, to gamble a little money for such high stakes, was short-sighted, cowardly, and even criminal.

Because he wanted to raise money for his proposed military expedition, and the London capitalists opposed his plans, and also by reason of certain personal quarrels with the Bishop of London over certain temporal and religious matters, personal irritation with London mobs, and a self-willed haughtiness that he had in his younger days, Gaunt allowed himself to be drawn into a feud with the ruling clique of London. He allied himself with the leaders of the mercers' guild (enemies of the victuallers) and with certain lesser magnates of the city. In particular, he championed the cause of two merchants, Richard Lyons (himself a heavy lender to the king) and John of Northampton—against Walworth, Philipot, and Brembre.

Since these merchants were intimately involved in Chaucer's controllership of the customs, a word about them is necessary. As for honest dealing, there was probably little to choose between the Walworth-Philipot-Brembre faction, and the Lyons-Northampton faction. Brembre, the victualler, turned out to be a political gangster and murderer, as well as a large-scale grafter, who was later hanged for his crimes; Lyons was an utter scoundrel who was beheaded by the peasants in the rising of 1381; Northampton was imprisoned for his lawless and dictatorial deeds as Lord Mayor (and £22, or $4,400, was paid to his enemy Brembre for conducting him to Corfe Castle!). Walworth and Philipot were far less crude operators than these three. Indeed, there is nothing especially heinous in the records of either. Yet Walworth kept a string of bawdy houses, was one of those who lent money to the government and, by devious means, secured an exorbitant rate of return, was the leader of a monopolistic group of food profiteers, influenced the government that was in debt to him to issue trading regulations that profited him and his clique enormously, was closely associated for years with Brembre, and (despite his extensive interests otherwise) found time to be a customs collector in a port whose mere wool trade alone grossed, in customs fees of various sorts, sums mounting up to $4 million annually. Philipot is also pictured in conventional history as an honorable man devoted to his country, and hostile to the evil machinations of John of Gaunt. But he too was a food monopolist, a lender to the king, a collector of the customs, and an associate of the unspeakable Brembre. As for enmity toward Gaunt—Philipot was repaid, on November 7, 1379, by Gaunt himself on behalf of the king, £100 ($20,000) that Philipot had lent the king;[32] in October, 1380, he was paid by Gaunt another £100 ($20,000) for wine that he had sold Gaunt;[33] and on February 14, 1380, Gaunt himself borrowed 100 marks ($13,330) from Philipot.[34] (One cannot help wondering whether the £100 Gaunt delivered to Philipot in October of the same year was not a repayment of the February debt, along with Philipot's usual exorbitant interest—all of it masquerading as a huge purchase of wine by Gaunt.)

One of the trio of Brembre, Walworth, and Philipot was a collector of customs during all but two years of the twelve that Chaucer was controller. Chaucer's salary of £10 ($2,000) annually was paid by the collectors out of their immense takings in fees, and they divided certain fines and bonuses with him, apparently as they saw fit. Thus Chaucer was largely dependent on alleged enemies of Gaunt for his income from the customs. Nevertheless, he remained a controller not only under the Brembre-Walworth-Philipot regime, but also under Gaunt's faction for the year or two when it was in power. All the while, his wife was a lady-in-waiting in the court of Gaunt's wife, his sister-in-law was well known as Gaunt's mistress, and (as Miss Giffin points out) his "missions abroad from 1372 to 1378 show him in close touch with members of the Lancaster circle."[35]

What can the modern student make of all this?

Perhaps my own attitude is too cynical—but I cannot believe that public funds amounting to what would today be millions of dollars per year would fail to attract vultures, especially during one of the most corrupt periods in all English government. I cannot believe that busy millionaires and Lord Mayors of London, like Brembre, Walworth, and Philipot, would trouble themselves to be mere customs collectors unless they knew that it would be extremely profitable to themselves. I cannot believe that a weak government that was strictly dependent on Brembre, Walworth, and Philipot for financial support would inquire too closely into the dealings of those gentlemen. I cannot believe that Brembre would associate himself with any project for long without corrupting it. And I cannot believe that persons like Walworth and Philipot could associate themselves for long with Brembre without being, or becoming, corrupt.

In the midst of this swirl of corruption, where would Chaucer stand? There are several possibilities. (1) He was a simple-minded innocent who did not see that the people to whom he looked for his salary and his fees were corrupt. Or (2) he was himself thoroughly implicated in the corruption. Or (3) he was an upright and honorable man trusted by men of all factions to do the right thing. Or (4) he was a mere figurehead official enjoying a sinecure in which his chief duty was to stay clear of the whole intricate financial operation—on the one hand employed by a decadent government that did not want him to make trouble for Brembre and

Company, and on the other hand duly rewarded by Brembre and Company as long as he stayed discreetly clear.

I cannot believe that the first of the above possibilities applies to a man as shrewd and worldly as Chaucer. I will not believe that the second applies. And I do not think that Brembre and Company, or the government itself, would have endured for a moment a strong and upright watchdog over public funds. Consequently, I believe that the fourth possibility is the only one that is acceptable. Chaucer doubtless got his controllership through the influence of Gaunt (see below); and he retained it for years simply because Gaunt remained powerful, and Chaucer did as good a job as anyone else in cultivating his own garden, and letting Brembre and Company cultivate theirs. It seems, somehow, more like Chaucer to have been the shrewd, probably cynical, perhaps resigned, non-participating observer than the active partisan or agitated reformer.

A similar confusion of allegedly anti-Gaunt and pro-Gaunt personalities is evident in the Cecily Chaumpaigne affair (1380) in which Cecily released Chaucer from charges of "raptu meo"—a phrase that has been variously interpreted as "seizing me" (or "kidnaping me") and "raping me." The five witnesses of her release of Chaucer from the suit she had brought against him were a curious assortment: Philipot (powerful member of the grocers' guild, and allegedly Gaunt's enemy), John Morel (another grocer), Sir William Beauchamp, John Clanvowe, and William Neville. Philipot and Morel may have been Chaucer's personal friends—perhaps because Chaucer's father, as a wine importer, had been closely associated with the grocers' guild. But the last three witnesses mentioned deserve a closer look, in view of Hulbert's thesis that Chaucer's friends and associates had no connections with Gaunt.

Beauchamp, a younger son of the Earl of Warwick, had been a retainer of Gaunt's and a member of his household. Clanvowe was, according to Hulbert, "strongly opposed to John of Gaunt."[36] But Waugh (whose detailed study of "The Lollard Knights" is the authority for most of the following information about Chaucer's associates) says that Clanvowe supported Gaunt in the great quarrel with the Good Parliament in 1376, and served under the Duke as late as 1378.[37] In 1373 Gaunt made a gift to Clanvowe of "un peir de paternostres ove une fermail d'ore."[38] William Neville, a close friend of Clanvowe, likewise supported Gaunt in the Good Parliament, served with the Duke in 1378, and through the latter's influence was granted an annual pension of 100 marks ($13,330).

Hulbert includes Louis Clifford, a close associate and friend of Chaucer, as another of the men "strongly opposed to John of Gaunt."[39]   But Clifford served with Gaunt on the Great March through France (1373-74), and again under Gaunt on the naval expedition of 1378.   Gaunt made him an executor of his will; in March, 1373, Gaunt placed under his own protection "une honouree dame q'est taunte a nostre bien ame chivaler monsire Lowys de Clifford";[40] in April of the same year he made a gift of "une hanape d'argent" to Clifford;[41] and in May, 1374, he gave Clifford 100 marks ($13,330).[42]   For whatever it is worth, it should be added that Philip de la Vache, Clifford's son-in-law, to whom Chaucer addressed the envoy of his poem "Truth," received from Gaunt a gift of 50 marks ($6,650) in May, 1374,[43] and served under the Duke in 1378.   He was a friend of Sir William Beauchamp, that other good friend of Gaunt's, and was connected in some way with Alice Perrers, the king's mistress, who was (very probably) Gaunt's collaborator.   Vache was also one of the most active, most trusted, and best rewarded retainers of Gaunt's son, Henry IV.

Hulbert numbers Michael de la Pole, another associate of Chaucer's, among the "enemies of Gaunt."[44]   But de la Pole belonged originally to the retinue of Gaunt's father-in-law, Henry Duke of Lancaster; he served under Gaunt in 1370-72 on the Continent; and, according to the *Dictionary of National Biography*, "in domestic politics he attached himself to John of Gaunt," and in the troubled period of the Good Parliament "stood strongly on the side of ... the unpopular duke."   Later on, when de la Pole became a favorite of Richard II, and a powerful figure in his own right, he became less dependent on Gaunt, and more ardently devoted to his own enrichment.   But many of his enemies remained Gaunt's enemies, and there was never anything like a break between the two men.

Still another associate of Chaucer's was Richard Stury, a king's esquire who was a son of the marshal of Edward III's household and seneschal of Calais.   In some ways, the facts about him are the most remarkable of all.   He was the knight associated with Alice Perrers (mistress of Edward III) in the dubious distinction of having been banished by the Good Parliament for his part in cheating the realm through influencing the doting old King Edward.   He served

with Chaucer under John of Gaunt in northern France in 1369; he
and Gaunt and Alice Perrers virtually controlled the government
in the later years of Edward's reign; it was through Gaunt's influence that Stury was restored to the court after his banishment by
the Good Parliament; he went under Gaunt's command on the
expedition to Brittany in 1378. He is also distinguished in history
as the man against whom the Black Prince, on his deathbed, burst
into violent rage, crying, "May God forgive you, for I never will!"
But, strangely, a few years later, Stury appears as one of the most
trusted knights in the service of the Black Prince's widow—who
made him keeper of one of her castles at 100 marks ($13,330) per
year, kept him with her for her personal protection, and named
him one of the chief executors of her will. Stury was equally
favored by the Black Prince's son, Richard II, and he headed a
commission of which Chaucer was a prominent member.

Exactly what to make of all these interlacing relationships I do
not know. But a theory that would account for many of them is
this:

During the 1360's both the Black Prince and his brother Lionel
were away from England much of the time, leaving John of Gaunt
as chief aid to their father. Being rich and powerful in his own
right, as well as attractive personally and engaging when he wished
to be, John endeared himself to his father, and became (as most
historians believe) the old king's favorite child. Lionel died in
1368; and when the Black Prince returned from France (1370) as
an invalid unable to serve consistently in either war or government,
the king still had to rely on John. Then, as Alice Perrers began to
exercise her influence on the old man (in the late 1360's), Gaunt
managed to work with or through her to accomplish his purposes.
Except for the brief two-months interlude of the Good Parliament,
Alice and Gaunt maintained their control over the government till
Edward's death in June, 1377. They were at this time, as Trevelyan
says, "absolute masters of England." With the situation like this,
for anyone to believe (as Hulbert did) that Chaucer owed his advancement, during the years of Edward's decline, to the king alone,
and nothing at all to John of Gaunt, seems a bit naïve.

Edward was succeeded by his grandson, Richard II, a ten-year-old
boy. To govern the kingdom, a Great Council of magnates (powerful princes, lords, and churchmen), of whom John of Gaunt was
far the most powerful, appointed a continuing council of twelve men

to govern the state. Of these twelve, six were outright adherents of John of Gaunt, and four had been followers of the Black Prince or were friends of his widow.[45] Since the widow was a friend of Gaunt's, and Gaunt was the chief executor of the Black Prince's will, and the Prince's followers (their master dead) would hardly align themselves against the Prince's brother and executor, who happened also to be the most powerful man in England—Gaunt had, in effect, ten friends on the council of twelve that governed the state.

During the next two years, the personnel of the governing council changed several times. But no council was ever openly opposed to Gaunt. Nor was any Parliament ever again openly hostile or punitive toward him, as the Good Parliament had been. And even his relations with London had become correct and restrained.

Only the spoiled and temperamental young king himself was periodically unfriendly; but even his hostility manifested itself mostly as the occasional temper tantrums of a petulant youth under the influence of greedy and foolish favorites. Gaunt, who doubtless understood the mercurial nature of his royal nephew's moods, never swerved in his loyalty to the king—and the king never ceased calling on Gaunt in emergencies. It was only the king's favorites that Gaunt regarded as his enemies.

Meanwhile, the routine business of government, the day-to-day appointments of minor officials and their supervision and payment, was apparently conducted by those who would be regarded today as high-ranking civil servants who had the confidence of the king. Significantly, however, a very large number of these governmental administrators were *old friends of John of Gaunt.*

Thomas Beauchamp, Earl of Warwick, said by Walsingham to have been made guardian of Richard in 1380, was a friend and supporter of Gaunt from a long time back. In 1381 the Parliament appointed the Earl of Arundel and Michael de la Pole as governors of the king's person and household. Though Arundel and Gaunt quarreled over personal matters ten years later, Arundel in 1381 was a friend of Gaunt's; he had served with the Duke in two campaigns in France; and he was a cousin of Gaunt's first wife, Blanche. De la Pole has already been mentioned as a long-time supporter of Gaunt's. Indicative of the omnipresent influence of Gaunt is the chancellorship of England in 1382 and 1383. In the former year Richard le Scrope, who had previously engaged himself as a lifetime retainer of Gaunt's, was chancellor; but the king removed Scrope in 1383, only to elevate to the office another familiar friend of Gaunt's, Michael de la Pole. "Both Richard le Scrope," says Armitage-Smith, "who . . . was 'the Duke's friend and honest adviser,' and Michael de la Pole were moderates and retainers and friends of John of Gaunt."[46]

On a lower level of service, Richard Stury, already mentioned as one of Gaunt's old friends, became one of the "king's knights" in 1378, a knight of the king's chamber in 1381, later on a knight attending the king's mother, and a member of the royal council as soon as Richard assumed his full powers in 1389. Lewis Clifford, another of Gaunt's old supporters, was a "king's knight" in immediate service on the king in the late 1370's, and then a knight attending the king's mother, and, in 1389, a member of the Privy Council. Thomas Latimer, son of one of Gaunt's most loyal and persistent defenders, and himself a member of Gaunt's retinue, became a knight closely attending the king's mother. John Clanvowe, an old adherent of Gaunt's, grew steadily in the king's favor from about 1379, was a knight of the chamber in 1382, and was placed on the king's council in 1389. William Neville, another old Lancastrian, became a knight of the chamber in 1381, and a member of the royal council in 1389. Philip de la Vache, Chaucer's friend, and also a friend of the Lancastrians, was a knight of the chamber early in Richard's reign, and a particularly trusted servant. And the king's mother herself, who had much influence over her son until her death in 1385, was one of Gaunt's most constant friends, and in her later years was surrounded by knights who were Gaunt's friends.

Thus, even when Gaunt was not present at court, his policy made itself steadily, if indirectly, felt through friends and administrative assistants immediately surrounding the king. Only four times in thirty years was Gaunt's influence in the government even briefly eclipsed. Once was during the two months when the Good Parliament was in session, in 1376. The second was in the few months immediately following the Peasants' Revolt, in June, 1381, when things looked bad for the Duke, and rats began to leave the ship they thought was sinking. The third time was from early in 1384 to late in 1385, when the king's favorites made several determined efforts to destroy the Duke, and seriously poisoned relations between him and his nephew. And the last time was from July, 1386, to November, 1389, when Gaunt was voluntarily out of England. But even in this last period Gaunt's not unfriendly brother Gloucester controlled the government, and the Duke's son and heir was one of Gloucester's closest adherents. After this three-year interlude, the Duke returned to England at the king's urgent command and thereafter exercised once again a dominating influence on public affairs until within a year or two of his death in 1399.

The bearing of all this on Chaucer's career is obvious. If Gaunt and his friends had wanted to help Chaucer, they could have done so with the utmost ease at almost any time from the late 1360's till Chaucer's death; and if they had wanted to ruin him, they could doubtless have done that with equal ease. Apparently they wanted to help him—for he remained on the public payroll from his mid-twenties till his death. It is simply not true that his friends and associates were anti-Lancastrians. Most of them were ardent Lancastrians, and none was an open and confirmed enemy of John of Gaunt.

Chaucer's offices and rewards

Hulbert's third point is that Chaucer's advancements came "at times when John of Gaunt's influence would have been harmful rather than beneficial, or when John of Gaunt was not in England to exercise it."

I have already shown that there were only three short periods in Chaucer's career when his friendship with Gaunt might have been harmful to the poet: the two months of the Good Parliament in 1376; the few days of the Peasants' Revolt, and the few months following, in 1381; and the period of really serious trouble between Gaunt and the king lasting from early in 1384 to late in 1385.

As for Chaucer's receiving advancements in money or office when Gaunt was out of England—the records should be inspected.

It is true that when Chaucer first appeared on the king's payroll (1367) with the grant of 20 marks ($2,660) annually for life, Gaunt was out of the country. This, however, was one of the very few times when such a thing occurred; a possible explanation for it is suggested later in this chapter.

In July, 1368, Chaucer was granted a passport out of England, and expense money from the royal treasury. Gaunt was in England at the time, and (the Black Prince and Lionel being out of the country) was undoubtedly a powerful influence in the government and on the king.

In June, 1369, Chaucer was suddenly paid £10 ($2,000) on account of wages and expenses to be incurred in the war with France that was just being renewed. Gaunt was to be the leader of the troops sent to France, and Chaucer was to sail and serve with him. Under the circumstances, it is hard not to see Gaunt's hand in Chaucer's monetary windfall.

On June 20, 1370, Chaucer received letters of protection for a journey to places beyond the sea. At the same time Gaunt was preparing to sail with a small army to Bordeaux. Whether or not there was a connection between the two circumstances is not known. But it *is* known that Gaunt was in England, and was taking a leading part in public affairs when Chaucer was granted his commission.

In November, 1372, Chaucer was commissioned to go to Italy, and receive £66 13s. 4d. ($13,333) on account for wages and expenses of the trip. John of Gaunt was in London at the time, had become the lover of Katharine Swynford (Chaucer's sister-in-law) some months previously, and was now the most powerful figure in the government. Doubtless Chaucer went to Italy on Gaunt's orders, or certainly with his consent.

From July, 1373, till April, 1374, Gaunt was out of England, conducting his Great March through France. I cannot determine the exact day in April when he returned to England. But on April 23, 1374, Chaucer was granted a pitcher of wine daily for life. Two and a half weeks later (May 10) he was granted a free lifetime lease on the house above Aldgate; four weeks after that he was appointed Controller of Customs and Subsidy of Wools, Hides, and Wool-fells for the Port of London; four days after that he was made Controller of Petty Customs of Wines for the Port of London; and the following day he was granted a lifetime annuity of £10 ($2,000) by the Duke. All these events happening right on the heels of the Duke's return do not indicate that Chaucer received his most important governmental employment "when John of Gaunt was not in England."

During the first few months of 1377 Chaucer was given several letters of protection, made several trips to France on official business, and received, by way of expenses and wages, £94 2s. 8d. ($18,826), of which at least £20 ($4,000) was outright salary—all this at a time when the old king was slowly dying, and John of Gaunt was present in London, and was "absolute master of England."

The day after the old king died, Chaucer was confirmed by the Great Council in his office as controller of customs—a confirmation that could not possibly have come except with Gaunt's approval.

Late the following March (1378) Chaucer was confirmed in Edward III's old grant of 20 marks ($2,660) a year; and in April he was granted another 20 marks ($2,660) a year in lieu of his daily pitcher of wine. Gaunt was in London at this time. Perhaps it should be said here that, all the while, Chaucer was receiving £10 ($2,000) a year from Gaunt's treasury; that his wife was receiving 10 marks ($1,333) a year from the king's treasury, and £10 ($2,000) a year from Gaunt's treasury; and that Chaucer was receiving a regular £10 ($2,000) a year as salary from the customs, plus a minimum of £10 ($2,000) a year in bonuses from the customs—a total in excess of $14,000 annually, to say nothing of many other perquisites such as fines, special fees, and wardships. There remains a record of a single fine, levied on one John Kent, merchant, from which Chaucer received the sum of £71 4s. 6d. ($14,245); and a single wardship he is known to have held, over Edmund Staplegate, brought him £104 ($20,800). It is incorrect, therefore, to think of Chaucer as a poor drudging civil servant deriving his principal means of livelihood from laboring over account books day and night.

In the spring and early summer of 1378 Gaunt was making preparations for a naval expedition that sailed in early July. He had experienced some difficulty in persuading the Parliament to vote funds for the expedition; and doubtless feeling that still more funds would be required in the immediate future, he must have been altogether responsible for sending a mission to Italy seeking a loan from Bernabò Visconti, tyrant of Milan, "for expediting the king's wars." Chaucer went with this expedition.

On May 1, 1380, Cecilia Chaumpaigne released Chaucer from further legal action on account of "raptu meo." The trouble with Cecilia may have resulted in Chaucer's having to give her money. If so, ten days later Gaunt came to the rescue with 100s. ($1,000) due on Chaucer's annuity; on November 28 Chaucer was abruptly paid, from the royal treasury, £14 ($2,800), said to be due for expenses on his Italian trip two years previously; and on March 8, 1381, he received a gift "from the king" of £22 ($4,400) as compensation for wages and expenses dating from trips to France he had made *four years* previously. Gaunt was in England all this time, and was a power in the government.

Perhaps the sudden unsteadiness of Gaunt's position during the Peasants' Revolt, and in the months immediately following, as well as his long absence in the North during those months, accounts for several items in the Life Records at this time. On June 19, 1381, immediately after the Revolt, Chaucer sold his old family home in London; on August 1, 1381, he asked for and received an advance of 6s. 8d. ($66) on his annuity from the government; and on November 16, 1381, he asked for and received a similar advance.

A record dated September 29, 1382, is tremendously suggestive—yet I cannot find that any Chaucerian biographer has referred to it. On that date, one John Hyde and Chaucer were paid for acting *successively* as controllers of the customs during the preceding year. This might indicate (*1*) that Chaucer was ill or incapacitated for a while in 1381—except that his presence at the Wool-quay had never before seemed necessary for the conduct of business. Or it might indicate (2) that, with John of Gaunt in danger, and stranded in the North, Chaucer himself temporarily relinquished an office where his known connections with Gaunt might be perilous. Or it could mean (*3*) that enemies of Gaunt, thinking the Duke now safely out of the picture, dared at last to turn against an old friend of the Duke's and relieve him of a public office that was not only lucrative for the controller, but was also an observation post from which a check could be made as to where the customs fees were going. If Chaucer was removed because he was a friend of Gaunt's, the enemies of Gaunt acted prematurely. Late in the year the Duke's power seemed greater than ever. Not only was his candidate for Lord Mayor of London, John of Northampton, elected about the beginning of November, 1381, but the session of Parliament beginning about the same time saw Gaunt's most powerful enemies forced to eat crow and beg his pardon for deserting him in the dark days of the Revolt. The following year, with Northampton as Mayor and Gaunt restored to his accustomed influence, Chaucer was *reappointed* to his controllerships (April 20 and May 8). If this interpretation of the record is correct, the incident is a dramatic illustration of the close linkage of Chaucer's fortunes to John of Gaunt.

I shall now summarize Gaunt's career to the late autumn of

1389—and then see how Chaucer's career dovetails with Gaunt's ups and downs.

After the Peasants' Revolt matters moved with comparative smoothness for both Gaunt and Chaucer until 1384. But in the Parliament at Salisbury, April 29 to May 27, 1384, there were violent personal quarrels and misunderstandings on every side, and the king's favorite, Robert de Vere, Earl of Oxford, all but succeeded in having Gaunt murdered. Matters were smoothed over, however, and Gaunt went abroad to try to patch together a peace treaty with the French. He failed—and returned to present his unsatisfactory agreement to a surly and captious Parliament sitting at Westminster, November 12 to December 24, 1384. Six weeks later, the Earl of Oxford was hatching another plot against Gaunt's life. It came to a head on February 24, 1385, when Gaunt, wearing chain mail under his robe, and accompanied by armed men, went to the palace of Sheen (across the river from London) where the king was staying, posted men at every door of the palace to prevent anyone's entering or leaving, strode into the king's chamber with his armed friends at his side, lectured the king severely on his advisers, and strode out again. A few days later the king's mother managed to get her son and Gaunt together for a formal reconciliation—but Gaunt, still mistrustful, left immediately afterward for his well-fortified Pontefract Castle in the North, where he remained until the king found it necessary to ask him for aid against the Scots, in July, 1385.

This Scottish adventure, mismanaged by the king, ended in another violent quarrel promoted by Oxford. But once again a reconciliation was effected—and Gaunt lent the king £100 ($20,000) in November, 1385.[47] Not long after this, Gaunt's often postponed and long dreamed of project of invading Spain and securing the Spanish throne for himself began to materialize. He sailed for Spain in July, 1386, taking with him the king's blessing and some of the king's solid cash. The reconciliation of the two was apparently complete and sincere; indeed it is likely that the young man and his uncle would always have been friends had it not been for the machinations of Richard's foolish and envious favorites.

Gaunt was away until November, 1389. In the intervening three years his brother, the Duke of Gloucester, seized the government from the king, exiled or executed some of the king's favorites, and ran matters to suit himself—until Richard dared to assert himself and assume the kingship (May 3, 1389). Immediately thereafter he "sealed Gloucester's political fate for good, for he recalled the Duke of Lancaster" from Spain.[48] When the Duke finally reached home, he was welcomed with general rejoicing by all factions. The king himself rode out two miles from town to greet his uncle with the kiss of peace; and for seven years thereafter Gaunt stood at the king's right hand, and was, in influence on the government and the nation as a whole, the greatest power in England.

These years from 1384 to 1389 are a kind of storm center in Chaucer's career—or at least in scholarly speculations about his career. Why did he lose his controllership? When did he lose it? Did he actually lose it, or did he relinquish it voluntarily? Did the rise of the Duke of Gloucester to power in 1386 force Chaucer out of office? What happened to him between the time when he was replaced at the Wool-quay (December, 1386) and the time he became Clerk of the King's Works (July, 1389)?

While the angry Parliament was sitting at Westminster, November-December, 1384, to hear Gaunt's explanation of his failure with the French treaty, Chaucer was granted a license (November 25, 1384) to be absent from his duties as controller for one month, on condition that he appoint a deputy. Three possible interpretations may be given to this leave of absence granted at this particular time: (1) Its occurrence just when Parliament was meeting, and was giving Gaunt a hard time, may have been a mere coincidence. (2) It may have resulted from a *bona fide* request by Chaucer to be absent at this critical time—either to attend the Duke and support him in his difficulties, or to get safely out of the way (perhaps on the Duke's own advice) in case lightning should really strike the Duke. (3) Or it was a move by someone hostile to Gaunt and his people—an attempt by someone in authority either to force Chaucer out of his position by the subterfuge of a leave of absence, or to harry him with unacceptable bureaucratic regulations from which he had previously been free. Since the license is written in formal governmental Latin, and is noted as being "Per ipsum Regem" (the first such Chaucerian record under Richard), and since subsequent events tend to confirm the third interpretation, this interpretation may be correct.

A few weeks after the time stated for the expiration of the former leave of absence, and just as the anti-Lancaster murder plot of February, 1385, was reaching its climax, another petition by Chaucer (or ostensibly by Chaucer) appeared. It was a mere note in French reading (I translate literally): "Petition to our lord the

King to grant to Geoffrey Chaucer that he be able to have, in the office of controller of the Wool-quay in London, a competent deputy, such as for whom the said Geoffrey is willing to be responsible, during the term that the said Geoffrey shall be controller of the customs of our said Lord in the port mentioned."[49] In other words, the petition is for permanent leave from the controller's office. The petition has the notation, "Le Roy lad grante."

Taken at face value, this looks like a request by Chaucer to be permanently relieved of his controllership, and a gracious acquiescence on the part of the seventeen-year-old king. *But the petition is signed by the Earl of Oxford.* It is immediately followed (February 17, 1385) by an official Latin note, "Per ipsum Regem," granting the original petition. The fact that Oxford approved the petition, that Oxford was Gaunt's most vindictive enemy, that an attempt on the life of Gaunt was being planned by Oxford at the very moment he signed the paper, and that Chaucer was closely connected with Gaunt—all this suggests that Oxford was having Chaucer permanently suspended from his controllership under subterfuge of granting him a permanent leave of absence that Chaucer may, or may not, have asked for. Doubtless Oxford was not so much interested in the fact that Chaucer might continue drawing his annual salary of £10 ($2,000) as controller, as in the desirability (from Oxford's point of view) of placing a friend of Oxford's in a position from which he could view the eventual destination of thousands of pounds (millions of dollars) being collected as customs fees.

This explanation seems all the more plausible when we remember that John Philipot (who had long been a customs collector, and had worked out a modus vivendi with Gaunt) had died the previous summer, and that William Walworth (also a long-time mayor and customs collector who had likewise perfected a working agreement with Gaunt) had virtually retired from public life early in 1385 (probably from ill health) and was to die before the year was out. Their departure from the scene had left the unspeakable Brembre to dominate the City and the customs collections, and to work with Oxford for their mutual profit. A friend of Gaunt's would not fit into this pattern; therefore Chaucer was suspended permanently. Admittedly, all this is conjecture. But the conjecture depends on a chain of highly significant circumstances, and it would perfectly explain a situation that has always mystified biographers of Chaucer.

The only trouble with Oxford's plotting against Gaunt was that it failed: Gaunt was not killed, his influence was not permanently destroyed, and the rift between him and his young nephew was soon closed. If the interpretation I have given of Chaucer's suspension is correct, the king now found himself in a quandary. Oxford wanted to keep Chaucer away from the customs records; yet Chaucer, as a friend of the powerful Gaunt, could not be brusquely dismissed from public service. The king's solution was an old one: he kicked Geoffrey upstairs.

Miss Galway has, I think, very convincingly analyzed the events of Chaucer's life from 1385 to 1389.[50] She believes that, while he was still on permanent leave from the Wool-quay, he was appointed by the king to be the steward of the palaces of Eltham and Sheen, in Kent, just across the river from London. Moreover, the king, as greatest lord and chief landholder in the county, mollified Chaucer (and Gaunt) for suspension from the controllership by appointing Chaucer Justice of the Peace (October 12, 1385, just when the king and the Duke were becoming friendly again, and just a month before the king borrowed $20,000 from the Duke!). This last advancement of Chaucer, it should be noted, occurred while Gaunt was in England, and while his influence would not have been harmful.

It may be assumed that Gaunt, even after he left England for Spain, kept in close touch with matters at home. He had too much at stake in the way of property, power, and parliamentary support for his enterprises, to neglect the home front. It may be assumed also that the king was quite aware that Gaunt would hear of the appointment, by the king himself, of Chaucer to be a knight of the shire and to sit in the Parliament of August, 1386. This was the Parliament in which Gaunt's brother, the truculent Duke of Gloucester, seized power. For Chaucer, a known friend of Gaunt's, to be sitting in this Parliament representing the king certainly did the king's cause no harm with Gloucester, or with the far-off Duke, who would learn with interest and approval of Chaucer's appointment.

In the next three years, during the supremacy of Gloucester, Chaucer, as a friend of Gaunt's, was left unmolested—even though the customs collections in which he had been involved were closely investigated, and his old collector Brembre was hanged. During these years Chaucer's annuities from the royal treasury (which Gloucester controlled) were paid regularly, as was his controller's salary up to the time his successors were appointed (December, 1386). But he lost the controller's fat fees and other perquisites, and accordingly seems to have experienced some financial difficulty in 1387 and 1388.

On May 3, 1389, Richard announced that he was assuming the full powers of kingship. He displaced Gloucester and immediately sent for the Duke of Lancaster. But the Duke, remembering the king's former instability, was cautious and suspicious. The king sent him repeated messages. And, no doubt to convince Gaunt of his sincerity, he began showing special favors to Gaunt's old friends. Stury, Clifford, Clanvowe, and Neville were named to the Royal Council; and Chaucer was given the important position of Clerk of the King's Works (June 12, 1389). Hulbert is literally correct in saying that this advancement of Chaucer's occurred "when John of Gaunt was not in England"—but it occurred under the prospect of Gaunt's imminent return to England. Moreover, the appointment continued after Gaunt's arrival, and was followed by numerous other royal favors that could have been granted only with Gaunt's consent—or perhaps at Gaunt's instigation.

The conclusion seems inescapable. Every circumstance of record suggests that Chaucer's public career was closely linked with the fortunes of John of Gaunt. Perhaps it is not literally correct to call Gaunt a "patron" of Chaucer—if we define the word *patron* in a certain limited sense. But Gaunt was a loyal friend who saw to it that Chaucer prospered steadily as long as Gaunt was alive, and whose son and heir saw to it that Chaucer prospered as long as Chaucer was alive. Gaunt was the enormous brilliant sun of public life around which Chaucer's small asteroid of an official career revolved for more than thirty years.

John of Gaunt and Chaucer's private life

Let me say at once that, in all probability, no more than four or five people ever knew the truth about matters to be glanced at in the following brief review of a complex situation—and these four or five people died centuries ago, presumably without revealing their darkest personal secrets (if they really had any) to anyone else. Therefore, all we can do today is to guess—and to guess under the clear realization that we may be mistaken in every detail.

The question may well be asked whether, under such conditions, guessing is profitable. Perhaps not. Nevertheless, it is intriguing, and just possibly it may hit the mark.

The lost six years] We know that Chaucer was a courier for Prince Lionel in May, 1360. After that, he vanishes from all records until September, 1366, when one "Philippa Chaucy," a damoiselle of the queen, is mentioned in the records. Whether or not this woman was Chaucer's wife, we cannot say. Presumably she was, for, in many subsequent records, the name of his wife is given as Philippa, and in several records (e.g., *John of Gaunt's Register, 1379-1383,* Items 608, 1056) she is mentioned as having been in the service of Queen Philippa. Though the pieces are few, they fit.

In the June following the mention of "Philippa Chaucy" Chaucer himself reappears as a "valettus" of the king. Where he was, or what he was doing, between 1360 and 1367 is a mystery. Prince Lionel went, with his wife Elizabeth, to Ireland as its governor in 1361. Elizabeth died there in 1363, and Lionel returned to England in 1366. The dates roughly correspond to Chaucer's lost years; and it has been suggested that he went to Ireland with Lionel. On the other hand, evidence either in governmental records or in Chaucer's works that Chaucer ever saw Ireland is completely lacking—nor do many scholars believe that he was there. Actually, the reference to "Philippa Chaucy" is dated September 12, 1366, whereas Lionel did not return to England till November, 1366. This discrepancy in dates might be accounted for in several ways, even if Chaucer had gone to Ireland; but its general tendency would be to discount the theory that he was there.

In his "Retractions" Chaucer says that, in his youth, he made "many a song and many a lecherous lay." Perhaps he should be taken literally when he uses the word *song.* The well-educated middle-class and upper-class Englishman of the fourteenth century was almost always thoroughly trained in music, and could sing and play an instrument. Perhaps Chaucer, in his youth, wrote songs and sang them as his contribution to the entertainment of the company on those long afternoons and evenings when the entire household of castle or palace would gather in the great hall to entertain one another. In any event, if we may judge by the number and variety of his friends later on, as well as by his apparent popularity at court, and what we may surmise about him from his works, Chaucer must have been a likeable young man. Moreover, if we may judge by such mathematical exercises as the *Astrolabe* and the *Equatorie of Planets*, and by his employment as controller of customs and Clerk of the King's Works, Chaucer was doubtless handy with figures; he could have made himself useful in helping keep household accounts. We may imagine, therefore, that, after some initial service in ordinary capacities in the Countess Elizabeth's household, he was soon recognized as a rare and gifted personality.

If, then, when Lionel and Elizabeth were sent to Ireland, and young Geoffrey (his parents being still alive in London, and Ireland being generally regarded as a wild bogland) did not care to go along—nothing would have been more natural than for the Countess Elizabeth to recommend the bright and accomplished Geoffrey to her young cousin and only sister-in-law, Blanche, Countess of Richmond. As Hulbert has pointed out, such transfers of employees from one household to another were common.

When Blanche died in 1369, Chaucer wrote a poem in her memory and hinted at an "eight years' sickness" of love that he had suffered. Though the hint may be only an artificial courtly gesture, the number of years is probably correct. The number corresponds exactly to the time that Chaucer would have been associated with Blanche if he had been transferred to her household in 1361. We know that he did make a connection with the Lancasters sometime in the 1360's, and we might accept his word that it was made eight years before 1369.

What Chaucer did in the first six of those eight years we can only guess (see Chapter IX). But let us look a little more closely at the records and relationships of 1366 and 1367.

On September 12, 1366, "Philippa Chaucy" was granted a lifetime annuity, from the royal treasury, of 10 marks ($1,330), in addition to her regular wages as a lady-in-waiting. Perhaps the annuity was granted on the occasion of her marriage to Chaucer. If Chaucer himself was an employee of the king at this time, he could not have been employed very long; for there exists a very full list of members of the king's household who were granted robes in the summer of 1366, and Chaucer's name is not on the list. But if he was not with the king in the months before September, 1366, and not with Lionel in Ireland, he may well have been with John of Gaunt, or with Blanche. The fact that Gaunt (who had not been out of England since 1360, except for a brief diplomatic mission to Flanders in 1364) was preparing, in September, 1366, to leave England on an extended military mission is suggestive. Perhaps Chaucer, doubt-less no fiery warrior, transferred from employment with the Duke to employment with the king when the Duke was leaving for an in-definite and perilous stay abroad. But, whatever the circumstances, Chaucer was an employee of the king the following year when, on June 20, 1367, he was granted, in addition to his regular salary, a lifetime royal annuity of 20 marks ($2,660) for services he had rendered, and was to render, the king. All these dates dovetailing together so neatly may be interpreted as evidence that Chaucer was employed by Gaunt, or by Blanche, until Gaunt left the country in November, 1366, and that thereafter Chaucer (like many other persons formerly employed by Gaunt) was in the employ of the king.

Chaucer's marriage] Dark rumors have long hung about Chaucer's marriage. It is hinted that John of Gaunt was Philippa's lover, and that Chaucer married the girl as a favor to Gaunt. The cir-cumstantial evidence responsible for these rumors follows:

Philippa was the daughter of Sir Payne (Paon) de Roet,* Guienne King-at-Arms (and father of Gaunt's famous mistress

* There was a time when this relationship of Chaucer's wife to Sir Payne was questioned; at present, however, I know of no Chaucerian scholar who doubts the relationship. The matter is virtually clinched by the recorded facts about Thomas Chaucer. This man, who became a prominent figure in the government, and about whom there are many records, used Geoffrey Chaucer's heraldic arms, and is universally recognized as Geoffrey's son, or putative son. But on Thomas's tomb the Roet arms appear in a position showing that Thomas' mother was a Roet. Russell Krauss, who has studied the matter ("Chaucerian Problems," in *Three Chaucer Studies*, ed. Carleton Brown, 1932) more thoroughly than anyone else, writes that above Thomas' effigy on his tomb, and "occupying the dexter position, are the Roet arms alone. This is proof that Thomas assumed the Roet arms as his own. Being obviously not a Roet himself, nor married to a Roet, he could have taken them only if his mother was a Roet *heiress* with no surviving male heir between her and her father's estate. The important point here is that Thomas' mother must have been not only a Roet but a Roet heiress. Since we know beyond question that Katherine Swinford was such, we can hardly escape the conclusion that another Roet heiress of the same time must have been co-heiress with her and consequently her sister" (pp. 36-37). Krauss adds, "Proof will pile upon proof when we come to the examination [in the remainder of his study] of the collateral arms." Obviously, it follows that, if Thomas Chaucer claimed Goeffrey as his father and a Roet heiress as his mother, and if Geoffrey's wife was named Philippa —Geoffrey must have been married to Philippa Roet. That this Philippa Roet was related to Katharine Swynford is indicated by the fact that the arms of Katharine appear on Thomas Chaucer's tomb, and also the arms of Katharine's four children that she had by John of Gaunt. It would seem beyond doubt, therefore, that Philippa Chaucer was the daughter of Katharine Swynford's father, Sir Payne de Roet.

Katharine Swynford), who had accompanied Queen Philippa when the latter had come to England to be married to Edward III. Sir Payne served Queen Philippa for many years, and afterward returned to Europe and served the queen's sister Margaret, Empress of Bavaria.[51] When Sir Payne left England, he seems to have left his two daughters at the English court under the supervision of Queen Philippa—who had brought up as fosterlings many other highborn girls, including both Elizabeth of Ulster and Blanche of Lancaster. Philippa Roet eventually became a damoiselle of the queen, and was rewarded in 1366 with the annuity already mentioned—possibly as a wedding gift. At any rate, nine months later Chaucer himself was granted an annuity. Since Elizabeth Chaucer, probably the daughter of Philippa,[52] was apparently born about this time, it is possible that the grant to Chaucer was a routine gesture recognizing his new parental responsibilities.

But a darker interpretation is also possible. Chaucer's father was alive in January, 1366, but dead by May 6, 1367, when his widow (Chaucer's mother) remarried.[53] To give that lady the benefit of every doubt, Chaucer's father must have been dead at least a year before his widow took another husband; that is, he was dead when we first find Geoffrey a married man. Though John Chaucer had thriven as a merchant, most of his property seems to have come to him through his wife, and to have remained with her at his death. Accordingly, Geoffrey was not a wealthy young man. Nor was he of high birth; nor did he hold a prominent position in the king's household (being only a "valettus," the lowest non-menial rank, at least a year after he was married); nor, seemingly, had he been long in the king's service; nor was his annuity very handsome.

In contrast, Philippa's family was prominent; it had long been associated intimately with the court and with the queen; and it must have owned property, for Philippa's nephew, Thomas Swynford, later on sued for land in Hainault that he had inherited through his mother, Philippa's sister Katharine. Something of the family's status may be gathered from the fact that Katharine had married into the old, landed, aristocratic Swynford family. Why, then, should Philippa, the senior daughter, have married an undistinguished "valettus" like Chaucer? One answer is, of course, that she may have loved him. But love seldom cut much figure in the marriage of fourteenth-century heiresses. Besides, Chaucer himself, in poem after poem, professes that he has never experienced happy or successful love. His insistence is so frequent, so emphatic, and apparently so sincere that, as Hales says, "It seems impossible to put a pleasant construction on these passages. It is incredible that they have no personal significance. The conclusion clearly is that Chaucer was not happy in his matrimonial relations."[54]

How can we explain all these contradictory circumstances—that Chaucer's marriage does not seem to have been a love marriage, that the marriage of any fourteenth-century heiress was regularly a marriage of convenience, and that the marriage of an heiress like Philippa Roet to a "valettus" like Chaucer could not have been a marriage of convenience? The most frequent explanation offered is that Gaunt (who had a contemporary reputation as being notably amorous as a young man) got Philippa with child, and persuaded (or hired, or forced) Chaucer to marry her.

Gaunt, as I have said, was preparing to leave England (on a great military expedition into Spain) in the same September that Philippa is recorded wedded to Chaucer. It would have been in keeping with the character of the Duke (whose record of unswerving loyalty to friends and dependents is almost without parallel in his time—or any time) to provide for his mistress by seeing that she received a pension. Supplying her with a husband was also necessary—for Philippa was not just an ordinary wanton, but the daughter and heir of an old friend of the queen's and a protégée of the queen herself. It should be stressed that mere seduction of an unmarried woman by a great lord in the fourteenth century was itself no special cause for scandal—witness the several illegitimate children of the Black Prince, and John of Gaunt's own illegitimate daughter born before his marriage to Blanche. But seducing a girl who was a damoiselle and ward of the queen was another matter; it was an affront to majesty, and also to Gaunt's own mother. Such a girl could not be left casually with her troubles.

If the Duke really did seduce Philippa, nothing would have been more natural than for him to persuade one of his retainers (by bribes, promises, and appeals to loyalty, friendship, or a sense of gratitude for past favors) to marry the girl. Moreover, if Philippa was to bear the Duke's child, it was altogether in character for him to have made provision, in case he was killed in Spain, that his own flesh and blood not starve. Thus the pension Philippa received on the eve of the Duke's departure, and the larger pension Geoffrey received when the Duke's child was born, may be explained. Philippa's and Geoffrey's pensions were not only rewards for them, but also means of providing for the Duke's own offspring. Whether such procedures were common in this corrupt court, I do not know; but there is a teasing little record of one of Chaucer's fellow employees in the court, Edmund Rose, being granted a royal annuity "because he has taken to wife Agnes Archer, Damoiselle of the Queen's chamber."[55] The wording is suggestive—and Agnes retained her maiden name.

Of course all this is speculation, without proof; and the most that can be said of it is that it represents a likelihood, or perhaps only a strong possibility. But there are many pieces in the puzzle: Chaucer's sudden appearance in the king's court, the probability that he was married in September of 1366, the birth of Elizabeth Chaucer in the summer of 1367, Chaucer's receiving a pension about the time Elizabeth was born, Philippa receiving a pension about the time she is supposed to have been married, Gaunt's departure from England at about the time Philippa was married and received her pension—all this together with the facts that Chaucer was certainly one of Gaunt's men in 1369 (when he accompanied Gaunt on an expedition to France), that he may well have been (if we take seriously the reference to the "eight years' sickness" in the *Book of the Duchess*) an employee of Gaunt from 1361 to 1366 or 1367, and that, though he went on military expeditions both before and after 1366, he was left at home in 1366. There are many pieces here; and they all fit together to suggest the explanation of Chaucer's marriage that has been given.

An alternative explanation is that Chaucer himself seduced the heiress Philippa, and then married her as a duty, or under compulsion, or for her property, without loving her. But before accepting this alternative explanation, we should consider several other facts. First of all, when Philippa's daughter Elizabeth was fourteen years old, and entered the convent of Barking to become a nun, Gaunt presented the convent with £51 8s. 2d. ($10,290) as a gift and for "various expenses" incurred. This considerable sum of money may have been contributed because Elizabeth was the niece of Gaunt's current mistress Katharine Swynford, or it may have been contributed because Elizabeth was the daughter of Gaunt's friend Geoffrey. But the sum was so large that one cannot help suspecting that Gaunt had a more intimate interest in Elizabeth.

For another thing, the records suggest that Gaunt had an interest in Philippa that was independent of his interest in Chaucer. In

August, 1372, he granted Philippa an annuity of £10 ($2,000) "by our special favor, and for the good and agreeable service" which she had done and was to do for "our very dear and much loved companion the Queen."[56] Since Gaunt had become the lover of Katharine Swynford about four months earlier, this pension to Philippa may have been granted at the behest of Katharine, and to please her; or it may have been granted as a kind of peace offering from Gaunt because he had deserted Philippa for her sister.

In June, 1374, Gaunt granted Chaucer himself an annuity of £10 ($2,000) not only for the good services of "our well-loved Geffray Chaucer," but also "for the good service that our well-loved Philippa, his wife, has done to our most honoured lady and mother the Queen, whom God pardon, and to our much loved companion the Queen."[57] Paying Chaucer for his wife's services to a lady who had been dead nearly five years seems doubly odd. Shortly before his departure on the Great March, in 1373, Gaunt made out an order bestowing gifts on his sister, his father, his wife, his daughters, Alice Perrers, Philippa Chaucer, and others. Something of his esteem for Philippa may be guessed from the fact that he gave his wife, Queen Constance, four gold buttons, and Philippa a "buttoner" with six silver buttons worked with gold.[58] On New Year's Day, 1380, he gave Philippa a silver cup worth 31s. 5d. ($314);[59] in 1381 he gave her another silver cup, worked with gold, which was one of a pair costing £10 14s. 2d. ($2,141);[60] and in 1382 he gave her another silver cup.[61] Gifts of this sort were not extraordinary in Gaunt's household; but they do indicate an interest in Philippa that was not associated with her as the wife of Geoffrey Chaucer—who received no such gifts. On February 19, 1386, Philippa was admitted to the fellowship of Lincoln Cathedral—along with Gaunt's sons Henry Bolingbroke and John Beaufort, Katharine Swynford's son Thomas Swynford, Robert Ferrers (soon to be Gaunt's son-in-law), and several other retainers of Gaunt.[62] The fact of Philippa's admission along with this rather exalted company is not so significant as the fact that Chaucer himself was not of the company. To her contemporaries, Philippa was something more than the wife of Geoffrey Chaucer.

Geoffrey received more or less public monetary marks of the Duke's favor, but (so far as the records show) was not *personally* favored, as was Philippa. But, of course, it is possible that Gaunt and Chaucer were so close that expressions of the Duke's regard for the poet may never have reached the formality of records.

A few other curious items hint at Philippa's being regarded as something besides Geoffrey Chaucer's wife. On May 21, 1379, at a time when John of Gaunt was in full control of public affairs in Lincoln, the Sheriff of Lincoln sent Philippa and one Mary St. Clair (another pensioner of Gaunt's) the sum of £26 13s. 4d. ($5,333)[63]—for what purpose I do not know. Another curious fact is that, from 1381, certain receipts from the customs were not paid entirely to Geoffrey, as controller, but were divided between him and Philippa. For example, on December 21, 1381, the sum of £10 ($2,000) went to him and Philippa together;[64] on July 22, 1382, 5 marks ($665) went to him, and 5 marks to Philippa; on May 5, 1383, 20 marks ($2,660) went to Geoffrey, and 5 marks ($665) to Philippa; on April 30, 1384, £15 6s. 8d. ($3,066) went to Geoffrey and Philippa together; on November 18, 1384, £16 13s. 4d. ($3,331) went to Geoffrey and Philippa together; on April 24, 1385, 17 marks ($2,261) went to Geoffrey, and 66s. 8d. ($666) went to Philippa; on November 3, 1385, 20 marks ($2,660) went to Geoffrey, and 5 marks ($665) to Philippa; and on June 22, 1386, 10 marks ($1,330) went to Geoffrey, and 5 marks ($665) to Philippa. Also, there is a curious document (December 9, 1384) in which money from the customs is assigned to "Ph[ilipp]o Chauc[er]"—evidently a scribal error by someone who had been told that Philippa Chaucer was to receive money.

What to make of these records I do not know. Possibly the division of fees recognizes the fact that Chaucer and Philippa were not living together after 1380—as they had not been living together before the lease on the Aldgate house in 1374. But whatever the explanation, the records make it clear that Philippa was considered a person in her own right, and not merely Geoffrey's wife. The point is significant because it re-emphasizes the strangeness of the marriage of an independent woman like Philippa to a man like Geoffrey, who was so completely dependent on John of Gaunt, and who (if we take him at his own word) did not love his wife.

Thomas Chaucer] In 1932 Russell Krauss made an extensive and detailed study of "The Paternity of Thomas Chaucer." Though he had started out to disprove that Gaunt could have been Thomas' father, he concluded, after considering all the evidence, that, in all probability, Gaunt was indeed Thomas Chaucer's father, and Philippa Chaucer his mother.[65] Many anguished reviews followed the appearance of Krauss' study; but it must be said that the criticisms of Krauss' thesis are no more convincing than the work they criticize. Perhaps the sanest of all the reviews (and the one to which the reader is referred for a summary of Krauss's arguments, as well as a summary of opposing arguments) appeared in the London *Times Literary Supplement*, December 29, 1932, p. 986. About all I have to add here is a comment on a couple of points made by Manly and one by Professor B. J. Whiting. Manly sets much store by the fact that Thomas Chaucer is known to have used Geoffrey Chaucer's shield (coat of arms) on certain official documents, and that that circumstance proves that Thomas considered himself to be Geoffrey's son.[66] Manly does not seem to remember that, if Thomas was legally (if not actually) Geoffrey's son, there was no other shield that he could have used legally. Certainly, if he had tried to use Gaunt's arms, he would have been subject to trial for high treason.

Whiting alludes ironically to Chaucer's "pretty role as a contented cuckold."[67] But it should be remembered (*1*) that Chaucer never expressed contentment with his married life or his love life— quite the contrary; (2) that if he really married Philippa at Gaunt's behest in 1366, he went into the arrangement with his eyes open, and had no cause to feel deceived; (*3*) that he was well remunerated; and (*4*) that he may actually have regarded it as a high honor to be so closely connected with the royal house of England, and the kingdom's greatest nobleman. Alice Perrers' husband accepted with excellent grace his wife's role as mistress to the king, along with the incidental perquisites to himself; and many a subsequent husband of the royal mistress in France and in England has managed to view a similar situation with philosophic aplomb. The moral perspective in which we ourselves view such goings-on has been vastly altered by generations of Puritan influence and Victorian patterns of thought.

Another point that Manly makes against Krauss's argument is that Gaunt's marrying Katharine after he had had carnal relations with her sister would have violated canon law. This is not convincing. Universal rulings about impediments to marriage had not been formulated in the fourteenth century; indeed, the modern *Catholic Encyclopedia* states that, even to this day, "No official list of impediments has ever been promulgated." The entire problem of Gaunt's marrying one sister (Katharine) twenty-five years after he had cohabited with another sister (Philippa), and eight years after this latter sister's death, was so unusual and so complex, with so many unique features, that no ready-made rule could possibly have been applied. Nothing resembling a formal marriage contract, or agreement, or relationship, between Philippa and Gaunt was ever involved; nor had there been any formal recognition of Philippa's children as Gaunt's children (if they actually were his children). At most, Philippa was only a mistress of Gaunt's younger days, and she was long dead when Gaunt married her sister. There is considerable difference, in canon law, between marriage before and marriage after the death of a former sexual partner. If there was actually an affair between Gaunt and Philippa before the latter's marriage to Chaucer, the offense occurred as mere fornication—to be confessed privately, and to be forgiven once and for all—not to be made a matter of canonical disputation.

On the whole, then, it seems likely that any carnal relationship between Gaunt and Philippa would have constituted no absolutely insurmountable barrier to his marrying Katharine. Besides, the Duke had private confessors in his own household, and abbots and even bishops dependent upon him for livelihood, position, and power; nothing would have been easier than for him to obtain from one of these ecclesiastics, in this unprecedented borderline case, an opinion favorable to his marrying Katharine even though he had cohabited with her now dead sister many years earlier. He had doubtless long since received complete absolution for that early episode (if it occurred at all) that had ended before he began cohabiting with Katharine. His petition to the Pope for permission to marry Katharine was necessary only to legitimize the children she had borne him while he was married to Constance. Philippa and her children were simply not involved.

Just possibly, carnal relationships carried on contemporaneously with two sisters, one of whom subsequently became the man's wife, may have smacked of incest. But the evidence suggests that no such contemporaneous relationship existed. Gaunt returned from his French raid in November, 1369, shortly after Blanche's death; he left England for France and Spain in late June, 1370; he returned to England in November, 1371; and his liaison with Katharine commenced in the spring of 1372. From November, 1369, to June,

1370, he may have begot on Philippa the child who became Thomas Chaucer; or (if he took Philippa with him to France) he may have begot the child while there; or he may have done it after his return to England, between November, 1371, and the spring of 1372. But there is no hint of evidence that he and Philippa were lovers after the spring of 1372.

Where would Chaucer stand in such a matrimonial complex? If Gaunt and Philippa cohabited either before or after the latter's marriage to Chaucer, the offense occurred with the full knowledge of the husband—which would have made a serious difference in the offense of the lovers, according to common interpretations of early canon law. Furthermore, ample restitution was made to the wronged husband (in the form of Gaunt's lifelong patronage)—which also would have made a difference in many medieval interpretations of the law.

In conclusion, I may say that I hope that this discussion has not left the impression that I think the Gaunt-Philippa relationship has been proved. Most emphatically, it has *not* been proved. On the other hand, the existence of such a relationship has not been *disproved,* either. But there are enough odd circumstances concerning the entire relationship of Geoffrey, Philippa, Gaunt, and Katharine to make us wonder. If a Gaunt-Philippa relationship, such as has been described, really did occur, it would help clarify a good many facts about Chaucer's life and poetry that are otherwise mysterious.

Whatever the explanation of the Gaunt-Chaucer linkage, there can be no doubt that Chaucer's public life and private life were long, uninterruptedly, intimately, and significantly related to the public life and the private life of John of Gaunt. Any other view does not accord with the facts.

Before leaving the subject of the man-woman relationships involved in the matters just discussed, we should, perhaps, try to guess how those relationships affected the day-to-day lives and personal contacts of the people involved. First, however, we should disabuse our minds of any notion that the typical medieval marriage, especially among the upper classes, was characterized by anything like the "togetherness" that is the ideal of modern marriage. Medieval marriage might, or might not, be accompanied by what we regard as romantic love. Most often, apparently, it was not so accompanied. The devoted wife in the "Franklin's Tale" seems to be a remarkable case even in Chaucer's eyes, and she is hardly typical of other wives in the *Canterbury Tales*. Even Emily, of the "Knight's Tale," accepts Arcite or Palamon indifferently, and Griselda, of the "Clerk's Tale," is much more like a faithful servant than a companionable wife. The widely prevalent system of courtly love recognized the fact that husband and wife were not expected to be personally compatible; they married for reasons of property or family, cohabited sufficiently to have children, worked together if they belonged to the lower classes, managed the business together if they were tradesmen, and may have had no other communion, mental or spiritual, with each other, except in the conduct of daily routines.

I have already said that Philippa seems to have been generally regarded as something more than Geoffrey's wife—witness her acceptance into the fellowship of Lincoln Cathedral without Geoffrey, the granting of Gaunt's pension to Geoffrey partly on account of her, and her sharing in the money due Geoffrey from his customs-house work. To November 22, 1368, she drew her own pension from the king's treasury without benefit of Geoffrey; and on November 7, 1369, she let one John Hermesthorp, not Geoffrey, draw her pension for her. The records do not show that she drew her royal pension at any time in 1370 or 1371. These were years when Gaunt was out of England. Gaunt's absence and Philippa's failure to draw her pension may be a coincidence; on the other hand, the fact may be interpreted as indicating that Philippa's pension was really dependent upon Gaunt's favor, or even that Philippa failed to draw her pension because she was in France with Gaunt. Later on, in July, 1374, when she received arrears on her pension, she was paid only from the beginning of 1372.

Apparently Chaucer and Philippa had no home until Chaucer was granted a lease on the house above Aldgate in May, 1374. For a few years thereafter the two probably lived together, since (from July 6, 1374, to November 27, 1376) Philippa's royal pension was paid into the hands of Chaucer himself. But in May, 1379, her pension went to one John Yerneburgh, and in May, 1380, to William Bagot. Subsequently her pension was paid sometimes to Chaucer and sometimes to her; and after 1383 a portion of it was paid to Chaucer and a portion "assigned"—to Philippa or to some person unknown. Meanwhile Philippa was drawing Gaunt's pension, ostensibly, at any rate, for serving Gaunt's wife, Queen Constance.

If Philippa was really with the Queen, she must have been away from London and from Geoffrey much of the time. And, of course, Geoffrey himself made many protracted trips out of the country.

What all this means is that, from 1366 or 1367, Philippa and Goeffrey led "semi-detached" lives. Their marriage itself was almost certainly not a marriage of love; during most of their married life they had no home together; their financial affairs were often separate; and they lived apart for long periods. The evidence we have indicates that there was only a minimum of spiritual or intimate personal communion between them. If there had been such communion, Chaucer's attitude toward, and his poems about, extramarital love might have been different.

What was true of Chaucer's marriage must have been even more pronounced in the marriage of Gaunt and Constance of Spain. This marriage was strictly political. In marrying Constance, Gaunt merely seized the opportunity to obtain a title (of sorts) to the throne of Spain; and in marrying him, Constance merely seized the opportunity to get a powerful protector at a time when her very life was in danger. At the time of the marriage, Gaunt was thirty years old; Constance was sixteen. She was not beautiful; and all her life she was motivated by two obsessions: determination to regain the Spanish throne, and a morbidly religious devotion to the memory of her murdered father. Under the circumstances, it is easy to see why Gaunt took a mistress. It is also easy to see why his taking a mistress might have been a matter of indifference to Constance—indeed, it is not impossible that she was glad to have her husband's sexual attentions directed away from herself. At any rate, she had no more children by him after 1374, though she was only twenty years old at the time, and lived twenty years longer. Perhaps she even blessed the affair of Gaunt and Katharine; for though she could not have been ignorant of the liaison between the two, she named her own daughter Katharine. Moreover, the contemporary artist who painted the frontispiece of the most famous manuscript of *Troilus and Criseyde* seems to have shown Constance embracing Katharine.[68] In short, we have no reason to believe that Constance was a jealous wife who exercised a diligent supervision over her husband's extramarital personal life—any more than Philippa Chaucer supervised Geoffrey's private life, or censored his poems.

Finally, what about the personal relationship between Gaunt and Chaucer? The records show that both Gaunt and Gaunt's son, Henry IV, showered favors on Chaucer. It is possible that Chaucer was in Gaunt's employ from 1361; and it is certain that Chaucer was a follower of Gaunt on the French expedition in 1369—Chaucer's name being very high on the list of persons who went with Gaunt on that expedition. Chaucer knew Gaunt well enough to write a poem on the death of Gaunt's first wife, and in the poem depicts himself speaking in intimate and affectionate, though respectful, terms to Gaunt. In the poem "Fortune" Chaucer refers repeatedly to his "beste frend"—some noble personage who is able to help him to a "beter estat," and who has been identified by most Chaucerians as Gaunt. In addition, Chaucer was the brother-in-law of Gaunt's mistress of twenty years and third wife. There can be no doubt that Chaucer and Gaunt were on friendly terms.

It must be remembered, too, that, though medieval society was not democratic, the personnel of a medieval castle or palace mingled daily on democratic terms hardly conceivable today. It would have been entirely possible for Chaucer to have rubbed elbows daily with the great Duke, and also to have talked with him frequently, and to have become his personal friend. Since Chaucer was learned, knowing in the world's ways, evidently diplomatic, witty and humorous, a good story-teller, and (increasingly during his life) a celebrated poet—and since he was beholden to Gaunt in many ways, to say nothing of being a virtual kinsman through Katharine—it would have been surprising if something like friendship had not risen between the two men.*

Perhaps Chaucer was to Gaunt something like the personally ambitionless confidant that many a great man has. (One thinks of President Franklin Roosevelt's Louis Howe, President Woodrow Wilson's Colonel E. M. House, General Eisenhower's Captain Butcher, and even President Kennedy's brother Robert.) Perhaps he was the kind of friend who admired Gaunt, praised him, advised him, sympathized with him, celebrated him in poetry, and still could jest lightly with him or about him, and even criticize him on occasion. Gaunt was not a paranoiac tyrant, and Chaucer was not a shallow sycophant. Both were great men—one in power and place, and the other in personality and genius—and there is every reason to believe that they lived on terms of close, perhaps even intimate, friendship for at least thirty years.

* If, in addition, Gaunt was beholden to Chaucer for having married Philippa, and for being the foster father of Gaunt's child, or children, by Philippa, the relationship between Gaunt and Chaucer would have been permanently cemented— especially in view of Gaunt's undeviating loyalty to anyone toward whom he felt a sense of obligation.

Chapter III. What is the *Complaint of Mars*?*

If one glances at the index of almost any book about Chaucer written in the last seventy-five years, there is an excellent chance that he will find no listing of the *Complaint of Mars*. Or, if it is listed, the commentary in the text itself will probably be something like this: "a poem of inferior merit,"[1] or "witty, though arid,"[2] or "has little claim to attention,"[3] or "nothing more than an ingenious astronomical allegory, used to diversify a highly conventional theme."[4] The best that Skeat can say for it is that "The poem is remarkable for its astronomical allusions."[5]

The poem purports to be words sung by a bird on St. Valentine's Day. The bird tells that Mars fell in love with Venus, and this love made him a better man. But on one occasion when the lovers are in bed together, Phoebus discovers them. Frightened, Venus flees to the refuge of "Cilenios tour," but, not finding Cilenios at home, she goes into a cave close by the tower. Mars follows her, and then makes his formal "Complaint," in which he praises Venus, tells of the hardships lovers suffer, and begs all hardy knights and faithful ladies to sympathize with him and Venus, and to be kind to her.

The *Complaint of Mars* has long been one of Chaucer's mystery poems. The old copyist Shirley stated that the poem had been written "at the commandement of the renommed and excellent prynce my lord the duc John of Lancastre"; and he added that "some men sayne" that the poem concerns "my lady of york doughter of the kyng of Spaygne and my lord huntington."[6] Actually, "my lady of york" was not Gaunt's daughter, but his sister-in-law, wife of his brother Edmund, and sister of his own wife Constance—and there is no record of any affair between her and Huntington, who was John Holland, half-brother of Richard II. But Gaunt's daughter Elizabeth did suddenly break off her engagement to the Earl of Pembroke, and marry John Holland. Brusendorff,[7] Cowling,[8] and others have thought that the poem refers to this affair, and that the angry Phoebus represents John of Gaunt. But, aside from the fact that this theory leaves many peculiar details of the poem unexplained, there is no evidence that Gaunt was enraged by

* A slightly different version of this chapter appeared in the *Journal of English and Germanic Philology*, LVII (1958), 167-73.

his daughter's sudden change of plans, no reason why Chaucer should have wanted to write an apology for the two young lovers (especially if he knew that Gaunt disapproved), and no likelihood that he would present Gaunt as unsympathetically as he portrays Phoebus in the poem. As Robinson says, "the whole theory remains very doubtful."[9]

Some attempt has been made to pin down the allegory by reference to dates suggested by the astronomical events described in the poem. But Manly made a detailed study of these events, and, in the words of Robinson, "proved the astronomical conclusions to be erroneous, and showed further that the exact conditions demanded by the poem were not fulfilled at any time between 1369 and 1400 ... he concluded that it would be hazardous to draw any inferences from the astronomical data."[10] Despite the unreality of the astronomical situation, however, Manly decided that the poem must be regarded as "a mere exercise of ingenuity in describing a supposed astronomical event in terms of human action and emotion."[11] My own belief is just the opposite of Manly's. That is, I should like to consider the poem as an exercise in describing human action and emotion in terms of a supposed astronomical event.

The lack of astronomical realism in the poem argues against its being a mere astronomical exercise; and many details of statement and diction argue for its being a fanciful depiction of a real flesh-and-blood love affair. The lovers are thoroughly human, not celestial: "unto bed thei go" (l. 73), and they reign, not in heaven, but "*as* in hevene" (l. 50). They retire to a "chambre" (l. 79); Venus flies to a "tour" (l. 113); and she hides in a "smokyng" "cave" (l. 120)—all terms unknown to astronomy. Mars himself declares in so many words, "This is no feyned mater that I telle" (l. 173).

Almost at the beginning of the poem Chaucer seems to offer clues as to its interpretation. Exactly as he refers to "Saint Johan" near the end of the *Book of the Duchess* in order to connect that poem unmistakably with John of Gaunt,* so in line 9 of the present poem he advises lovers "with seint John to borowe" (that is, let John be their guide or surety). Insertion of this Christian reference into a poem about pagan divinities could not have been accidental.

In lines 29-31 Mars is called the "thridde hevenes lord," "As wel in hevenysh revolucion / As by desert." Before Prince Lionel's

---

* See subsequent chapters on the *Parliament of Fowls* and *Troilus and Criseyde* for other examples of Chaucer's use of Saint John as a means of identifying Gaunt.

death in 1368, John had been the king's third son; after Lionel's death, John was the third male heir in line for the throne; he was the third most celebrated military figure in the kingdom after 1370; he was the third most powerful man in the kingdom until the Black Prince's death in 1376; and even after the Black Prince's death, John was third in royal rank until the death of Edward in 1377, when John moved up to second place. If Chaucer ever read these lines in public, either at Gaunt's court or at King Edward's court, his hearers would have had no difficulty recognizing the man who "by desert" and "by hevenysh revolucion" occupied a singular position of "thirdness" in the realm. The applicability of the reference to a human "Mars" becomes all the more apparent when we remember that the planet Mars was supposed to lie, not in the third celestial sphere outward from the earth, but in the fifth, and in the fourth sphere if we count inward from the Primum Mobile.

If, then, we begin with the hypothesis that the Mars of the poem represents John of Gaunt, we must test the hypothesis by discovering whether it is consistent with other details in the poem, and helps explain them.

If Mars is John of Gaunt, the identity of Venus becomes obvious. Gaunt's only serious extramarital affair that was well known, the only one for which he was bitterly censured, and the only one, very probably, about which Chaucer would have written a poem, was the affair with Katharine Swynford, sister of Chaucer's wife. Knighton and Walsingham were scandalized by the affair, and wrote scurrilously of Katharine;[12] the affair contributed no small part, in the 1370's, to what Armitage-Smith calls Gaunt's reputation as an "abandoned libertine";[13] and we may assume that the open liaison of a great prince (who was also titular King of Spain) and a waiting-maid furnished gossip for every courtier's tongue in England.

The actual "Complaint" of Mars, for which the entire poem is constructed, is essentially a plea for tolerance of Mars's illicit love that has been harshly rebuked. In making his plea, Mars points out the "gret excellence" of his mistress (ll. 169-81), and says that he loves her because he cannot help it (ll. 218-71). Harsh criticism has forced his mistress to leave him; and Mars says flatly, "The poynt is this" (l. 212) that "My right lady, my salvacioun, / Is in affray" (ll. 213-14). He then reminds all "hardy knyghtes" (l. 272) that "I am your patroun" (l. 275), and prays them not to ridicule him for this affair (l. 277) but to sympathize with him (l. 276); and he

begs all "ladyes that ben true and stable" (l. 281) to remember how
kind his mistress has been to them (l. 292), and to pity her and do
her "sum kyndnesse" (l. 298) in return.

The fundamental situation revealed in the "Complaint" is entirely consistent with everything we know, or can reasonably surmise, about the Gaunt-Katharine affair. John (who must have had
more than a passing affection for Katharine, since he eventually
married her, and went to considerable trouble and expense to
legitimize the children he had had by her) must have been hurt and
angered by the vilification to which both she and he were subjected
at court.* It is likely, furthermore, that Chaucer (brother-in-law
of Katharine and friend of Gaunt) would have been eager to
mollify court opinion about the liaison, and that Gaunt would have
welcomed Chaucer's effort to make the affair more acceptable at
court. Perhaps Shirley's remark that the poem was written at the
request of Gaunt has an element of truth in it, after all.

Whether Katharine was ever forced to flee from Gaunt, as the
poem depicts Venus fleeing from Mars, we shall probably never
know. But universal criticism must have made the lovers nervous
about their relationship in its earlier years. Chaucer includes a
precise date—"This twelfte daye of April" (l. 139)—when Venus's
flight occurred. On the authority of Manly, this date has no conceivable connection with any genuine astronomical event; therefore,
it must represent some actual date in the affair between the man
and the woman whose love is here recounted. Our problem, then,
is to discover the year in which this particular twelfth day of April
fell. But the solution of this problem depends upon the solution of
another.

Venus is reported as fleeing to "Cilenios tour" (l. 113). If Venus
does stand for Katharine, and if Katharine was compelled by public
scandal to leave Gaunt temporarily, where would she be most likely
to go? Her father had returned to Europe[14] and her mother had
doubtless either gone with him, or was dead; her husband was dead
in 1371; her husband's relatives would have been unlikely to look
with sympathy on a widow who was having an illicit affair with

---

* It is virtually impossible for us, in the twentieth century, to see with the eyes
of the fourteenth century. But it seems likely that the royal court condemned the
Gaunt-Katharine affair not merely because it was immoral, but because Gaunt had
elevated this woman of low birth to a position of influence over him and in his
court. The immorality of the affair was only a handy excuse for the court's
resentment against a waiting-maid who had been lifted high.

another man less than a year after her husband's death; she was evidently (judging by this very poem) in some disgrace, if not actual danger; she had no brothers, so far as is actually known; she had no sister but Philippa Chaucer. In a word, Chaucer's house was the most likely place in London to which she would retire, on separating herself from Gaunt. If this reasoning is sound, it follows that Cilenios (Mercury) represents Chaucer himself.

Certain peculiar facts make this identification seem highly probable. The Wife of Bath says (*Canterbury Tales*, D 699) that the children of Mercury love "wysdom and science"; they are bookish scholars—and Chaucer was a bookish scholar rather than a lover or a warrior. Mercury was the messenger of the gods, and the god of commerce—and Chaucer had been a royal messenger, and he was involved in commerce as a controller of customs. If he was to be symbolized by any god, it would have had to be Mercury. Doubtless no great lord would have liked being identified with the commercial Mercury; a man of the middle class, like Chaucer, was a much more likely candidate. The poem tells that Venus fled, in fear of Phoebus, to the "tour" of Mercury. After May 10, 1374, Chaucer lived in what may be called a tower above Aldgate. When Venus fled to the tower, she found "no maner wyght" (l. 116) there. Accordingly, she hid herself for an entire day within a dark and smoking "cave" that stood "two pas within the yate" (l. 121). The nonastronomical language and the precise details about the "cave" irresistibly suggest a real place, and equally irresistibly suggest Chaucer's residence at Aldgate. Chaucer's lease on this place mentions not only "the dwelling-house above the gate of Aldgate, with the rooms built over" (evidently something of a tower), but also "a certain cellar beneath the same gate, on the south side of that gate."[15] This cellar, perhaps used as a kitchen according to the custom of the time, and certainly not well ventilated, could have been the dark and smoking cave two paces within the gate where Venus waited till Mercury returned home. The sensational nature of such an incident can be guessed if we imagine a celebrated modern film star visiting, say, a well-known government official, and having to spend the day in his kitchen basement because he was not there to receive her. In any event, when Mercury did return home and found Venus there, "he salueth and doth chere / And her receyveth as his frend ful dere" (ll. 146-47).

To be sure, there is no evidence (outside this poem) that Katharine ever went to Chaucer's house under the circumstances suggested; but even if she did, it is extremely improbable that any written record of the occurrence would have been made, or would have survived. All we know is that Katharine was loathed among certain important factions in England in the early 1370's, that her affair with John of Gaunt was a public scandal, that her only friendly relatives in London were Chaucer and his wife, that her lover was a friend and patron of Chaucer, that the house where Chaucer lived fits perfectly the rather peculiar details that describe the place to which the Venus of the poem fled, and that the public character of Chaucer corresponds to that of Mercury, master of the house where Venus took refuge. These facts do not absolutely prove the interpretation offered here; but the extraordinary consistency with which so many of them fit together, and fit many other details to be mentioned immediately, is impressive.

If Katharine did flee to Chaucer at Aldgate, it must have been after he moved there in May, 1374. And it must have been before King Edward III died on June 21, 1377—for this death would have left Gaunt second, not third, in power in the kingdom. Accordingly, the "twelfte daye of April" on which Venus (Katharine?) fled must have been in 1375, 1376, or 1377. In 1375 Gaunt was out of England from about March 10 to July 10;[16] therefore April 12, 1375, is probably not the date meant.

Something may be said for April 12, 1377. The poem speaks of Mercury "rydinge in his chevache" (l. 144) just before he returns to his "tour"; and Chaucer had returned from a mission in Flanders on March 25, 1377. On the other hand, the phrase "rydinge in his chevache" is very obscure, and could imply a horseback excursion of any duration from a few hours to many years. Furthermore, in April, 1377, the king was old and sick, Prince Richard was only nine years old, the Parliament that had met in February had been altogether under Gaunt's thumb, and Gaunt was in complete control of the entire national situation. Neither he nor Katharine would have felt the need for separation at this time. On the whole, therefore, April 12, 1377, is probably not the one meant in the poem.

Thus April 12, 1376, is left as a possibility. Extremely significant events were occurring in that April. The famous Good Parliament was assembling, and officially opened its first session on April 28, 1376. This was the Parliament that was bitterly hostile to John of Gaunt, his friends, and everything he stood for; it attacked his position in the government, punished his immediate friends and subordinates, and deprived him of much of his power and influence. Perhaps the shadow of these coming events had gone before, and persuaded Gaunt to clean house literally, if only temporarily, just sixteen days before the Parliament met. At any rate, it is entirely credible that, with matters developing so dangerously, and with Gaunt unquestionably the most unpopular man in England, both Katharine and Gaunt might have felt it expedient that they separate until the storm passed. Here again we are merely speculating; but when so many of these speculations fall into a consistent pattern with one another and with Chaucer's poem, they must be heeded.

In the poem it was the enmity of Phoebus which caused the lovers to separate. Thus the question arises as to who or what is symbolized by the character of Phoebus. Chaucer indicates something of the identification early in the poem:

> Fleeth, lest wikked tonges yow espye!   (6-7)
> Lo! yond the sunne, the candel of jelosye!

Phoebus represents "wikked tonges." He searches out every fearful lover (l. 28); he comes knocking on the door of the lovers Mars and Venus (l. 84); fear of him compels Mars to send away his mistress. Phoebus is gossip, slander, public opinion.

It is possible also that he represents some individual who was particularly active in persecuting the lovers. This individual could hardly have been the king, who was himself consorting with a mistress at that very time, the notorious Alice Perrers, and was in no position to point a finger of scorn at his son; and it could not have been the Black Prince, for Mars is shown, in the poem, seizing sword, spear, and buckler to do battle with Phoebus (ll. 92-102)—and Gaunt would never have allowed himself to be represented as militantly resisting either the king or the Black Prince. That would have been treason.*

At this time the people of London had a very special animosity toward Gaunt; and William Courtenay, Bishop of London, was just developing into one of Gaunt's severest critics and most formidable enemies. In the church convocation of 1373 Courtenay had spoken

---

* Neither would John Holland have allowed himself to be represented militantly resisting his father-in-law, John of Gaunt. Indeed, Gaunt and Holland seemed to get along very well; Gaunt appointed his son-in-law to a high office right after his marriage.

loudly and angrily against what he considered the government's abuses; and the Good Parliament appointed him a member of its council of advisers. Again he vigorously attacked the government (which now meant John of Gaunt); and measures he advocated were enacted by the Good Parliament with the express purpose of curbing Gaunt. Feeling between the two men was so high that, within a year, Gaunt was threatening to drag the Bishop by his hair from St. Paul's Cathedral, and within less time than that Gaunt was taking vengeance on Courtenay's brother bishop in the Good Parliament, William of Wykeham, by taking away the latter's temporalities and forbidding him to approach within twenty miles of the court.[17] If no open move was made against Courtenay at this time, it was probably because London was in an ugly mood, and Gaunt did not venture to attack its bishop. In any event, as the Good Parliament convened, no love was being lost between the Bishop of London and John of Gaunt.

I do not know whether there is a specific record of the Bishop's condemning Gaunt's affair with Katharine; but considering the notoriety of the affair, the hostility of the Bishop toward Gaunt, and the fact that the Bishop, as a churchman, would certainly go on record as condemning immorality in high places, we must conclude that the Bishop was a party to public criticism of the affair. Consequently, if Phoebus in Chaucer's poem represents any real individual, this individual may well be William Courtenay, Bishop of London. I do not wish to press this identification too hard; yet several interesting points bear mentioning.

First, Chaucer is known to have indulged in frequent puns.[18] For example, there are two well-known and long-recognized puns near the end of the *Book of the Duchess*, where Chaucer writes of a "long castel" when he means *Lancaster*, and of a "ryche hill" when he means *Richmond*. Second, Phoebus is described as bearing "firy torches rede" (l. 27), and his "torche" is referred to twice more in the poem (ll. 83, 91). Finally, the Courtenay arms are distinguished by three red *torteaux* (that is, three red disks).[19] If we may imagine that Chaucer read this poem aloud at some social gathering of Gaunt's partisans, we may even imagine that he pronounced the word "torche" to resemble "torteau." A generation as sensitive to the lore of heraldry as our own generation is sensitive to advertising slogans, or to the stock symbols of the cartoonist, could not have failed to catch the innuendo—the fiery disk of the sun (Phoebus), the fiery disks of the Courtenay arms, the thrice repeated play on the words *torche* and *torteau.*

Several other phrases in the poem have a special significance in view of the interpretation being offered here. The poet says that Mars "tok gretter ire" (l. 132) from being separated from Venus "Then fro al his brennyng in the fire" (l. 133). This "brennyng in the fire" is an aptly worded description of what happened to Gaunt in the Good Parliament. A few lines farther on, Mars exclaims, "O lady bryght, Venus, alas! / That evere so wyd a compas ys my spere!" (ll. 136-37). If Mars and Venus do represent real lovers, it is obvious that this exclamation implies that the great sphere of place and power in which the man moves is interfering with the love affair.

Certain other lines or allusions in the poem may refer to incidents involving two human lovers, or may be mere attempts to make the astronomical allegory more convincing. The passage (ll. 54-56) in which Mars hurries into "hir nexte paleys" and there waits for Venus to come to him may be intended as a realistic astronomical detail. Fitting it into the Gaunt-Katharine frame of reference, however, would not be too difficult. It is on record that, in 1377, Gaunt granted Katharine two manors from his immense properties; and it is certainly probable that, if she had already been his mistress for four years in 1376, and had borne him two children, he would have provided a place for her to live in London, or nearby. That is, she could really have had a "paleys" in which he visited her. On the other hand, for a great public figure to go to his mistress' house and wait there for her seems a little odd. "Hir nexte paleys" may mean "their nearest palace"; or (since a medieval final *s* looks much like an *r*) it could have originally read "his nearest palace."* In either case, one thinks of Gaunt's magnificent palace, the Savoy, lying just outside London's west wall. From this palace it would have been easy, and natural, for Katharine to retire to Aldgate.

If the palace is the Savoy, the following mysterious lines become immediately clear.

* None of the MSS have "his." But (as examples of MS variants) in l. 67, where Robinson has "her," several MSS have "hir," and two (Harlean 7333 and Arch. Selden B, 24) have "his." In l. 70, where Robinson has "he," four of the eight MSS (Pepys 2006, Hand E; Arch. Selden B, 24; Longleat 258; Tanner 346) have "she."

[Mars] dwelleth in solitude til she come—
For hyt stod so that thilke tyme no wight
Counseyled hym ther, ne seyde to hym welcome.   (65-67)

These lines would imply that Gaunt's wife Constance (a twenty-one-year-old woman of no special beauty or charm to whom he, now a man of thirty-six, had been married five years) had deserted the Savoy, and left him alone there. I cannot find out where Constance was in April, 1376; but her usual place of residence was at Hertford.[19] If she was there, instead of at the Savoy with her husband during the troubled times of the Good Parliament, the lines just quoted would be peculiarly apt. They would be Chaucer's method of justifying Gaunt for loving another woman.

All this is (admittedly) highly speculative and conjectural. But, after nearly six hundred years, speculation and conjecture must play a major role in all Chaucerian scholarship. The most significant thing about the speculation and conjecture here offered is that it holds together so consistently, that so many details fit together to form the pattern, and that it illuminates the poem as a whole, all of its important elements, and most of its minor details. Furthermore, as will be pointed out later, it parallels interpretations that will be given to many other portions of Chaucer's work. Finally, it makes this poem (often considered hardly worth study) assume considerable importance as a possible account of some of Chaucer's personal relationships, and also as a picture of an intensely interesting moment in the lives of three famous personages.

A word about the date of the poem. It must have been written between April 12, 1376, and June 21, 1377—when King Edward died, and Gaunt moved up to second place in the kingdom. If, as hinted in the second stanza, it is a St. Valentine's Day poem, it must have been written for St. Valentine's Day, 1377. An additional comment may be worth while. If the poem is concerned with the marriage of John Holland and Elizabeth of Lancaster, the date would have to be no earlier than 1386, when these two were married. But the very subject of the poem, to say nothing of its artificialities of language, allegory, and allusion, would seem to place it in a period much earlier than 1386.

Chapter IV. Who were Troilus, Criseyde, and Pandarus?*

At first glance, Chaucer's *Troilus and Criseyde* looks like a mere retelling of Boccaccio's *Il Filostrato*—with certain minor variations due to personal whims or tastes of the new teller. The story was already old in Chaucer's time: Troilus, a prince of Troy, falls in love with a young widow, Criseyde, and she with him; their affair is consummated through the machinations of Criseyde's uncle, Pandarus, and the lovers are happy for a while. Then Criseyde must go to her father, Calchas, who is in the Greek camp. She promises to return to Troilus immediately; but instead, she delays, falls in love with the Greek Diomede, and never returns to Troilus. That is the simple plot of this famous story.

But many mysteries are concealed here. As Tatlock says, Chaucer's version, unlike any older version of the story, "is a poem of people, their personalities and feelings, and incident is only for their expression."[1] Why did Chaucer choose to emphasize character so strongly, and thus transform a trite old story into the greatest narrative poem in English?

Again Tatlock remarks that "inexperienced modern readers naturally ask why Criseyde and Troilus should not marry, and the answer is that if this were history there would be no reason. Many medieval love stories do end in marriage, and there would be no reason in medieval social prejudice why a royal prince should not marry a patrician subject."[2] Why did Chaucer let them love each other, live together two years, and still never marry?

Chaucer changes the Italian Cressida from a rather bold wanton to a woman "more innocent, less experienced, less sensual, more modest than her Italian prototype."[3] Why?

Boccaccio's uncomplex, though scheming and lecherous, Pandaro becomes, in Chaucer, a complicated human being who has good intentions and an acute sense of honor. Why this change?

Why the constant reiteration (altogether absent in Boccaccio) of the honorableness of Troilus' love?

* A considerably different version of this chapter appeared in *Studies in English Honoring George Wesley Whiting, The Rice Institute Pamphlet,* XLIV (1957), 126-46.

Why did Chaucer do all he could to excuse Criseyde for her unfaithfulness, even in a period when unfaithfulness in love was about the worst crime a hero or a heroine of romance could commit? "The charity of Chaucer toward Cressida," says Chesterton, "is one of the most beautiful things in human literature."[4]

Why, as Lowes points out, does Chaucer end the *Troilus* "in an access of personal feeling without parallel elsewhere in his work"?[5]

How is the mysterious Epilogue of the poem (about which so much has been written) to be explained?

What accounts for the many changes, additions, and omissions (some of them to be noted later) that Chaucer effected in his rendition of Boccaccio's stanzas?

Is Robinson's suggestion that "Perhaps there were living models"[6] for the chief characters in the poem worth following up?

These questions, and many more besides, are considered in this chapter and the Appendix of this book. The answers to be suggested may reveal that there exists in this poem a hidden world that has lurked there unnoticed for centuries.

Some general probabilities

In the Proem of *Il Filostrato*, from which the *Troilus* is adapted, Boccaccio announces plainly that the chief characters in his poem represent himself and his mistress. He says that, before he undertook the poem, he began "to turn over in my mind with great care ancient stories, in order to find one that would serve, in all color of likelihood, as a mask for my secret and amorous grief." His Troilo's fortunes, Boccaccio tells his mistress, are "in conformity with the facts in my case"; and "things praiseworthy in a lady written of Cressida you may understand to be said of you."[7] With this testimony before him, Chaucer could hardly have avoided considering, at least, the introduction of personal allegory into his own poem.

In the Prologue of the *Legend of Good Women* (F, ll. 366-67) Chaucer hints that he wrote the *Troilus* at the behest of some powerful personage. The powerful personage with whom Chaucer was most intimately associated for many years was, of course, John of Gaunt. Accordingly, when Chaucer hints that he was doing the bidding of some powerful personage, we think immediately of Gaunt.

Obviously, this is only a guess. But the guess seems strengthened by evidence from one of the earliest manuscripts of the poem—the one known as Corpus Christi College, Cambridge, MS. 61.[8] This manuscript was evidently planned as a superb treasure of art and literature. Most significantly, it was owned by the Countess of Westmoreland, granddaughter of John of Gaunt and Katharine Swynford. Brusendorff surmises that the Countess "had the Corpus Christi MS. transcribed from a family copy of Chaucer's *Troilus*"; and he adds that "the lavish execution, regardless of cost, makes it unlikely that the original was a presentation copy from the poet to John of Gaunt; rather it was ordered from a firm of publishing copyists by the Duke himself."[9] In any event, it seems likely that John of Gaunt and his granddaughter through Katharine Swynford had a very special interest in this poem. Moreover, it has recently been shown that, in all probability, the famous illumination serving as frontispiece of the Corpus Christi MS portrays certain personages prominent in the life of Gaunt—including Gaunt himself and Katharine.[10]

Evidence of the Beaufort family's interest in the poem calls to mind a real-life situation within that family which overpoweringly suggests the situation in the poem. I refer to the love of a king's younger son for a young widow beneath him in rank. The situation in the poem is a perfect replica of the liaison between Gaunt and Katharine—a king's younger son in love with a young widow beneath him in rank. This unique parallel between the fictional situation and the real-life situation is almost enough, of itself, to suggest that Troilus and Criseyde may represent Gaunt and Katharine. It would have been strange indeed if Chaucer and his contemporaries had not thought instantly of the parallel.

Criseyde's unfaithfulness to Troilus does not, so far as our ignorance permits us to say, belong to the history of the Gaunt-Katharine liaison. Nevertheless, it is likely—if human nature in the fourteenth century was like human nature today—that Gaunt and Katharine quarreled on occasion, and separated. As a matter of fact, it is of record that Gaunt and Katharine did separate temporarily in 1381;[11] and she bore him no more children after 1379, though she was only twenty-nine years old at that time. If, indeed, she did separate from Gaunt in 1381, it is possible (and human) that she would have gone to Europe to visit her father, or perhaps to take possession of property left her there on her father's death. (As I have said previously, it is known that she did have property in Hainault.)   A trip to see her father could actually have been opposed by Gaunt, and could have been the basis of the episode in which Chaucer's Criseyde deserts her lover to go to her father in the foreign camp.

All this is speculation, however, and is really somewhat beside the point.   A good writer seldom forces his allegories to fit actual fact down to the last detail; and medieval writers were notoriously inconsistent in such matters.   Even Boccaccio, having said that *Il Filostrato* symbolizes real-life characters and incidents, explains that other matters unsanctioned by reality are included "only because the story of the noble young lover requireth it."[12]   Chaucer too says that he refrains from speaking of Criseyde's unfaithfulness "Further than the storye wol devyse" (V, 1094).

I have already mentioned Chesterton's remark about "the charity of Chaucer toward Cressida"; and Tatlock comments on the same characteristic of the poem.   He says that Chaucer, having spent as much time as possible on the love affair itself, "can no longer defer what must happen in the familiar story."   Criseyde "had to do just as her original had done."   But Chaucer himself "has not the heart to watch the steps of her decline."[13]   He finishes off the story hastily and with little originality.

In short, if Chaucer's poem is actually an allegory of the liaison between John and Katharine, Criseyde's unfaithfulness does not necessarily reflect a similar unfaithfulness of Katharine.   This unpleasant part of the story may be forced on a reluctant Chaucer by his "auctor," or by "the dramatic necessities of the action,"[14] or by some literary convention.[15]   Chaucer's paramount interest is, quite clearly, the love affair itself, and not its decline.   When, for whatever reason, he is compelled to present Criseyde unfavorably, he apologizes for her:

> Ne me ne list this sely womman chyde,
> Forther than the storye wol devyse.
> Hire name, allas! is punysshed so wide,
> That for hire gilt it oughte ynough suffise.
> And if I myghte excuse hire any wise,
> For she so sory was for hire untrouthe,
> Iwis, I wolde excuse hire yet for routhe.   (V, 1093-99)

As will be shown in the Appendix, it is likely that Chaucer read only the first three books of his poem to the court; the two last books, showing Criseyde's unfaithfulness, he may have finished privately (and reluctantly) only because he, like Boccaccio, felt that the story required it.

Chaucer's extreme care to portray Criseyde as favorably as possible is most peculiar. Why should he hesitate to condemn a traitress in love—especially at a period when treachery in love was an unforgivable sin in romance—if the traitress were only another fictional character? Chaucer's delicacy here can be explained only if we assume that Criseyde had some real-life original whom the poet wished to defend. If this original *was* Katharine, Chaucer's kindness toward Criseyde would be entirely understandable. Otherwise, it remains a mystery.

Specific evidence

Boccaccio says plainly that his Cressida had neither son nor daughter.[16] But Chaucer, who could have avoided complications by going along with Boccaccio, states carefully:

> But wheither that she children hadde or noon,
> I rede it naught, therefore I late it goon. (I, 132-33)

There must have been a reason for this singular alteration of Boccaccio. Was the reason the fact that Katharine Swynford was the mother of a son and a daughter by Hugh Swynford when the affair with Gaunt commenced—and that Chaucer did not feel that it would be either realistic or diplomatic to deny the existence of these children? It is a seemingly trivial change; but, in the 1380's, it would have been a key to the allegory.

An extremely interesting departure from Boccaccio involves Hector. In *Il Filostrato* Hector appears in two stanzas (I, st. 13-14) as Cressida's protector, and thereafter is mentioned only half a dozen times, and then very casually. Chaucer, however, not only includes Boccaccio's references to Hector (often in elaborated version), but mentions Hector more than twenty times, and goes out of his way to insert laudatory comments about Hector that do not appear in Boccaccio or in any other source of this particular story.

Boccaccio has Pandaro tell Cressida: "I do not believe that [God] ever put a *more perfect soul in anyone* than in the soul of him who loveth thee.... He is lofty in soul and speech, very virtuous, and jealous of honor, wise in natural sense *beyond any other*, and *without a superior* in knowledge.... I do not believe that there is in the world *any man more worthy*...."[17] Nowhere does Boccaccio suggest that Troilo is the inferior of Hector, or of anybody else.

Chaucer, on the other hand, forces Hector into the picture, ranks him unmistakably the first among men, and declares repeatedly that Troilus is only "Ector the secounde" (II, 158), or just below Hector in worthiness:

> Of Ector nedeth namore for to telle:
> In al this world ther nys a bettre knyght
> Than he, that is of worthynesse welle. (II, 176-78)
>
> For out and out he [Troilus] is the worthieste,
> Save only Ector, which that is the beste. (II, 739-40)
>
> He [Troilus] was, and ay, the first in armes dyght,
> And certeynly, but if that bokes erre,
> Save Ector most ydred of any wight. (III, 1773-75)
>
> As he [Troilus] that was withouten any peere,
> Save Ector, in his tyme, as I kan heere. (V, 1803-4)

The fact that all this praise of Hector is quite without authority in Boccaccio makes us suspect that Chaucer was being especially cautious about not claiming too much for Troilus. What was the reason for this caution, this obvious eagerness to exalt Hector above the real hero of the story? The answer to the question may lie within the contemporary political situation.

It seems clear that, if Troilus does stand for John of Gaunt, Hector, King Priam's oldest son, must stand for Gaunt's older brother, Edward Prince of Wales (the Black Prince), who was idolized in England when the Gaunt-Katharine affair commenced, and whose memory was worshiped long afterward. Moreover, in the 1380's, when Chaucer's poem was probably written, a very large number of Englishmen suspected that John was plotting to seize the throne from the late Black Prince's son, the little Richard II. Under the circumstances, any suggestion by Chaucer that Troilus (Gaunt?) was in any way superior to Hector (Edward?) would have amounted, in that touchy time, to virtual treason. It would have been dangerous, if not fatal, to Chaucer, and almost equally dangerous to Gaunt.

All this may not actually prove that Hector stands for Prince Edward; but it is the only reasonable explanation that presents itself for Chaucer's very remarkable divergences from Boccaccio in this matter.

One of Chaucer's most notable inventions, about which there has been a great deal of scholarly speculation, is the entirely original passage in which the eagle seizes Criseyde's heart out of her breast, and leaves his own in return (II, 925-31). Perhaps we may explain this passage if we remember that the poem was written in an age when heraldic symbolism carried a vital meaning and importance to everybody.*

In at least one poem (*Book of the Duchess*, l. 1319) and probably in another (*The Complaint of Mars*, l. 9; see preceding chapter), Chaucer alludes symbolically to John of Gaunt as "Saint John." Now, the traditional symbol, used regularly in medieval sculpture and painting, of Saint John the Evangelist was an eagle.[18] Furthermore, "Edward III used an eagle as an extra crest, and passed it on to John of Gaunt, from whom, through the Beauforts, it descended."[19] But the Beauforts, it will be remembered, were Gaunt's descendants through none other than Katharine Swynford. Actually, the eagle seems to have been commonly recognized by contemporary writers as a symbol of John himself. Thus Gower refers to Henry Bolingbroke as "aquile pullus"[20] ("offspring of the eagle"), and Adam Usk likewise calls Henry "pullus aquile, quia filius Iohannis."[21] (It may be worth noting that the canopy of Henry's tomb "is powdered with Eagles volant, Crowned, within the Garter."[22])

In a word, this gratuitous episode in the poem, wherein a widely recognized symbol of John of Gaunt is linked with Criseyde, can hardly have been an unpremeditated outburst by Chaucer. If it has significance (and undoubtedly it does), the significance probably lies within the heraldic implications of the eagle.

In a passage original with him (II, 666-79) Chaucer defends Criseyde against the "envious jangle" that she fell in love with Troilus too lightly and too soon. He returns to this topic later on (II, 1291-98), and has Criseyde argue that it is "ek to soone" for her to love Troilus, and has Pandarus grumble that "this nyce opynyoun / Shal nought be holden fully yeres two" (II, 1297-98).

---

* Witness the tremendous furor of the Scrope-Grosvenor controversy, a national *cause célèbre* that dragged on for years, wherein the only point at issue was which of two families had a right to bear a certain not-very-distinguished coat of arms, and John of Gaunt's bitter feud with the City of London because certain rioters had reversed Gaunt's arms hanging before a building in a London street.

Apparently Chaucer felt that he had to defend Criseyde against charges that she fell in love with Troilus too soon after being widowed. It has been argued that Chaucer, in so defending her, was merely deferring to a convention of courtly love demanding long resistance by the lady. If Criseyde, however, was only a fictional character, Chaucer could easily have pictured her holding out the required time, thus making his elaborate apologies superfluous.

But if she really stands for Katharine, reasons why he showed her yielding soon, and therefore needing defense and apology, become immediately apparent. Gaunt returned to England with a new Spanish wife late in 1371. This wife (chosen for dynastic reasons only) was a morbidly religious, unattractive girl with a single-minded devotion to the memory of her murdered father. Sir Hugh Swynford, Katharine's husband, had been killed in France in November, 1371. Now Gaunt's grants of cash, pensions, and lands to Katharine show a sudden and marked increase in early May, 1372.[23] Probably, therefore, the liaison between them began about then. (Chaucer has the Troilus-Criseyde affair begin in April—I, 155-56.) But if the real-life liaison began in April-May, 1372, there must have been a great deal of unfavorable gossip about Katharine's taking a new lover so quickly after her husband's death. Chaucer's wish to defend Katharine from the gossip would perfectly explain his eager and otherwise perplexing defense of Criseyde for her quick capitulation. His motive here is exactly the same as it was in the *Complaint of Mars*, as that poem has been explained in the preceding chapter. The court gossiped about Gaunt and Katharine; Gaunt did not like the gossip; and Chaucer tried to defend the lovers.

A famous passage, entirely original with Chaucer, in which the poet defends Troilus' love occurs in Book I, ll. 232-59. Having told of Troilus' overwhelming love, Chaucer takes time out to lecture those "wise, proude, and worthi folkes" who scorn love—exactly as Mars (Gaunt?) pleads with all hardy knights and loyal ladies, in the *Complaint of Mars*, to show sympathy for his love. In the *Troilus* Chaucer reminds his hearers that love makes good men better still, and that it is well known that the wisest and strongest men are the greatest lovers. He repeats his conception of the ennobling power of love in Antigone's song (II, 855-61) and Troilus' song (III, 1744-71)—all of it a restatement of what he had said in the *Complaint of Mars* (ll. 263-98).

If we remember that contemporary opinion, worldly and clerical, in the court and in the City, condemned Gaunt for his long and open devotion to Katharine, we may see in all the passages just cited a meaning extraordinarily rich and appropriate. They constitute not only a poetic defense of love, but a poet's brilliant defense of a friend against public criticism.

The same purpose may inspire the lines (also original with Chaucer) near the beginning of the poem (I, 38-52), in which compassion is asked for lovers that "falsely be apeired [injured] / Thorugh wikked tonges, be it he or she." The only conceivable reason why Chaucer would take it on himself to defend his fictional lovers from gossip and slander is that they must represent real persons who have been victims of gossip and slander. Whether these real persons were Gaunt and Katharine we cannot say for certain; but it would be consistent with everything else in the poem if they did represent those two.

In a very important departure from Boccaccio, Chaucer pictures Troilus as never having been in love previously. One reason for this departure may have been Chaucer's desire to defend Troilus himself against the slander of light and hasty love. Furthermore, if Troilus does stand for Gaunt, Chaucer could not possibly have followed Boccaccio in having Troilo regard his former love as a "great folly" and "an accursed fire." To have done so would have damned both the dead Blanche and the living Constance (and, possibly, Philippa Chaucer also). If Troilus is Gaunt, Chaucer did the only discreet thing: he simply ignored Gaunt's former loves. Again, this does not prove that Troilus represents Gaunt, but it is one more item neatly consistent with that hypothesis, and hard to explain otherwise.

Chaucer invents entire the long episode in which Pandarus persuades Deiphebus to help defend Criseyde from her creditors (II, 1414 ff.), the dinner at Deiphebus' house (II, 1555 ff.), and Troilus' singular confession that he loves Deiphebus best of all his brothers (II, 1396-98). If there was a historical parallel (in Katharine's life) for the dinner, no one would be likely to know about it now. That the young widow Katharine must have been harried by creditors— in an age when widows and orphans were considered a legitimate source of income, even by Chaucer himself—is certain. But Troilus' special love for Deiphebus needs explaining.

John of Gaunt had four brothers. Lionel died in 1368, before the affair with Katharine commenced; the Black Prince and Gaunt were on friendly and mutually respectful, but not intimate, terms;

Thomas, later Duke of Gloucester, was a brutal, violent man very different from the polished and politic Gaunt. This leaves only Prince Edmund. He was an easy-going man who always remained friends with Gaunt, aided him in his ambitious continental enterprises, and married the sister of Gaunt's wife Constance. If Troilus represents Gaunt, and Hector the Black Prince, then Deiphebus must represent Edmund; and Chaucer's having Troilus declare that he loves Deiphebus best of all his brothers becomes natural and understandable. Without some such explanation, Chaucer's reason for having Troilus express a preference among his brothers is quite unaccountable.

In describing the lovers (V, 806-40) Chaucer creates a composite made up of phrases drawn from many sources (Joseph of Exeter, Dares, Benoit, Guido, and even Boccaccio). It would seem reasonable that he drew from many sources, instead of merely copying from one source, because he had in mind two precisely visualized images of the persons he was describing: not just any generalized picture would do. Once more, nothing can be actually proved; but this detail fits perfectly into the hypothesis that Chaucer modeled his characters on actual persons with whose appearances he was familiar.

We do not know enough about Katharine to judge whether Chaucer's description of Criseyde fits the real woman. But perhaps his comment, "trewely, I kan nat telle hire age" (V, 826) would have been necessary, or discreet, only if he had been speaking of a real woman; he could have given a fictional woman any age he pleased.

The description of Troilus fits John of Gaunt perfectly. Gaunt was a typical Plantagenet—tall, fair, and handsome; and Fernão Lopes, describing John at about the age of fifty, pictures a "well-formed man, tall and erect, with not so much flesh as his height required."[24] This tallies well with Chaucer's picture of the young Troilus:

> And Troilus wel woxen was in highte,
> And complet formed by proporcioun
> So wel that kynde it nought amenden myghte;
> Yong, fressh, strong, and hardy as a lyoun.   (V, 827-30)

Gaunt's biographer, Armitage-Smith, speaks of him as a man "whose conversation was reserved and had something of what with an enemy would pass for haughtiness and with a friend for dignity."[25] This description is reflected perfectly in Chaucer's own praise about Troilus: "His heighe port and his manere estraunge" (I, 1084). On the other hand, when love transformed him, Troilus became the "frendlieste man / Of gret estat, that evere I saugh my lyve" (II, 204-05), gentle, generous, brave, provident, chivalrous (I, 1070-85).

The only item in Troilus' character that seems not to fit the usual conception of Gaunt is Troilus' early scorn of love. On the other hand, Gaunt's reputation for amorousness seems to have been largely due to the Katharine affair itself. And I have already shown that, if Troilus does represent Gaunt, Chaucer was virtually compelled by circumstances to ignore the young man's earlier loves.

More than half of Chaucer's alterations of and additions to *Il Filostrato* in his own poem serve to make Pandarus a more prominent figure. The tendency of older scholarship, with its roots in Victorianism and its values colored by the unsavory connotations of the modern word *pander*, was to regard the role of Pandarus as "one of infamy and dishonor."[26] But modern scholarship leans more to the opinion that "Chaucer intended Pandarus's role as intermediary, uncle, and friend to be ideal, and wholly commendable."[27] He is neither a villain nor a mere piece of machinery necessary for the plot. As Coghill has said, "Pandarus is Chaucer's first creation of a piece of actuality...the first grown-up in English, the first worldling, the first figure of *Canterbury Tales* dimension.... He is on a Shakespearian scale."[28] With acute discernment, Coghill goes on to say that Pandarus "seems to offer a speaking portrait of his own creator, Geoffrey Chaucer.... Perhaps this partial self-portraiture was entirely unconscious, but it is striking and may well be a reason why Pandarus is so lively and lovable."[29]

Indeed, if Troilus stands for John of Gaunt, and Criseyde for Katharine Swynford, Pandarus can hardly stand for anyone else but Geoffrey Chaucer. Even the mere factual alterations that Chaucer makes in Boccaccio's Pandaro bring the character into close conformity with the Chaucer-Katharine relationship. By making him an uncle instead of a cousin of Criseyde, Chaucer gives Pandarus a right to be something of a guardian and elder adviser of the young widow. At the same time, however, he keeps Pandarus young enough[30] to be adventurous, unconventional, and somewhat sensual.

This rather peculiar pattern of relative ages, deliberately altered from Boccaccio, fits the peculiar circumstances in the age relationships of John, Katharine, and Chaucer. Gaunt and Chaucer were about the same age—Gaunt was born in 1340, and Chaucer in or near that year (see first chapter of this book); and Troilus and Pandarus are about the same age.[31] Yet Pandarus was clearly older than Criseyde, just as Chaucer was about ten years older than Katharine. In contrast, in Boccaccio all three are about the same age. When the Gaunt-Katharine affair commenced, in 1372, John and Chaucer were a little over thirty years old, and Katharine was a bit over twenty. ("Personally," says Kirby, "I am sure Pandarus is still in his early thirties."[32]) That is, Chaucer was just the right age to be (like Pandarus) an elder relative of Katharine, but not so old as to be sedate and conventional. In other words, Chaucer's alterations in the relationship and the relative ages of Pandarus and Criseyde make the situation fit the Chaucer-Katharine situation with amazing neatness.

As Coghill says, Pandarus startlingly resembles the Chaucer whom we know. Pandarus is a man of proverbs—and so was Chaucer. Pandarus was something of a diplomat and "fixer"—and so, apparently, was Chaucer in his various official missions, and perhaps in his work as controller of customs. Pandarus is a familiar in the royal court—and so was Chaucer for years. Pandarus is well acquainted with at least two royal princes—and Chaucer was well acquainted with at least Prince Lionel and Prince John. Pandarus is something of a practical philosopher—and so was Chaucer. Pandarus has humor, sophistication, and shrewd understanding of human nature—and so had Chaucer. Pandarus is a man deprived of happiness in love[33]—and Chaucer frequently professed himself (even in this very poem) to be one whom love has passed by.[34]

Pandarus is an amateur astrologer (II, 74-77); Boccaccio's Pandaro is not. Yet Chaucer's interest in astrology is well known.

Pandarus gives Troilus some pointers on the art of writing, and is evidently an expert in the field (II, 1023-43); Boccaccio's Pandaro has no such literary talents. Thus Chaucer's Pandarus resembles still more the father of English literature.

In talking with Criseyde, Pandarus banters with her, and tells his "beste japes" till "she for laughter wende for to dye" (II, 1167-69). Boccaccio's Pandaro is no such jester. Thus again Chaucer has made Pandarus resemble the greatest humorist in English literature.

These resemblances between Pandarus and Chaucer are so abundant, so apt, and so peculiar that it is virtually impossible to regard them as merely coincidental. Nor should we be surprised that Chaucer introduces himself into a poem: he did it often—in the *Book of the Duchess*, the *House of Fame*, the *Parliament of Fowls*, the *Legend of Good Women*, and the *Canterbury Tales*.

So far, I have discussed the *Troilus* in relation to historical fact only; but now I wish to mention one literary relationship that has a bearing on the problem.

That Dante had a considerable influence on Chaucer is well known. Clark writes: "A cursory survey of the notes in Robinson's edition produces references to at least eight very probable or certain instances of the direct influence of the *Divine Comedy* on *Troilus and Criseyde* (*outside* the epilogue), and at least eighteen further very possible ones."[35] Clark goes on to the conclusion that "almost every detail of the epilogue of *Troilus and Criseyde*" could have been suggested to Chaucer by a reading or a recollection of *Paradiso* XIV and XXII.[36] Reading on a little farther in the *Paradiso* reveals, however, an even closer relationship to Chaucer's epilogue, as well as to the passage in Boccaccio's *Teseida* (XI, st. 1-3) from which it has been usually assumed that Chaucer took the materials for his epilogue.

The epilogue describes Troilus' spirit mounting to the eighth heavenly sphere,[37] and looking down on the earth and his own body. After this description, Chaucer finishes the poem with two stanzas contrasting heavenly and earthly love. All this irresistibly suggests the last twenty lines of *Paradiso* XXV, and the first sixty-six of *Paradiso* XXVI. In these lines Dante pictures himself mounting to the eighth heavenly sphere, meeting Saint John (called here *aguglia di Cristo*, "Christ's eagle"), hearing Saint John explain how his (John's) body now lies on earth, listening to John's brief sermon on heavenly love, and himself contrasting this heavenly love with earthly love.

It seems to me beyond question that this part of the *Paradiso* influenced the epilogue of the *Troilus*, and thus inevitably associates Troilus with Saint John. But in at least one, and probably three, other poems[38] by Chaucer the name of Saint John is used to help identify John of Gaunt. The epilogue is, therefore, probably an important key by which the real-life original of Troilus may be identified. The eighth sphere, the eagle, the body on earth and the spirit in heaven, the discourse on earthly and heavenly love, and the name of John cannot all be merely accidental.

Chaucer's motivation

What were the probable motives for Chaucer's writing a poem like this about John and Katharine?

One motive, of course, would be flattery of Gaunt, Chaucer's long-time friend and benefactor.

Another would be (if Chaucer really did have a part in bringing Gaunt and Katharine together) a desire that Gaunt should not forget who had been indispensable in the match-making.

A third would be to defend Gaunt against critics of his affair with Katharine.

A fourth would be to excuse Katharine (if she really ever left Gaunt) for her temporary defection—by showing that, after all, she was only a weak and bewildered woman, "slydynge of corage" (V, 825).

And a final motive (to be noted in fuller detail in the Appendix of this book) was to keep reminding Gaunt that he was honor-bound to Katharine. Once we start noticing it, Chaucer's insistence on the honorable obligation of Troilus to Criseyde seems to leap from almost every page of the poem. Reasons for this insistence are not hard to imagine.

Between 1380 and 1386 (a period to which the writing of the *Troilus* is usually assigned) Gaunt was moving heaven and earth in an attempt to create an expeditionary force that he could lead to Spain in an effort to seize the Spanish throne. It must have been obvious to Chaucer that Gaunt could not risk offending Spanish proprieties by taking along with him his well-known mistress—in case Gaunt did manage to get away to Spain. Katharine would simply have to be left in England. Moreover, if Gaunt succeeded in his undertaking, and really became King of Spain, he would doubtless remain there for life, and never return to Katharine. He had to make a choice between a crown and Katharine—a dilemma worthy of the protagonist of a heroic tragedy. But from Chaucer's point of view, the tragedy lay in the fact that the chief support and mainstay of Katharine, Philippa Chaucer, and Geoffrey himself would be withdrawn. The outlook for all three of them, with Gaunt out of England, might become desperate. Only Gaunt's sense of honorable obligation to Katharine stood between them and possible disaster.

The fear that Gaunt's wall of honor might crumble seems to have been almost an obsession with Chaucer. In the *Troilus* he anxiously reiterates, over and over, the high honorableness of the relations between Troilus and his mistress. If Troilus does represent Gaunt, Chaucer has no intention of allowing the Duke (always sensitive to the demands of chivalric honor) to forget that he is honor bound to Katharine. Chaucer's insistence on this point sometimes seems almost morbid. And not only in the *Troilus*, but in many other poems as well (*Anelida and Arcite*, the *Legend of Good Women*, the first book of the *House of Fame*, the "Squire's Tale," the "Wife of Bath's Tale," the "Clerk's Tale") he betrays his anxiety about women cast off by their husbands or lovers. He seems to be waging a one-man campaign in the English court against any man who would forget his honorable obligation to his mistress. Doubtless Chaucer's own sense of honor, chivalry, and pity inspired this campaign; but it must have been reinforced by an acute sense that Gaunt's desertion of Katharine would leave Chaucer and his family in a very uncomfortable, not to say dangerous, situation.

Certainly, I do not mean to say that Chaucer wrote the *Troilus* merely to remind Gaunt of his obligations to Katharine. People seldom do anything for only one reason. No doubt Chaucer was moved by a pure creative impulse to write his poem. But the creative impulse must have some subject to work with—and the subject of the love between Troilus and Criseyde was attractive not only as a romantic story, but also as a device by means of which the poet could flatter Gaunt, picture Katharine and himself favorably, memorialize in verse a great romantic love affair of the century, and influence Gaunt not to desert Katharine. Chaucer, it must be remembered, was not only a poet, but also an astute courtier who knew how to make his way in the world.

* * *

In this chapter I have suggested only the main outlines of the proposition that *Troilus and Criseyde* is a fictional, or allegorical, version of the love affair between John of Gaunt and Katharine Swynford. Of course (it hardly needs saying) the poem is much besides. Nevertheless, in its main characters and in its essential narrative plot it seems to be a personal allegory. I have not included *all* the evidence for this proposition. To have done so would have made the chapter unwieldy and incoherent. But in an Appendix to this book I have collected a very large number of details that seem to substantiate what is suggested by the relatively few details presented here.

Chapter V. The *Parliament of Fowls* — a three-part mystery

ew of Chaucer's shorter pieces have given rise to so extensive and controversial comment as has the *Parlement of Foules*."[1] In the article just quoted, Professor Lumiansky did a service to all Chaucerians by summarizing the interpretations of the poem, "with pertinent bibliographic references," that had been offered until the time of his writing, in 1948. Instead of duplicating Lumiansky's work, I shall merely summarize his summary, and add comments ("with pertinent bibliographic references") to the interpretations that have appeared since 1948.

Until about thirty years ago, the *Parliament* was, as Lumiansky says, "almost invariably termed inartistic because of lack of unity." The poem consists of an introduction (ll. 1-28), and three parts as follows: (*1*) a summary of Cicero's *Somnium Scipionis*, as edited by Macrobius; (2) a tour through the Garden of Love and the Temple of Venus; and (*3*) a dispute among a group (a parliament) of birds as to which of three male eagles a lovely female eagle should take as her mate.

Until quite recently, most commentators have felt that the eagles in the third part represent certain historical personages, and that the other birds disputing together represent certain contemporary social classes or intellectual attitudes. These commentators have occupied themselves chiefly with speculations as to the real-life originals of the allegorical eagles. Among those who have approached the poem from this angle, Lumiansky mentions Tyrwhitt (1775), Koch (1877, 1879, 1890, 1921), Emerson (1910, 1911), Moore (1911), Lange (1916), Rickert (1920-21), Reid (1923), Douglas (1928), Patrick (1930), Langhans (1930), and Braddy (1931, 1932, 1933). But, as Lumiansky points out, the identifications offered have been widely divergent, filled with admitted inconsistencies, and never satisfying to many Chaucerians. As a result, no doubt, of the general failure of this approach, attempts to explain the historical or personal allegory have died down of late, and there has developed a strong tendency to deny that a personal allegory exists—and that if it does, it is no concern of the critic.

A second group of critics have regarded the poem all along as hardly more than a conventional genre poem celebrating St. Valentine's Day (Manly, 1913, 1935; Langhans, 1918), or depicting a love-debate of a kind familiar in folklore (Farnham, 1917, 1918, 1920; Brewer, 1958[2]).

A final type of criticism, and that the most recent, has turned away from the historical method, and has attempted to discover an intellectual or an aesthetic unity in the three parts of the work (Bronson, 1935; Goffin, 1936; Lumiansky, 1948; Stillwell, 1950;[3] Owen, 1953;[4] Bethurum, 1955;[5] Emslie, 1955;[6] McDonald, 1955;[7] Frank, 1956;[8] Bennett, 1957[9]). Bronson sees a humorously ironic attitude toward love as pervading the poem; Goffin sees the poem as an exposition of the nature of heavenly love and earthly bliss; Lumiansky sees it as an account of "Chaucer's unsuccessful search for a way of reconciling true and false felicity"; Stillwell, sharing the attitudes of the preceding group, regards the poem as "a comedy of medieval manners and ideas adapted to the framework of the love-vision"; Owen says that it represents "the victory of impulse and passion, frustrated though they be, over the idealism suggested by" the poet's reading; Bethurum believes that the poem's theme is "specifically courtly love," and that its unifying principle is the "medieval tolerance for encyclopaedic works" that to moderns would seem incoherent; Emslie believes that "the poem gives us a brief epitome of the courtly love code" and demonstrates dramatically how this bookish, unnatural code "is related to certain levels of society"; McDonald thinks that its unity consists in its exhibiting "an entire spectrum of varying types of love experience which the poet is trying to define and analyze"; Frank finds that the very disharmony of the poem's three parts was "deliberately intended by Chaucer" so as to make the conflicting attitudes toward love "look slightly ridiculous" by being juxtaposed; Bennett (if I understand him correctly) argues that in the poem Chaucer presents a "synthesis" of medieval "love-doctrine" by means of a technique that "shows a synthesis of modes" (pp. 13-14).

Clearly we have not only a problem that is tremendously complex, but also one that lends itself to a very wide range of critical speculation. If the following study is also complex and speculative (but in a very different way, I hope), the reader need not be surprised.

Disunity in the poem

Two kinds of disunity are recognizable in the world. One may be called the disunity of *difference*, and the other the disunity of *discord*. The first involves the lumping together of items that are merely unlike; the other involves the lumping together of items that actually clash or conflict with one another. As a medieval artist, Chaucer did not mind, it seems, indulging in the first type of disunity—witness the "Squire's Tale," the "Monk's Tale," the *Legend of Good Women*, the intrusion of the Ceyx and Alcione story into the *Book of the Duchess*, the medley of themes in the *House of Fame*, and the three different parts of the *Parliament of Fowls*. But the second kind of disunity—the one involving inner discrepancies, contradictions, incongruities, and inconsistencies—is not what any artist would deliberately plan.

Recent criticism, starting with the premise that Chaucer can do no wrong even according to contemporary critical standards, has devoted itself to demonstrating that unity actually does exist in the *Parliament of Fowls*. In the present study, however, the unregenerate position adopted is that the older scholars were right, and that the poem does possess a fundamental disunity, of both the first and the second types just mentioned.

Disunity of sources] The sources of the three parts of the poem (the dream of Scipio, the Love Garden, and the true Parliament of Birds) are different and exclusive; that is, no overlapping of sources is apparent from part to part.

The first part is a free translation and summary, with certain omissions, of Macrobius' version of Cicero's *Somnium Scipionis*.

The transitional stanzas (ll. 85-112) between this part and the poet's dream of the Love Garden are said (by Robinson, Brewer, and others) to contain echoes of Dante. And certainly the account (ll. 120-75) of the guide leading the poet to the gate of the Love Garden, and the description of the gate itself, are obviously influenced by Dante.

The second part of the poem, the Love Garden, is a rather close translation of a portion of Boccaccio's *Teseida*.

The third section, however, shows no trace of Italian influence. It is largely original, though it shows some dependence on the Frenchman Alanus de Insulis, and on a limited number of well-known folktales, as well as ordinary folklore and proverbial lore that were the common property of the age. The general spirit and tone of this section are those of the courtly and romantic French poems that influenced Chaucer's early work. As a matter of fact, Chaucer concludes this part of the poem with a French roundel, which, he says in so many words, "imaked was in Fraunce" (l. 677).

The stanzaic form of the entire poem is French, Guillaume de Machaut in particular having made extensive use of the form. (Chaucer may have met and associated with Machaut at a very early and impressionable period in the English poet's life.[10]) The form appears in some of Chaucer's early love poems, and it is an easy simplification of the stanza of the very early "An A B C."

Disunity of dates] Since Macrobius was known to Chaucer as early, at least, as the *Book of the Duchess* (ll. 284 ff.), and probably much earlier (the work being a standard moral treatise of the century), not much can be determined from this quarter concerning the date of the first part of the *Parliament of Fowls*. Brewer, however, may have a point worth considering. He writes that "a mistake in the *House of Fame* about 'King Cipioun', who was not a king, points to the *House of Fame* being earlier than the *Parlement*, where 'Cipioun' is properly understood."[11] Though this can hardly be considered absolute proof, it suggests that the first part of the *Parliament* was written relatively late in Chaucer's career.

The transitional stanzas between the first part and the Love Garden part, as well as the introduction to the Love Garden, being influenced by Dante, were almost certainly written after Chaucer's return from his first trip to Italy, which occurred in 1373, and probably after his second trip, in 1378.

The same thing is true of the second part of the poem, the Love Garden. As a translation from Boccaccio, it must date from after the first Italian visit; and since Chaucer was busy with the *Teseida*, for the sake of his tale of Palamon and Arcite, in the late 1370's or early 1380's, this part of the *Parliament* was probably written within a year or so of 1380.

The third section, however, is entirely French in source, style, and mood. If scholars were in possession of this third part only, they could not do otherwise than place it among Chaucer's early works, as an excellent example of the sort of thing he was writing in his "French period."

In short, evidence from sources, as well as from style and mood and comparison with other works, suggests that the first part of the *Parliament* may have been written rather late in Chaucer's career. The second part, the Love Garden, was probably written not far from 1380. The third part was written before Chaucer first went to Italy. This conclusion about different times of composition for the three parts is consistent with what we know (and what was mentioned in the first chapter of this book) about Chaucer's habit of subjecting many of his works to major alterations, excisions, additions, and adaptations.* It is consistent, moreover, with what will be pointed out immediately concerning the structural disunity and disjunctions within the *Parliament*.

Structural disunity] From a mere Johnsonian, common-sense angle, anyone can see that, as R. W. Frank (himself a "unifier") has said, "Each part of the poem differs from the others in its sources, content, mode of treatment, and tone."[12] The first part is a serious, somber, religious, moral, consolation-for-death poem; the second is a luscious, sensuous, almost sensual description; and the third is a broadly satirical, half-humorous and half-courtly, dramatically handled story of a love-dispute. If these three elements had come down to us in three separate manuscripts, nobody could possibly believe that the two last belong together, or that the last has any relation to the first; and the only connection between the first and the second is the use of the name "Affrican" (Scipio) at the very beginning of the second part.

Moreover, the extreme disagreements among the many different unifiers raises the suspicion that the poem's unity is an individual creation of each critic, and not of Chaucer himself. It would be difficult to believe that Chaucer could have written *that* obscurely.

Finally, certain specific details in the poem itself suggest that it is a composite made up of a complete poem and two fragments (or of two complete poems and one fragment) that were written separately, at different times, and later united into the poem we know. An examination of some of these details follows.

1] After a short proem (ll. 1-28), the first part of the *Parliament*, extending through ll. 29-112, consists of a synopsis (with much of the original omitted) of the *Somnium Scipionis*, and a transitional

* See also the discussion of the "Epilogue" of *Troilus and Criseyde* in the Appendix of this book.

introduction (ll. 85-112) to a dream of the poet that is to be narrated. In this transitional passage we may note a kind of loose-gripped fumbling that suggests a major break in the continuity. In l. 93 the poet writes that he was "For wery of my labour al the day"; and in l. 112 he mentions the "labour" of reading the "olde bok"— yet, in l. 27, he has spoken not of weariness and labor, but of delight: "To rede forth hit gan me so delite." In l. 89 he says that he is "Fulfyld of thought and busy hevynesse"—but in l. 28 he has said that "al that day me thoughte but a lyte."

In ll. 95-98 he explains that

> in my slep I mette, as that I lay,
> How Affrican. . .
> Was come and stod right at my beddes syde.

And eight lines farther on he absently repeats the same information: that "Affrican . . . made me to mete that he stod there" (ll. 107-8).

This passage plainly states that Scipio "made me to mete"; but l. 115 directly contradicts the preceding by having it that Venus "madest me this sweven for to mete." Furthermore, an entire stanza invoking Venus is here inserted as a sudden interpolation without (as Bronson shows[13]) any pertinence to what has gone before or comes after.

Finally, this very stanza indicates as clearly as possible that Chaucer has written the poem at two different times:

> As wisly as I sey the north-north-west,
> Whan I began my sweven for to write,
> So yif me myght to ryme and ek t'endyte!   (117-19)

What Chaucer is saying here is this: "As surely as I saw thee in the north-northwest when I first began to write of my dream, so give me power to write the rhymes that I am now about to compose." Two dates of composition are clearly implied.

2] Leaving the first part of the poem, and its transition to the second, or Love Garden, part, we find a very peculiar situation right at the beginning. In the first part, Scipio Africanus the Elder conducts his grandson, in a dream, through heavenly spaces, and speaks to him gravely of death, the soul's immortality, and right-living. In the second part, this same Africanus appears to the poet in a dream, and conducts him to, and into, the gate of the Garden of Love. We observe at once three strange things about this introduction: (*1*) A more unlikely and inappropriate guide than the stoical Publius Cornelius Scipio Africanus the Elder to a world of romantic love and sensual delight can hardly be imagined; (2) this Africanus, who is concerned with romantic love, and jokes with the poet about being too dull to love (1. 162) and too lacking in cunning to write about the love scenes he is to be shown (1. 167), is a completely different personality from the grave and moral Africanus of the first part who deplores the sins of "likerous folk" (1. 79); (*3*) though the Scipio of the dream is called a guide (1. 153), and promises to show the dreamer love topics to write about (1. 168), and leads the dreamer by the hand into the Garden (ll. 169-70), he disappears suddenly, without a word of explanation, and never reappears.

The first two of these peculiarities indicate a clashing disunity, or disjunction, between the first part of the poem and the second; and the third peculiarity suggests a disunity between Chaucer's announced intentions and his actual performance—for nothing suggested by the creation of African as a guide is realized in the poem itself.

The two inscriptions on the gate by which the dreamer entered the Garden of Love bear out the suggestion of unrealized promise just mentioned. On one side of the gate an inscription promised a "blysful place" where "grene and lusty May shal evere endure" (ll. 126, 130); and on the other side, "mortal strokes," "Disdayn and Daunger," and a world where "nevere tre shal fruyt nor leves bere" (ll. 135-37). It would seem, from these two inscriptions, that Chaucer was planning to describe a garden in which both these aspects of love were revealed—as in the *Roman de la Rose*. He does, indeed, describe the Love Garden in its first aspect—sensuously beautiful and romantic, and sensually exciting. But he never gets around to describing the other aspect in any detail. The nearest he comes to it is just fourteen lines before he abandons the Love Garden altogether. Here he turns momentarily to the more unhappy aspects of love—but merely to mention by name certain miserable lovers whose images are painted on a wall. He does not carry out the implied promise of the two inscriptions on the gate.

In connection with viewing the pictures of the miserable lovers, Chaucer makes another promise. He says that these lovers offer "many a story, of which I touche shal / A fewe" (ll. 285-86). But despite this outright promise, he tells no story at all about any of the lovers he has listed. Instead, he drops the whole topic of Love Garden, Venus, miserable lovers, Scipio, and everything else that has occupied him up to his point, and moves on abruptly to something altogether new and different.

3] The third part of the poem, the true Parliament of Birds, just begins—without transition of any kind from the previous part. The dreamer is inspecting the wall paintings in the Temple of Love, when suddenly he says:

> Whan I was come ayeyn into the place
> That I of spak, that was so sote and grene. (295-96)

The rest of the stanza goes on to describe the goddess Nature. But in one of the earliest and best manuscripts (Harleian MS. 733) all of this stanza except the first of the two lines just quoted is omitted, together with the first line of the next stanza.

Abruptly in this new section the reader perceives that he has entered an entirely new world—with new scene, new story, new characters, new tone, new style. Sensuousness gives way to courtly decorum, description to drama, personified abstractions to concrete personages, dreamy atmosphere and langorous tone to crisp dialogue and humorous caricature.

The reader will note also many specific inconsistencies between this part and the preceding—though both are ostensibly continuous elements of the same adventure. The second part occurs in "grene and lusty May" (l. 130); but the third part occurs in February, on "seynt Valentynes day" (l. 309). In the second part, the Garden is pictured as a timeless place where spring "shal evere endure" (l. 130), and where there is always day and never night (ll. 209-10); but the third part ends with the promise of a decision to be made within a year—not within the timeless scheme previously envisioned. In the Love Garden part, the birds are thus described:

> On every bow the bryddes herde I synge,
> With voys of aungel in here armonye. (190-91)

But in the third part the birds are pictured as pressing forward into the presence of the goddess Nature:

> And that so huge a noyse gan they make
> That erthe, and eyr, and tre, and every lake
> So ful was, that unethe was there space
> For me to stonde. (312-15)

One gets the impression here of a huge assemblage of birds noisily crowding on the ground about Nature, with nothing like the beauty and harmony suggested in the previous part. In the Love Garden section the birds bring out their young beside them (l. 192); but in the third part the birds have not yet taken their mates, much less hatched out young. These varying pictures of the birds in the same garden are so inconsistent that it is hard to believe that any poet visualizing his work as a single unit could have included both pictures.

What does all this mean? If we consider together the obvious disunity of subject matter, style, and mood among the three parts of the poem—the sharply etched disunity of sources—the statement in the Cytherea stanza about two periods of composition—the incongruities involved in having Scipio act as guide to the Love Garden—the unrealized promise of the two gate inscriptions—the unrealized promise that the poet will tell stories about unhappy lovers—the self-contradictions in many details from part to part of the poem—the complete disjunction between the second and the third parts—the junction forced (by the use of Scipio as a guide) between the contrasting first and second parts—if we consider all this, the *Parliament of Fowls* seems to be clearly a patchwork of three separate pieces joined together not too skilfully. Moreover, it would seem (if we judge by sources, tone, and manner of writing) that the last part, the true Parliament of Birds, belongs to a considerably earlier period in Chaucer's career than the first two parts.

The last part of the poem

Let us adopt, for the moment, the hypothesis that the last part of the *Parliament* (or at least some version of it that may have undergone subsequent revision) was written before the Italian period. This hypothesis opens the door to brand-new conjectures that have been closed to us because we have so long assumed that the last part, like the middle part, belongs to Chaucer's "Italian period" —that is, the years after 1373 or even after 1378.

Personal allegory] In particular, our new conjectures may center upon the identity of the historical characters who may be represented by the four principal birds in the poem. Until fairly recently it has been assumed that a personal allegory is actually involved in the four birds and their dispute, even though the identity of the persons allegorized has remained a mystery. Lately, however, many critics have adopted a kind of sour-grapes attitude that "an allegorical interpretation seems neither absolutely necessary nor, at present, very probable."[14] On the other hand, certain of the older critics, who may be more historically oriented than the recent critics, believe with Robinson that "The theories of allegory are not unreasonable in themselves, and they find support in the literary practice of Chaucer's age."[15]

This third part of the poem tells about a beautiful female eagle whom Dame Nature is offering in marriage to one of three male eagles. Each of the three male eagles states his claim to the female. The other birds standing about then dispute among themselves as to which of the three the female should accept. But she finally stops the debate by announcing that she will make no decision until a year has passed.

Both Tyrwhitt[16] and Godwin[17] decided long ago that the female eagle represents Blanche of Lancaster, whom John of Gaunt married, and the first of the male eagles to speak represents Gaunt himself. The identity of the other two eagles, however, "it is impossible for us at this distance to determine" (Godwin, I, 444). Since the marriage of Blanche and Gaunt "was solemnized in May, 1359, the date of the poem falls obviously upon the year 1358" (Godwin, I, 435).

Later scholarship, however, has completely rejected this entire theory—largely because the evidence of Italian influence in the Love Garden section indicates a date after the death of Blanche, after the remarriage of Gaunt, and after the courtship of Blanche and Gaunt had ceased to interest people.

The first discernible clue as to the precise date of the poem appears in the invocation to Venus that has been already mentioned:

> As wisly as I sey the north-north-west,
> Whan I began my sweven for to write.   (117-18)

Bronson's comment on this passage is succinct and sound: "The famous stanza invoking Cytherea is believed to indicate a position of the planet Venus which was most closely approximated—though never reached for Londoners—in the Spring (April-May) of the years 1366, 1374, 1382, 1390, 1398. The first two dates are thought too early in Chaucer's literary career, the last too late. *On this simple basis all the scholarly hypotheses depend,* and, although *no convincing historical parallel has yet been discovered* for the supposed allegory, these hypotheses by a circular influence react ... to create an almost universal confidence that the date of composition has been, if roughly, yet securely established.

"It is worth insisting, therefore, that nothing of the sort has been accomplished. . . . *Nothing in the sum of what we know of Chaucer would make it impossible for him to have* written a poem like this in any of the years mentioned above although probability is overstrained by a date as early as 1366."[18]

The only reason that probability might seem overstrained by a date as early as 1366, or even earlier, is that the second part of the poem (the Love Garden) was obviously written much later. But, I must repeat, evidence of date that applies to the second part need not apply to the last part.

Referring to the stanza invoking Cytherea, Manly shows that the planet Venus appears approximately north-northwest of London within a week or two of May 10 every eight years.[19] According to his figures, Venus would have been visible in the indicated position not only in the years mentioned by Bronson, but also in 1358. According to Manly's figures again, May 16, 1358, would be the precise date involved, provided we think a year so early is at all admissible. As a matter of fact, examination of the evidence for 1358, and the years immediately following, might prove profitable. So far as I am aware, this evidence has never been previously examined.

One of the male eagles in the last section of the *Parliament* is twice referred to as "royal"; yet the eagle was a royal bird *per se* in heraldry and medieval symbolism,[20] and was a second crest of Edward III himself.[21] At a later date (as has been said already in this book) the eagle gradually became a symbol for Gaunt; but he could hardly be represented by all three of the rival eagles—and besides, at the early period when this part of the poem was probably written, the eagle had not become fixed as Gaunt's crest. More probably, the poet means simply that all four of the eagles in the poem stand for persons of royal blood. The one referred to as "royal" may have been more intimately connected with actual kingship than the others.

Finding four historical personages and a historical situation matching the eagles and the situation in the *Parliament* has been a task which many a scholar, during almost two centuries, has strained to perform, but in which none has succeeded to the satisfaction of many other scholars. But if we permit ourselves to glance back as far as 1358 and 1359, we should be dull indeed if we did not instantly perceive a group of people and a historical situation exactly paralleling the conditions of the poem—and, furthermore, people and situation in which Chaucer would have been intensely interested.

In 1358 King Edward III had three sons of marriageable status. One was the most admired bachelor of all Europe, no less a personage than Edward, Prince of Wales (the Black Prince)—now twenty-eight years of age, idolized by every Englishman, unmarried and unbetrothed. The king had designs of marrying him to some continental grand lady. But the Prince, in 1358, was keeping a notoriously extravagant, gay, and wild court of his own, was busy fathering two illegitimate sons, and showed no disposition to get himself married.[22]

The Prince had two equally marriageable brothers. One was John of Gaunt, a handsome and promising Plantagenet now eighteen years of age. The other was the somewhat colorless Edmund of Langley, now approaching seventeen.

At the same time there lived at the royal court the most marriageable girl in the kingdom: Blanche of Lancaster.[23] She was of royal blood (her father was a second cousin of the king); her father, Henry Duke of Lancaster, was the greatest lord in England, the richest land-owner after the king himself, a famous warrior, a wise statesman, and an old friend of the king. Blanche herself was, by all accounts, both rarely beautiful and extraordinarily good. Living in a period when great heiresses were usually betrothed in childhood and married in their early teens, Blanche was now seventeen years old, and unbetrothed. It is true that, when she was a child, she had been betrothed, in a manner typical of the time, but this betrothal had been broken abruptly, and, in 1358, she had been for some years unattached.

This singular delay in the disposition of Blanche requires accounting for. Six years previously her older sister had been married off to the son of the Holy Roman Emperor, Lewis IV. It is only human to believe that Henry of Lancaster would have entertained hopes of marrying his one remaining child, Blanche, into a similarly high station. Why, indeed, should she not marry one of the sons of the King of England—perhaps the Prince of Wales himself? That such a marriage was not unthinkable is shown by the fact that the Prince eventually married a woman of exactly the same blood kin to him as Blanche, and that one of the Prince's brothers eventually married Blanche. At this distance, it would seem that a marriage between Blanche and the Black Prince would have been the absolutely perfect arrangement for all parties concerned. But, as Dunn-Pattison says, "The Prince, so dutiful in other respects, had his own ideas about marriage."[24] Though he could probably have had for wife any unmarried English woman that he chose—he did not choose Blanche.

The general outline of this whole situation fits so perfectly the general outline of the situation in the last part of the *Parliament,* that I wish to make the suggestion (radical in view of the almost universal opinion that this *entire* poem dates from after 1373, at least) that the female eagle in the *Parliament* represents Blanche, and that the three male eagles represent the three unmarried, and marriageable, English princes. The difference between this suggestion and the related one of Tyrwhitt and of Godwin is that I think the second eagle, not the first, represents John of Gaunt, and that only the last portion of the Parliament, not the entire poem, was written early, and probably not so early as 1358. As will be seen immediately, details of the poem bear out the implications of this general outline.

Here is how Chaucer describes the first of the male eagles—or has Dame Nature describe him to the female:

> The foul royal, above yow in degre,
> The wyse and worthi, secre, trewe as stel,
> Which I have formed, as ye may wel se,
> In every part as it best liketh me—
> It nedeth not his shap yow to devyse. (394-98)

Phrase by phrase, every word of this would fit the popular concept of the Prince of Wales—the perfect man, above Blanche in rank. Nature's own darling, so universally known that "It nedeth not his shap yow to devyse." Moreover, it is difficult to understand (even when allowance is made for courtly exaggeration) how the second line here could fit Richard II (as most scholars have insisted) when he was only something like ten to fourteen years old when marriage arrangements were being made for him. Finally, the wording of the stanza should be compared with the lines referring to Hector in *Troilus and Criseyde* (II, 158-61, 841-47)—where Hector probably represents the Prince of Wales.

The first male eagle begins his answer to Dame Nature by saying that he will take the female not for her own sake but for the sake of pleasing Dame Nature herself: "Unto my soverayn lady, and not my fere, / I chese" (ll. 416-17). This would be a surprising statement for any suitor to make—unless that suitor represents the Prince of Wales in these particular circumstances. What the male eagle is saying here is that, in choosing the female, he would be doing what was naturally expected of him. This is probably just about what the Prince of Wales would have said if he found himself being pressed to marry Blanche when he did not want to marry her. Though he goes on to make conventional protestations of love, he never says that he has loved her, but only that he will love her truly henceforth. Most significantly, he adds that the maiden has never pledged him her love (l. 436), and that he has no bond on her (l. 438). As plainly as possible, he is saying, "Though nothing of love has ever passed between this maiden and me, if Nature demands that I marry her, I shall marry her to please Nature, and shall love and be true to her."

The second eagle is "of lower kynde" (l. 449), that is, of lower rank. Since Dame Nature has previously said (l. 400) that the female shall choose "by ordre," this second male ranks next below the first. Of the unmarried royal princes who might have been considered as mates for Blanche, John of Gaunt ranked next below the Prince of Wales. At once this eagle swears "by seint John" (l. 451). This is precisely the oath used by Chaucer near the end of the *Book of the Duchess* (l. 1319) to help identify John of Gaunt; it is used for the same purpose, apparently, in the *Complaint of Mars* (l. 9); and Saint John is, presumably, associated with John of Gaunt in *Troilus and Criseyde*—both in the eagle episode of Criseyde's dream and in the "Epilogue" (see Chapter IV and the Appendix of this book). The second eagle's oath, therefore, may be a significant key to the allegory in the *Parliament of Fowls*.

This second eagle seems very much more ardent and excited than the courteously diplomatic first eagle. Unlike the first, he declares that he has loved the female a long time, and deserves her because of his long service:

> I love hire bet than ye don, by seint John,
> Or at the leste, I love hire as wel as ye,
> And lenger have served hire in my degre,
> And if she shulde have loved for long lovynge,
> To me fullonge hadde be the guerdonynge. (451-55)

These lines demand a commentary. Along with several other young women, Blanche of Lancaster, after her mother's death, had been largely brought up by Queen Philippa. John of Gaunt, being only a year older than Blanche, had grown up with her at the court. As a matter of fact, Chaucer has John saying, in the *Book of the Duchess* (ll. 1090-1105) that he had known Blanche since childhood, loved her with his "yonge childy wyt," and apparently associated with her daily. Moreover, the third eagle, in his speech immediately following, suggests that the second eagle has "ben languysshyng / This twenty wynter" (ll. 472-73) for the maiden. All this is perfectly consistent with the second eagle's plea, as quoted just above.

In contrast, the Prince of Wales, being eleven years older than Blanche, was already out in France fighting during Blanche's girlhood, and was probably never closely associated with the younger children at the court. In the speeches of these two eagles, therefore, we get the picture of a gallant man who will do his duty graciously, and of another man who has been long in love with a young woman, and fears he is about to lose her.

The third male eagle has nothing distinctive to say—merely that, though he loves the female eagle well, he has loved her only six months. In this remark, Chaucer was probably making a humorous contrast of such a love with a love that had endured "This twenty wynter."

One other suggestion must be made. In the picture of Dame Nature there may be some hint of Queen Philippa. She was one of the best of women. She had four daughters of her own; she brought up Elizabeth de Burgh, Chaucer's first employer; she brought up the daughter of this Elizabeth; she brought up Joan, who later married the Prince of Wales; she helped bring up Blanche of Lancaster; and she kept about her a large group of damoiselles for whom she provided.[25] Her court must have fluttered with maidens like so many birds. What is more, if we may judge from the shrewd way in which she married off her protégées, as well as from the fact that the marriage of an heiress like Blanche was actually a matter of state, we may assume that the queen took a

special interest in Blanche's destiny. She may have tried to influence her oldest son to marry this singularly desirable girl. At any
rate, the first eagle speaks to Dame Nature with great deference,
and calls her "my soverayn lady" (l. 416), while she calls him
"my sone" (l. 406). Nevertheless, this eagle gently reminds Dame
Nature that *the maiden does not love him* (l. 436).

This very point is the pivot of the whole story. Dame Nature
has said from the beginning that the female will be given only to a
suitor of her choice, for "This is oure usage alwey, fro yer to yeere"
(l. 411). The female eagle postpones her decision for a year. This
is exactly what happens in the *Book of the Duchess* (l. 1258) when
John asks Blanche to marry him. Though this coincidence of the
year's delay in the two poems may be (as is often alleged) only a
convention of courtly love, it is extremely interesting that the date
of May 15, 1358 (when Venus was to be seen north-northwest of
London) is just a year before the marriage of John and Blanche,
on May 19, 1359.

Contemporary historical evidence, as well as evidence drawn
from the *Book of the Duchess*, indicates that the marriage of John
and Blanche was really a love match. He had masses said for her
soul as long as he lived, and he ordered that he be entombed beside
her. In the third part of the *Parliament*, therefore, may be seen a
poetic and symbolic version of an attempt at royal match-making
that failed because of the Prince of Wales' stubbornness and the real
love that existed between Blanche of Lancaster and John of Gaunt.

This interpretation of the poem fits the text perfectly. There is
not a word or a phrase of the bird part of it that is inconsistent with
this explanation, or is not clarified to some extent by it.

(The theory of Miss Edith Rickert that the various other birds
who debate with one another about the female eagle's choice of a
mate represent certain social or intellectual classes in fourteenth-
century England[26] may not be accurate in every detail. Nevertheless, Miss Rickert's main thesis is undoubtedly sound, and is entirely consistent with the interpretation of the *Parliament* offered
here.)

The date of the last part] If Chaucer was strictly accurate in saying
that he began working on his poem when Venus was to be seen
in the north-northwest (ll. 117-19)—that is, about May 15, 1358—
we might assume that the romantic situation implicit in the presence

of Blanche and the three princes at court, together with royal plans and courtly gossip, must have stimulated his imagination even then. On the other hand, his knowledge about the year's delay, as well as the fact that he would have been most indiscreet to make his poem public *before* the actual marriage (since there is always a chance that plans will go wrong, and people who have taken things for granted may be seriously embarrassed)—this suggests that the poem was written *after* the marriage. At that time it would have been a complimentary masterpiece. It flatters Blanche by showing all the princes as her suitors; it flatters the Prince of Wales not only in its plain words but also in its implications of his romantic chivalry toward a girl who loved another; it flatters Gaunt by showing him winning over stiff competition; it flatters even Edmund by including him with his more exalted brothers; and (if Dame Nature stands partly for Queen Philippa) it flatters the queen by sincere deference throughout.

Since it would have been indiscreet of Chaucer to make his poem public before the marriage of John and Blanche, we may take May 19, 1359, as a probable early limit of the poem. A late limit is more difficult. Such a humorous poem about the courtship of Blanche would probably not have been written after her death; therefore, September, 1369, is the latest possible limit. Actually, the subject of the courtship of John and Blanche would have ceased to be of much interest, even to the participants, long before 1369. Possibly, the wedding of the Prince of Wales on October 6, 1361, may be a late limit; for this wedding would have discouraged Chaucer from depicting the Prince expressing devotion to another woman besides his wife. It is usually assumed that the poem was written for some St. Valentine's Day celebration. If this was the case, and if it was written between May 19, 1359, and October 6, 1361, it must have been written for one of the two St. Valentine's Days falling between the dates mentioned. But both Chaucer and Gaunt were in France on St. Valentine's Day, 1360 (and Chaucer was probably a prisoner at the time). Accordingly, if the poem was really written for a St. Valentine's Day, it was not written in 1360. That leaves St. Valentine's Day, 1361. This was the first St. Valentine's Day that the young married couple had spent together; the romance of their courtship must have been still fresh in their minds; and a gay poem memorializing their courtship would have been altogether appropriate. Perhaps this last part of the *Parliament* was written then.

One other minor point may be worth making. Moore[27] suggests that the last lines of the *Parliament* are a tactful plea for some reward:

> I hope, ywis, to rede so som day
> That I shal mete som thyng for to fare
> The bet, and thus to rede I nyl not spare.   (697-99)

If this part of the poem was written in 1361, Chaucer may have received a reward by being transferred (as I have already suggested) from the household of Elizabeth of Ulster to that of Blanche, Countess of Richmond, in 1361.

Dating this third section of the *Parliament* as early as 1361 is, of course, an extreme departure from the usual chronology. But though the date does violence to tradition, it is inconsistent with no known fact, and it is supported by all available facts—which is more than can be said of any other date heretofore assigned.

It may be objected that Chaucer was too young, in 1361, to have written the third section of the *Parliament* that year. But I have already shown (Chapter I) that Chaucer was at least twenty years old in 1361, and perhaps older. Nor is this light poem too "mature" for a twenty-year-old poet. Milton wrote "On the Morning of Christ's Nativity" a few days after his twenty-first birthday; Pope wrote his *Pastorals* before he was eighteen, and most of the *Essay on Criticism* before he had reached twenty-one; Byron had published four volumes of (admittedly poor) poetry before he was twenty, and wrote *English Bards and Scotch Reviewers* while he was still twenty; Shelley published *Queen Mab* when he was twenty. Nor is the third section of the *Parliament* a demonstrably better poem than any of these. Besides, the version we read today has undoubtedly had the benefit of a mature Chaucer's revisions.

The first part of the poem

As I have already said, there is no good evidence from sources to indicate when the first part of the *Parliament* was written. The amendment of the "King Cipioun" mistake, already referred to, suggests a rather late date, as does the grave and religious moral tone—comparable to that of "The Former Age," "Fortune," "Truth," "Lak of Stedfastnesse," and the *Troilus* "Epilogue"—all of them assigned to the late 1380's or the 1390's.

It is unlikely that any precise date can actually be proved. But if we tentatively assume that this part of the poem, like the last part, contains historical allegory, and that possibly (since Chaucer showed in the last part of this poem, as well as in many other poems, how intensely he was concerned with John of Gaunt) it has some reference to Gaunt—we may discover something very interesting.

Chaucer summarizes the *Somnium Scipionis* quite adequately—with only one highly significant omission. Here is the crucial passage in the *Parliament of Fowls*:

> Thanne telleth it that, from a sterry place,
> How Affrycan hath hym Cartage shewed,
> And warned hym beforn of al his grace,
> And seyde hym what man, lerned other lewed,
> That lovede commune profyt, wel ithewed,
> He shulde into a blysful place wende.   (43-48)

Between the third and fourth lines of this passage, Chaucer has totally ignored a short chapter in which Scipio the Elder makes predictions concerning the future of the grandson to whom he has appeared in a dream. After telling of various adventures that the young man will have abroad, the old man says that the younger will return to Rome: "Arriving at the Capitol in a chariot, you will find the commonwealth gravely disturbed because of the policies of my grandson. Then, Scipio, it will behoove you to display to your people the brilliance of your intellect, talents, and experience.... The whole state will take refuge in you and your name; the Senate, all good citizens, the Allies, and the Latins will look to you; upon you alone will the safety of the state depend; and, to be brief, as dictator you must needs set the state in order, if only you escape death at the hands of your wicked kinsmen."

With certain very minor changes, this passage could be a summary of the political situation in England during the last two years of Chaucer's life. Henry Bolingbroke, son and heir of John of Gaunt, after an adventurous life abroad, returned to England and settled there until he was banished to France for ten years in 1398. His father died in February of the next year, whereupon Henry's cousin, Richard II, immediately seized all the Lancastrian estates, and made Bolingbroke's banishment permanent. Meanwhile, all England was growing restless and rebellious under the wayward and corrupt rule of Richard. Henry Bolingbroke, disobeying the royal order, returned with armed forces to England in July, 1399, raised an army from Richard's many enemies, compelled the king to abdicate, and had himself named monarch, in September, 1399.

In the passage quoted from Cicero, if we go back and put John of Gaunt in place of Scipio the Elder, Henry Bolingbroke in place of Scipio the Younger, and "nephew" in place of "grandson"—we shall find that the entire passage is a marvelously accurate sketch of English history just at the end of the fourteenth century.

Was Chaucer versifying the *Somnium Scipionis* in 1399 or 1400? And did he ignore the passage quoted because of its extremely sensitive political implications? It would have been like Chaucer, who habitually steered clear of political topics and entanglements, in his verse at least, to have omitted it. Besides, with the entire political situation so delicately balanced that fortune might turn against Henry at any moment, any absolute commitment to Henry (as might have been implied had Chaucer used this passage) could have proved mortally dangerous. Even so, Chaucer does venture to make a gesture in Henry's direction. As both Margaret Schlauch and Howard Patch have pointed out, Chaucer was concerned with the medieval doctrine of the "common profit."[28] Henry IV, in assuming the crown, declared himself as supporting "the good purpose and the common profit of the realm." And Chaucer, in his summary of the *Somnium*, twice uses this phrase in assuring immortality to those who seek the "commune profyt" (ll. 47, 74).

I do not mean to say that I think Chaucer's omission of the significant political passage in the *Somnium*, and his references to the "commune profyt" prove to the hilt that he was writing this section of the *Parliament* in 1399 or 1400. But I think that the evidence, without being absolutely conclusive, points clearly in that direction.

In this same chapter that Chaucer omits, Scipio the Elder points to Carthage, and tells his grandson: "To take [that city] you have now come, ranking not much higher than a private soldier. Two years hence as consul you will conquer it, thus winning for yourself the cognomen which until now you have had as an inheritance from me." Though the reference to Carthage, instead of Rome, prevents this passage from fitting the historical situation so well as the passage previously quoted—the words about the younger man's coming to take the city, having a low rank, and being destined to win the name of his ancestor, perfectly fit the situation in which Henry Bolingbroke found himself on returning virtually alone to England, and there conquering his enemies and winning for himself his father's title.

Chaucer's summary, eschewing politics except in the phrases about the "commune profyt," is essentially an assurance of the soul's immortality. It is exactly the sort of thing a poet would write in memory of his old friend, and in trying to console the son of that old friend. It even consoles those who loved the deposed and murdered Richard; for the Elder Scipio assures his descendant that "breakers of the lawe" and "likerous folk" (the two major accusations against Richard) will eventually come, after many ages, "into this blysful place" which is heaven (ll. 78-74).

Finally, the description of Scipio the Elder ascending to a "sterry place," looking down on the little earth and all its sinful ways, hearkening to the music of the spheres, and making moral and religious observations is remarkably similar to the description in the *Troilus* "Epilogue" of Troilus ascending to the eighth sphere after death. But if Troilus represents John of Gaunt, then the Scipio who is created in almost the exact pattern of the dead Troilus doubtless also represents John of Gaunt.

All these signs pointing toward Henry IV and John of Gaunt can hardly be entirely coincidental.

The second part of the poem

If the last part of the *Parliament* concerns the marriage of John of Gaunt, and the first part concerns his death, it is easy to see why Chaucer would have felt no hesitancy about linking the two parts together into one poem.

The middle part, however, is much more troublesome. It seems, moreover, that any conclusions we draw about it must be based entirely on internal evidence. In view of the many discrepancies and discontinuities pointed out early in this chapter (especially the clear break between the second and the third parts, the altogether different sources for the three parts, and the complete change in Scipio's character from the first part to the second), we cannot discard the possibility that some "literary executor" of Chaucer may have joined together, to the best of his ability, three pieces left by the master at his death. On the other hand, if we assume that Chaucer himself joined the pieces together, we have to call to mind the working habits of Chaucer that were discussed in the first chapter of this book. There is some evidence that Chaucer sometimes inserted fugitive pieces (that he valued and that otherwise might have been lost) into more substantial works that had a better chance of surviving. Perhaps we are having to deal with some such situation here. Perhaps, as Root suggested, Chaucer translated the stanzas from the *Teseida* that make up the second part of the *Parliament* while he was working on his tale of Palamon and Arcite (which is also adapted from the *Teseida*). He then "thriftily turned them to account" by inserting them into this poem[29] between the part about Gaunt's death and the part about his youth.

My own belief, however, is that (if Chaucer himself really lumped the three pieces together), the process occurred in four steps.

First, Chaucer wrote the last part of the poem—the true *Parliament of Fowls.*

Next, and many years later, he planned to write a series of stories about unhappy lovers—something like the poem that actually did materialize as the *Legend of Good Women*. He got as far as writing a kind of Prologue to this projected poem—and this Prologue is the first two or three stanzas of the *Parliament* along with the Love Garden portion of the same poem. Evidence for this view is the passage in which Chaucer speaks "Of many a story, of which I touche shal / A fewe" (ll. 285-86), as well as the first two stanzas about the God of Love—stanzas that would be perfectly fitting for a group of poems about lovers, but are utterly inappropriate as an introduction to the *Somnium Scipionis.*

Next, John of Gaunt died, and Chaucer wrote the short poem that constitutes the first part of the *Parliament*. Since it was so short, and since its subject was the death of that "beste frend" about whom Chaucer had written his first major poem forty years previously, the thought of joining the two poems—the first and the last—must have come to Chaucer almost with the writing of the translation of the *Somnium*. Furthermore, the fact that Henry Bolingbroke was now king, and that Chaucer must have wanted to please him, would have had some effect in encouraging the poet to join together, for the king's pleasure, a poem about the death of the king's father, and another poem about the courtship of the king's father and mother. This step in the growth of the poem is easy to explain.

The final step is not so easy. Perhaps, indeed, there is no explanation except that it was an old man's whim as he fussed over his work during the last year of his life. Or perhaps the poet felt that the transition from Gaunt's death to Gaunt's courtship was too abrupt; and since he, as a court poet following courtly convention, had always previously written about Gaunt as a lover rather than as a warrior or statesman (*vide* the *Book of the Duchess, Complaint of Mars, Troilus and Criseyde*), Chaucer may have felt that the depiction of Gaunt ("Affrican") as a guide to the Temple of Love would be appropriate, and would serve as a transition between the death poem and the courtship poem. Therefore, he dug out the old Love Garden fragment that he had abandoned long before, changed the name (but not the character) of the original guide, and inserted it between the two other poems. In effect, he thus achieved a kind of biography-in-reverse of Gaunt. The poem as it stands begins with Gaunt's death and afterlife; it moves backward to picture him in his prime as a guide to love—"with seint John to borowe";[30] and it ends with him as a youthful lover.

Obviously, it is impossible for anyone to say whether or not this theory as to the manner in which the *Parliament* was composed is correct. But it does explain every one of those many puzzling facts mentioned earlier in this chapter. Viewed thus, the poem is revealed as a work that, though hardly unified by modern aesthetic standards, possesses a consistent and orderly pattern based on reverse chronology (not only as to times of composition of the three parts but also in the life of Gaunt) and on the personality of Gaunt. Any unifying principle in the poem is not aesthetic or philosophical, but strictly personal; and the person involved is John of Gaunt.

Chapter VI. The mysterious *House of Fame*

The *House of Fame* is one of Chaucer's most complex mystery poems—with fewer and vaguer clues for its solving than any of the other poems examined in this book.

Its Book I conducts the poet through the Temple of Venus, where he sees depicted in wall paintings the story of Aeneas' desertion of Dido, as well as desertions of many other women by faithless men, and brings him out of the Temple on to a lonely desert. Book II has the poet snatched up by an eagle who promises to take him to the House of Fame, where he may hear "tydynges" of love as a reward for the lovelessness of his own life; this garrulous eagle discourses at length on the physical properties of air, water, and sound, and tells how all talk ascends to the House of Fame. Book III shows Chaucer within the House of Fame, watching the arbitrariness of Fame's decrees, declaring that he himself desires no fame, turning away to observe the mad confusion of the House of Rumor—and ending at last in the middle of an uncompleted sentence.

Some interpretations

Root sees no great mystery in all this. According to him, the Temple of Venus "is the realm of poesy," from which Chaucer steps out into the world of reality, and "finds it a desert." The poet is then caught up by the eagle Philosophy. Fame, to whose palace he is transported, has two aspects: glory or reputation, and also "general report," or rumor. Chaucer philosophically rejects Fame in her first aspect, and turns to the other aspect in order to discover "more of human life and the deeds of men." In the House of Rumor "he can at least escape from the artificialities of conventional poetry, and mingle with men as an auditor and spectator, if not as an actor. He can thus keep himself in touch with reality, and not spend his life in dreams."[1]

Manly also finds no great difficulty in the poem. "If the reader will make due allowance for ... errors in proportion, the poem will be seen to be clear and simple in structure."[2] Nevertheless, as will be noted a little later on, what Manly sees so clearly bears not the slightest resemblance to what Root sees so clearly!

Other theories (mostly summarized in Robinson's notes, p. 779, to which the reader is referred) have it that the poem is an allegory of Chaucer's own unsuccess in life; that it was meant to celebrate the marriage of King Richard and Queen Anne; that it refers to the marriage plans of John of Gaunt's daughter Philippa; that it reprimands John of Gaunt for his public carrying-on with Katharine Swynford; and that it was meant to introduce a collection of tales about women (Manly's thesis). Kittredge thought that the poem is "a humorous study of mankind from the point of view of a ruling passion."[3] Baum says that in the House of Fame Chaucer found an "extravagantly brilliant décor, a crowd of worthy and unworthy followers of an erratic mistress, a medley of justice and injustice and folly"; and the poet "returns to his books, with the conclusion that in love, if not in all life, the poetic dream is preferable to the earthly reality"[4]—a conclusion exactly opposite to what Root saw in the poem. Ruggiers finds the poem "unified" because he sees Fortune, Love, and Fame as so similar that a poem involving all three (as does the *House of Fame*) is really a poem on one subject only.[5]

Tatlock remarks that "A striking but unfair case can be made out of any of these theories by picking out seemingly favorable evidence and disregarding all else and all proportion." He himself thinks that the "slowness of the poem in getting under way, and its especially marked tendency to digress, and the prolongation of the final book, and its very inconclusive breaking off, all justify doubts whether the *House of Fame* was begun with any clean-cut purpose or meaning, except irresponsibly 'for fun.' "[6]

Actually, none of the theories proposed answers all, or even many, of the questions the poem raises. Nor (may I add) am I under any illusion that the following hypothesis entirely circumvents Tatlock's generalized censure of all the others. I believe, however, that this hypothesis goes farther toward solving all the mysteries of the poem than any other so far proposed.

Structure of the poem

In examining the structure of the poem, I should like first to call attention to the beginnings and endings of the three "books" that make up the poem. Following the editions of Caxton (1483) and of Thynne (1532), modern printings of the poem mark off and label Books I, II, and III; Book I has a "Proem," an "Invocation," and a "Story" marked and labeled, even without benefit of Caxton or Thynne; Book II has a "Proem" and a "Dream," and Book III has an "Invocation" and a "Dream," all without authority from Caxton, Thynne, or any other primary source. The poem exists complete in its present form in only two early manuscripts, regarded generally as sisters descended from one earlier manuscript, now lost. In neither of these early primary manuscripts are to be found "books," colophons, subtitles, or labels of any kind: the poem runs straight from first to last without a break.

What is called the "Proem" of Book I discusses the nature of dreams for 58 lines in a well-rounded passage beginning, "God turne us every drem to goode!" and ending, "Turne us every drem to goode!" Appended to this are seven lines referring to a particular dream the poet had on "The tenthe day now of Decembre" (l. 63). But now appear several odd features. After 65 lines, we come suddenly on this: "But at my gynnynge, trusteth wel, / I wol make invocacion" (ll. 66-67). This long-delayed announcement of a beginning seems curious. Furthermore, the poet repeats, only 47 lines farther on, that he dreamed his dream "Of Decembre the tenthe day" (l. 111). Finally, Book II (coming after nearly 400 lines describing the poet's dream) tells us:

> Now herkeneth, every maner man
> That Englissh understonde kan,
> And listeneth of my drem to lere,
> For now at erste shul ye here
> So sely an avisyon. (509-13)

In other words, even after we have had a "gynnynge," and have heard all about a long dream, we are told that we are now going to hear *first* ("erste") about the same dream. This is disconcerting. A few lines farther in the same "Proem" the poet asks Venus to help him

> To tellen al my drem aryght.
> Now kythe thyn engyn and myght! (527-28)

This too sounds as if he were just beginning to tell about his dream.*

* In the "Invocation" at the beginning of Book I, the poet (in very similar lines) calls on the God of Sleep to help him
> My sweven for to telle aryght,
> Yf every drem stonde in his myght. (79-80)

All this is puzzling. Moreover, this "Proem," which marks the beginning of what we call Book II, does not fall, as one might expect, between dramatic scenes, but intrudes right into the midst of a scene. Actually, if the "Proem" and the two transitional lines following it were omitted, the poem would move right along without perceptible break in continuity.

Obviously, something peculiar is going on here. It looks as if we have the beginning of story about a dream after we have already been hearing a story about a dream, and several hundred lines after the announcement of the beginning of the story. All this doesn't make sense. But would it make sense if we assumed that the "Proem" of Book II was an original beginning of the poem, and the present beginning (at 1. 66) was composed for a major revision of the poem? In other words, did the poem begin, originally, with the dream about the eagle (somewhere near the beginning of Book II)? And was the dream about the Temple of Venus (most of Book I) subsequently placed before this part of the poem—either as new material or as a unit transposed from another part of the poem? The explanation suggested by these questions would account for the two separate announcements of a beginning, as well as for the apparently abrupt intrusion of the "Proem" of Book II.

The "Invocation" of Book III is most interesting. It calls on Apollo to help the poet master the "art poetical" in "Thys lytel laste bok." It seems strange that the poet would pray for the ability to write good verse only in the last book of his poem. Why not in the first two books also? It seems even more strange that he would refer to his "laste bok" when there were no "books" at all indicated, or previously mentioned, in the poem. Is it possible that Chaucer wrote this "Invocation" as a tentative introduction to the poem as a whole? And does "laste bok" mean "latest book"? Or could it mean (cf. Housman's Last Poems) that this is the last book the aging poet intends to write? And if this "Invocation" was really meant for the beginning of the poem, how did it get here at the beginning of what we call Book III? Did Chaucer himself insert it here, without anticipating the interpretation modern readers would give the phrase "laste bok"?* Or did some "editor" insert it there after Chaucer's death—not knowing what else to do with it, but wishing to preserve every scrap of the great man's verses? Questions abound; answers are scarce. My only reason for bringing up the

* See notes on Troilus and Criseyde, III, 1818 and IV, 26-28 in the Appendix.

questions is to suggest that the *House of Fame* may be an uncompleted, unperfected poem in more ways than are indicated by its
mere broken-off ending.

Perhaps we have in this poem the same sort of thing that we have
in the "Epilogue" of *Troilus and Criseyde* (see "Appendix" of this
book) and in the *Parliament of Fowls*—that is, revisions made at
different times (especially very late in Chaucer's life) and never
thoroughly mortised together or given final polish. We of the
twentieth century, with our paper cut to uniform sizes, our neat ball-
point pens, our typewriters, and our printing presses, may not quite
appreciate the difficulties of revision in an age when writers used
various scraps of paper, vellum, parchment, and even wax tablets for
their work, and scribbled with muddy ink, a feather quill, and no
professionally fitted spectacles, in the dim candlelight of drafty
closets. Under such circumstances, catching repetitions, inconsistencies, and self-contradictions (not easy even today) in revisions of
manuscripts was hardly to be expected. We should not be surprised,
therefore, if Chaucer did not produce flawless copy—even when he
thought he was finished with a manuscript.

Much more remarkable than the two beginnings of the poem,
together with the question raised by the various "books," proems,
and invocations, is the apparent lack of relationship between Book I
and Books II and III. Older Chaucerians commented frequently on
this discordancy; recent critics, however, feeling that Chaucer's
poems must be made to possess "unity" at any cost, have often tried
to show that Book I really is related to the others. But the very
pronounced disunity among the critics themselves suggests that any
unity the poem has may be a product of the modern synthesizing
mind, not the discursive mind of Chaucer.

Most of the first book is an account of the poet's dream in which
he thought he wandered into the Temple of Venus, and saw por-
trayed there the story of Aeneas and Dido. He tells this story (a
summary of Virgil) through about 250 lines in which (though the
entire poem is ostensibly about Fame) he mentions Fame (personified) only once (l. 349), and then in an almost literal translation of
the *Aeneid* (IV, 320 ff.). Not only do Chaucer's Aeneas and Dido,
in Book I, have little connection with Fame—but Fame, in succes-
sive books, has little connection with them. Dido, though her story
fills most of Book I, is not even mentioned in Books II and III; and
Aeneas is mentioned only once in those books, along with a whole

collection of other notables (1. 1485). In other words, and in plain
fact long recognized by all the older Chaucerians, there seems to be
absolutely no relation, as the poem now stands, between Book I and
Books II and III of the *House of Fame*.

There are still more peculiarities in the poem. Early in Book II,
the poet is promised that he will hear "tydynges" of love when he
reaches the House of Fame. But actually, once he is inside the
House of Fame (Book III), he hears no such love "tydynges"—or,
for that matter, "tydynges" of any sort. He turns away from the
House of Fame, and enters the House of Rumor. Here he does hear
many kinds of "tydynges"—but none of them specifically about love
—until, sixteen lines from the end of the poem, he notes, among
other thronging folk, a special group concerned with "love-tydynges"
(1. 2143). But the exact nature of these "love-tydynges" is never
revealed; the poem breaks off too quickly thereafter.

From all this "medley" (as Baum calls it) of double beginnings,
intrusive "Proem" and ambiguous "Invocation," unrelated narratives, unrealized promises, and broken-off ending, it seems absolutely certain that the poem, as we now have it, is not a work that
Chaucer finally completed to his perfect satisfaction and stored away
permanently without ever returning to it for revision. This view
is supported by the simple fact (even if there were no other cor-
roborating facts) of the broken-off last line. As I have said previously, there is ample evidence that Chaucer was a confirmed reviser of
his poems, and that he was frequently unable to let well enough
alone. It is possible that we have in the *House of Fame* a work that
was still undergoing major alterations and repairs during the last
years of his life.

A working hypothesis

A mere quick reading of the *House of Fame* reveals many
peculiarities that demand explanation: the two beginnings, the
"laste bok," the relation of the long story of Dido to the rest of the
poem, the function of the extensively described Temple of Love in
a poem ostensibly about the House of Fame, the significance of the
desert on which the dreamer emerges from the Temple of Love,
the apparently unfulfilled promise of "love-tydynges" made early
in Book II, the possible symbolic significance of the golden eagle
that carried off the poet, the broken-off and inconclusive ending,

the identity of the "man of gret auctorite" who appears without further comment in the last line of the poem. The hypothesis to be proposed immediately does explain all the foregoing items—and many more besides.

In offering this hypothesis, I should like to begin with the very last line of the poem: "A man of gret auctorite."

It has long been realized that the *House of Fame* is strongly influenced by Dante—to such an extent that some scholars have held that Lydgate's reference, in the *Fall of Princes*, to "Dante in Inglissh" means this poem. Robinson (p. 778) does not agree; he maintains that, though Chaucer "undoubtedly used a number of passages from Dante, and was under his influence at the time of writing ... there is no organic structural relation between" the *Divine Comedy* and the *House of Fame*. This conclusion is certainly true of the poem as it now stands. Nevertheless, Robinson may underestimate Dante's influence. Skeat says: "The influence of Dante is very marked." He then goes on to summarize the chief resemblances between the *Divine Comedy* and the *House of Fame* that were pointed out in a famous article by A. Rameau in 1880.[7] Though some of the twenty-odd parallels noted by Skeat[8] are strained or incorrect, enough authentic ones remain to show that Chaucer was indeed strongly influenced by Dante. Still more parallels (especially in phraseology) are noted by Robinson.

In another poem of Chaucer's, the *Parliament of Fowls*, the influence of Dante is also very apparent. An obvious parallel is to be noted in the fact that Dante is guided through a world of dream by a famous Roman personage (Virgil), and that, in the *Parliament*, Chaucer is guided into a world of dream by another famous Roman personage (Scipio). But the second part of the *Parliament* and Book I of the *House of Fame* bear an even closer resemblance: (*1*) the dream world of both is the Temple of Venus; (2) the adventure in the Temple of the *Parliament* ends with the poet's observing on the wall the stories of many unhappy lovers, and the adventure in the Temple in the *House of Fame* ends with the poet's observing on a wall the stories of many unhappy lovers; (*3*) among the unhappy lovers of the *Parliament* is Dido, and among the unhappy lovers of the *House of Fame* is Dido, though she is allotted much more space here than in the other poem; (*4*) in the *Parliament* the poet issues from the Temple of Venus, and finds himself in a glade "upon an hil of floures," and in the *House of Fame* he also issues from the Temple of Venus, but this time finds himself on a wide desert.

The parallels between the *Parliament* and Book I of the *House of Fame* are pronounced; and both poems are strongly influenced by Dante. The one important respect in which they differ in their narrative structure, and in which the *House of Fame* differs from Dante in this particular area is that (though the *Parliament* has a guide into the Garden of Love, and though Dante has a guide into the other world) the poet in Book I of the *House of Fame* has no guide into the Temple of Love. This lack of a guide is both unexpected and remarkable. It may be explained by the following hypothesis:

An eagle conducted Chaucer to the House of Fame itself; another person conducted him to the House of Rumor; Scipio conducted him to the Temple of Love in the *Parliament of Fowls*; Virgil conducted Dante through the other world. It would have been altogether consistent, therefore, for some guide to have conducted the dreamer through the Temple of Venus in Book I of the *House of Fame*.

Now I am going to make what must seem a very impudent assumption—but if this assumption leads to a rational conclusion that clarifies the mysteries and resolves the inconsistencies of the poem, the assumption may turn out to be more acceptable than, doubtless, it will first appear. I am going to assume that Chaucer did originally have a guide to conduct him through the Temple of Venus in Book I; and I am going to assume that the "man of gret auctorite" referred to in the last line of the poem as it now stands was that guide. If these two assumptions are accepted (and I shall show immediately why I think they should be), then it is clear that *the story about the Temple of Venus that now appears in Book I originally came last*—following right after the introduction of the "man of gret auctorite."

At first glance, of course, this hypothesis must look extreme. But reasons (some already mentioned) why it bears serious consideration are the following:

1] The beginning of the poem as it now stands is clearly the end-result of several revisions, or attempts at several different beginnings, with the Proem of Book II plainly offering a second beginning, as if it were the original start of the poem.

2] The end of the poem as it now stands is structurally incomplete and meaningless, and has been abruptly broken off in the middle of a sentence. Something of significance *must* have been intended to follow. Chaucer, the master story-teller, who, in the "Squire's Tale," shows how much he respects "The knotte why that every tale is toold" (F, 401), could not have meant to conclude a story in this pointless manner.

3] The absence of a guide through the Temple of Venus is such a unique departure from the precedent of Chaucer himself, in other poems, and of all his masters, that we must suspect some radical revision of the poem from its original form.

4] The example of Dante's having a poet for a guide might possibly make us suspect that Chaucer too contemplated having a poet for a guide. At any rate, Chaucer uses the exact phrase, "A man of gret auctorite," that Dante uses right after he has introduced the shades of great classic poets, and just before he introduces another group of shades, most of whom are writers: "di grande autorità ne' lor sembianti" (*Inf.*, iv, 113). The identity of Chaucer's hypothetical guide is, perhaps, of small consequence. But the strong influence of Dante on the poem, and the story translated from Virgil in Book I, suggest that Virgil himself might have been Chaucer's guide. On the other hand, perhaps Chaucer never firmly made up his mind on the matter; it is significant that a word (possibly *nevene*, "name") is omitted three lines from the present end of the poem, just before the "man of gret auctorite" is introduced, and just where Chaucer would have had to decide what to name his guide.

5] The most frequent observation and complaint of all readers of this poem is that the eagle promises Chaucer that he will hear, in the House of Fame, a multitude of "love-tydynges" (ll. 672-98); and Chaucer himself says that he has been promised such things (ll. 1884-95). Yet neither Chaucer nor the reader hears one small love-tiding, or any hint of one in either the House of Fame or the House of Rumor—until almost the end of the poem, when the single vague comment about "a corner of the halle, / Ther men of love-tydynges tolde" would seem to be a preparatory introduction, at last, to the long-postponed topic. But then the poem suddenly stops; and the eagle's promise about love-tidings (the actual motivation of the entire action in the poem) is left hanging in mid-sentence.

Since the poem breaks off so abruptly, with no reasonable conclusion in sight, some scholars have held that Chaucer planned to carry on the poem through actual love-tidings that would redeem the eagle's original promise. Manly sensed, long ago, "that this poem was intended to herald or announce a group of love stories and to serve as a sort of prologue to them."[9] Though no one (so far as I am aware) now agrees that Manly was literally correct in his supposition, he was undoubtedly on the right track in insisting that the poem, as it stands, is a prelude to love-tidings yet to come.

What no one seems to have noticed is that the love-tidings are already present in the poem—over four hundred lines of them, or almost an entire "book"—except that they now appear at the beginning of the poem instead of at the end. A moment's thought should convince any reader that, if the long story of Dido, and the brief stories of other unhappy loves that now appear in Book I were transferred to the end of the present Book III—all those scholars (including Manly) who have felt that the poem as it stands is a prelude to love-tidings would be vindicated. All those who have noted and complained that the eagle's promises go unfulfilled would be answered. All those who have felt that the central narrative motivation of the poem (the search after love-tidings) is disappointingly undeveloped and awkwardly unrealized would be satisfied. And all those who have wondered how the story of Dido in Book I is related to the rest of the poem would at once perceive the relationship.

6] Finally, the apparent lack of unity in the poem—a lack which most Chaucerians have sadly admitted or manfully tried to disprove for years—would be quite resolved if the Dido story came at the end. Placed there, it would fill out, with marvelous grace, the entire narrative structure and logical pattern developed in Books II and III.

Though the hypothesis just suggested seems to solve most of the major problems concerned with the structure, narrative unity, logic, and completeness of the *House of Fame*, several serious questions remain to be answered. The principal question is this: Why did Chaucer undertake to revise the poem so drastically? The answer may involve nothing more than the personal taste of the author; he may have felt that he could write a poem that would satisfy him better than did his original attempt. On the other hand there were

certain impelling personal reasons why he should revise this poem.
These reasons will be explained in the next section of the present
chapter.

But even if there were good reasons why he should revise the
poem—why should he revise it as he did, by transferring the story
of Dido from the end to the begining of the poem? Again, the
answer may involve merely the peculiarities of personal taste. On
the other hand, the broken-off ending and the second beginning in
Book II indicate very plainly that Chaucer had not finished working
on the poem. Doubtless he had further plans for it; but since we
cannot guess these plans, we cannot explain why he transposed the
Dido story. One thing seems certain, however; by removing the
Dido story from the end of the poem, Chaucer de-emphasized it.
No longer does it occupy a climactic place—"The knotte why that
every tale is toold." And, as will be seen later, Chaucer did not wish
(as the years passed) to emphasize the faithlessness of men like
Aeneas to their mistresses.

A more difficult question involves the dropping of the (hypothetical) guide to the Temple of Venus. The only explanation I can
think of would require that Chaucer must have revised the poem
very late in his life. In the previous chapter it was suggested that
the middle part of the *Parliament of Fowls* was written sometime
about 1380 as a Prologue for a projected series of stories about unhappy lovers. This project, however, never developed as originally
planned (it was replaced by the *Legend of Good Women*), and
therefore its prologue was discarded. Years later, however, Chaucer
dug out the old Prologue, and made it a part of the *Parliament*.
But meanwhile he had written the *House of Fame*, in which he used
the same motif (a guide conducting the poet through the Temple
of Venus) as appeared in the now resurrected old Prologue. The
similarities between the two poems were so obvious that Chaucer's
artistic conscience urged him to do something about it. His problem was to decide whether he would use the guide to the Temple
of Love in the *Parliament*, and go back and eliminate him from the
House of Fame—or keep him in the *House of Fame* and eliminate
him from the *Parliament*. For reasons of his own (maybe because
the death of Gaunt was so fresh in his mind, and because the new
king figured in the *Parliament*), he chose to keep the guide in the
Parliament. But this would necessitate his going back and elimi-
nating him from the *House of Fame*, an easy matter that would

require only a stroke of the pen and the writing of a couple of transitional lines. If this is not the explanation, I can think of no other reason, except his own personal whim, that would have caused Chaucer to drop the guide.

A final question is this: Why did Chaucer leave the poem in such an unfinished state? Having started revising the poem sometime after 1389 (see next section), he found himself so busy with the *Canterbury Tales*, to say nothing of his official work as a government employee, that he simply did not have time to finish revising the *House of Fame*. Or if (as suggested above) he set about revising the poem very late in his life, it is possible that, before he could finish the work, he was called away by the greatest "auctorite" of them all—death.

Again I must say that I am perfectly aware that factual evidence for the hypothesis that the story of Dido in Book I originally came last in the poem is admittedly meager; a great deal must be interpolated between a few points of reference. At the same time, I must repeat that *the hypothesis accounts for all the major mysteries of the poem*. It accounts for the broken-off end; it identifies the "man of gret auctorite" as a prospective guide to the Temple of Love; it shows the relation of the Temple of Love to a poem about the House of Fame; it shows the relation of the story of Dido, and the other unhappy lovers, to the rest of the poem; it shows how the eagle's promise of "love-tydynges" is actually fulfilled; and it presents a poem having a unified and well-rounded narrative structure in place of its former un-Chaucerian pointlessness.

Allegory

Though the hypothesis just outlined does solve many problems, others remain. Perhaps the major problem is this: Does the poem conceal any meanings behind its outer façade of personified, or concretized, abstractions? Is it more than a mere allegorical affirmation of the vanity of fame and the irrationality of rumor?

The answer to this question depends on the answers to several others. For example, exactly what does Chaucer mean when he says that the eagle promised him "tydynges" of love? Goffin argues convincingly for a special meaning for the word—which "scholars practically without exception [have construed] as equivalent to 'news.'" "There can be no question," he says in summarizing his discussion; "Chaucer is thinking of stories.... The equation of 'tiding' with 'story' in *The Hous of Fame* is well worth the making. It clarifies and reinforces the generally accepted 'allegorical', as well as the literal meaning of the poem. This is confirmed as essentially a search for, and a discovery of, stories: 'olde gestes' on the one hand, 'newe thinges' on the other.... It is not fame, but new material for his art that Chaucer wants."[10]

In seizing the poet, the eagle tells him that not only is he without tales of love from his own experience, but also he learns no such tales either from his neighbors or from any "fer countree" (ll. 639-51). Therefore, the eagle tells the poet, "I bere the to a place / Which that hight the Hous of Fame" (ll. 663-64), where he can learn a new body of love-tales to replenish his own dry fountain (ll. 670-75). It is clear, then, that the eagle thinks of the House of Fame as not merely the abode of the goddess Fame, but as a place where the poet may expect to hear famous love tales. Indeed, Chaucer himself tells a bystander in the House of Fame that the eagle had brought him there to hear new love-tidings, or love-tales (ll. 1884-95).

Chaucer's description of the House of Fame bears out this conception of it as the home of love tales. What impresses Chaucer is the host of "many thousand tymes twelve" minstrels, harpers, and other musicians; famous magicians and clerks who know love charms, exorcisms, and incantations; and, looming above all the others, the writers Josephus, Statius, Homer, Dares, Dictys, "Lollius," Guido, "Englyssh Gaufride," Virgil, Ovid, Lucan, and Claudian—all famous tellers of tales. Clearly Goffin is right: both Chaucer and the eagle envision the House of Fame as essentially a fountainhead of song and story.

But is there a second layer of allegory beneath this first? Perhaps so. The eagle lifts Chaucer and takes him over city, mountain, and sea to the House of Fame—evidently to that "fer countree" (l. 647) from which Chaucer has been receiving no love-tales. Is this "fer countree" from which Chaucer is to derive his stories only an imaginary country, or is it real? If it is real, it must represent either France or Italy, the two countries from which Chaucer derived so many of his tales. Probably France is not meant; for Chaucer had been deriving tales from France since he was a very young man. But could it be Italy? And could Chaucer's journey to the House of Fame in order to learn new tales be meant as a representation of his journeys to Italy, where he gleaned so much fresh poetic material?

Such an interpretation is supported by a certain amount of evidence. With the exception of "Gaufride" (l. 1470) (who may be Chaucer himself[11]) and two other Britons (ll. 1208, 1277), all the persons named in the poem belong to the Greco-Roman-Italian world. Not one of them belongs to that French world of letters (de Meun, de Lorris, Machaut, Deschamps, Froissart, Alanus, Deguilleville, Graunson, and others) who were Chaucer's principal masters before he went to Italy. It seems altogether plausible that Chaucer is saying, in the *House of Fame*, that he went to Italy (mentally, and probably physically) to find Greco-Roman-Italian sources for fresh narrative materials to be used in his own tales.

Perhaps a desire to call attention to the part Italy plays in the poem is one reason why Chaucer was willing to shift the Roman writer's story of Aeneas and Dido to the beginning of the poem. Aeneas "cam, thurgh his destinee," to Italy (ll. 145-47); he "seyde he moste unto Itayle" (l. 187); he sailed "Towards the contree of Itaylle" (l. 196); he "wende fro [Dido] to Itayle" (l. 298); the god "Bad hym goo into Itayle" (l. 430); and the poet sees pictured on the wall of the Temple of Venus "the aryvale / That Eneas had in Itayle" (ll. 451-52). The effect of all this is to make the reader emphatically aware of Italy.

Moreover, Italy was the one part of medieval Europe where fame was recognized as an incentive and a reward surpassing even political power and material wealth. In his great book on *The Civilization of the Renaissance in Italy* (first English translation, 1878), Jacob Burckhardt has a chapter entirely devoted to "The Modern Idea of Fame" as it existed in medieval and Renaissance Italy. In other countries, he says, "the different classes of society lived apart, each with its own medieval caste sense of honor." But the Italians had early achieved a social integration unknown in the North, and in addition had zealously studied the Roman writers— who were "filled and saturated with the conception of fame." Dante was always conscious of, if not actually obsessed by, the concept of fame; so was Petrarch; so was Boccaccio—all in a manner quite unknown in England. "History and the new topography were careful to leave no local celebrity unnoticed. At the same period the Northern chronicles only here and there, among the lists of Popes, emperors, earthquakes, and comets put in the remark that at such a time this or that famous man 'flourished.' " But in medieval Italy, "It was a point of honor for the different cities to possess the bones of their own and foreign celebrities; and it is most remarkable how seriously the Florentines, even in the fourteenth century—long before the building of S. Croce—labored to make their cathedral a Pantheon. Accorso, Dante, Petrarch, Boccaccio, and the jurist Zanobi della Strada were to have had magnificent tombs there erected to them."[12] Root too recognized the preoccupation of Italy with fame. The inevitable result, he says, of the "Petrarchan Renaissance" was "the desire for glory and fame"; "Fame was that goddess for which all Italy was sighing."[13] If Chaucer thought of the House of Fame as anything more than an abstract tradition of great history and song—he must have thought of it as the living Italy which had supplied so much of that tradition, and in which so much of it was still preserved.

Finally, Chaucer gives (twice in the version of the poem that we have) the date when he had his wonderful dream of being transported to the House of Fame. The date is "Of Decembre the tenthe day" (ll. 63, 111). Scholars have taken this date as a key to the date of the poem itself. Skeat seems assured that the date indicated for the composition of the poem is December 10, 1383;[14] Robinson (p. 779) makes out a plausible case for "a date about 1379-80"; and Baum says, still referring to the date of the poem, "One could make out a very plausible case for a date sometime in the 1390's."[15] Actually, however, the date when Chaucer dreamed his wonderful dream may have no precise relation to the time when he wrote about it. The December 10 that he specifies could have been years, or decades, before he wrote the poem itself.

In view of the suggestion that Chaucer's imaginary trip to the House of Fame may symbolize a real trip to Italy, certain dates in 1372 (when he first started for Italy) are significant. On November 12, 1372, he was commissioned to go to Genoa on the king's business. But medieval bureaucracy moved slowly. It was not until December 1, 1372, while Chaucer was in London, that he received money from the king's treasury, apparently as expenses for the trip. With the money at last in his hand, he probably spent the next few days outfitting himself for the journey. Therefore his last day in London, when he slept "Ryght ther as I was wont to done" (l. 113), could easily have been December 10. Some years later, when he wrote the *House of Fame*, he may have remembered this date as one of the most significant in his life—a day when one epoch of his career ended, and another began.

An objection to choosing December 10, 1372, as the "Decembre the tenthe day" that Chaucer mentions is that the eagle speaks of Chaucer going home from the labor of his "rekenynges" (ll. 652-53), and that this reference may mean his work at the customs, which did not begin till 1374. But, as was said in a previous chapter, there is an excellent probability that Chaucer, with his knowledge of figures, had long been employed as a kind of accountant, or auditor, in either Gaunt's household or the king's. It is hardly likely that he would have been sent to Genoa in 1372 to conclude a commercial treaty, and then on to Florence to talk with Florentine bankers, as seems likely, about the English king's borrowing money from the bankers, if he had not already been proved competent at "rekenynges." Accordingly, this reference really proves nothing about the date of the poem. So far as "rekenynges" are concerned, "Decembre the tenthe day" could have been in almost any year between 1360 and 1399.

A bit of circumstantial evidence having some bearing on the matter is involved in a curious passage at the very beginning of "The Story" of Book I:

> [I] fil on slepe wonder sone,
> As he that wery was forego
> On pilgrymage myles two
> To the corseynt Leonard,
> To make lythe of that was hard.   (114-18)

"Corseynt Leonard" is usually taken to mean St. Leonard's convent that lay just two miles east of Aldgate, the easternmost gate of London. Though Chaucer occupied this gate after 1374, it had been there long before. As Chaucer indicates in these lines, it was customary for suppliants to make the short pilgrimage on foot from Aldgate to ask the Saint for favors. Robinson suggests (p. 780) that "St. Leonard was the patron saint of captives and might therefore be expected to release the wretched who were in the prison of married life." This interpretation is obviously strained; and just how it is related to the poem is unclear.

Perhaps we might do better to remember that St. Leonard was also supposed to help pregnant women through confinement (see

Catholic Encyclopedia). If Chaucer is referring to a pilgrimage made for the purpose of asking St. Leonard's intercession in a childbirth, the line (hitherto quite unexplained), "To make lythe of that was hard," becomes immediately clear. Moreover, the suggestion that a person would be forgone with weariness after a mere pilgrimage of two miles sounds ridiculous—unless, perhaps, the pilgrim was a pregnant woman. In other words, this "Decembre the tenthe day" of Chaucer's is probably associated with childbirth in Chaucer's mind. It is generally believed that Chaucer's (or Gaunt's) son Thomas Chaucer was born in 1371 or 1372; Katharine, Gaunt's first child by Queen Constance, was born in 1372; and Joan Beaufort, Gaunt's first child by Katharine Swynford, was born early the next year (which was still 1372 by old reckoning). Thus, the year 1372 was a kind of *annus mirabilis*, for births, in the Gaunt ménage; and this very passage, so curious and seemingly so out of place in the poem, may be Chaucer's way of telling the year when his "Decembre the tenthe day" occurred.

To sum up, the eagle's bearing Chaucer to a "fer countree" to learn new tales of love; the thronging of Greco-Roman-Italian (no French) poets, romancers, and historians about the House of Fame; the emphasis, in the Dido story, on Italy; the obsession of all Italy with the idea of fame; the date of December tenth, and the probabilty that the year was 1372, coinciding with the beginning of Chaucer's first trip to Italy—all this suggests that the House of Fame that Chaucer visited in his dream was (in at least one of its aspects) Italy.

If the conclusion just recorded is sound, several other minor, but very knotty, problems in the poem may be solved.

1] It has been noted that "Repeatedly in his poem [Chaucer] emphasizes the fact that he owed his journey to the House of Fame to the favor of the thunder-god Jupiter"[16] (ll. 609-10, 632, 661-62, 2007-9). This fact has served to connect the poem with Thor, and therefore Thursday, and thence a theory about a December tenth which falls on Thursday—all of which seems to be forced reasoning. But it seems pretty obvious that, if this poem may be interpreted as (partly) an account of Chaucer's official trip to Italy, then his Jupiter, king of the gods, who sent him on his journey, is none other than Edward III. Chaucer's stressing the fact that Jupiter is responsible for the whole trip is probably the poet's way of rendering thanks to the king.

2] If Jupiter is Edward III, who is the great golden eagle who actually transports the poet to the House of Fame? It has been proposed that the eagle represents philosophy, or knowledge, or thought, or some other abstract quality. Steadman says that Chaucer, by using the eagle, "emphasizes the purely intellectual character of his journey, the fact that his aerial visit is essentially a flight of thought."[17] This is true—insofar as a search for literary example and inspiration is intellectual and thoughtful. But for several reasons it seems insufficient to regard the eagle as a mere abstract symbol. First, the eagle in Dante (whom Chaucer closely imitates in this episode) was not an abstract quality, but a real person, Santa Lucia (*Purgatorio*, IX), who had assumed the form of an eagle. Next, the eagle speaks not only "In mannes vois" (l. 556), but also "Ryght in the same vois and stevene / That useth oon that I koude nevene" (ll. 561-62).* Evidently the eagle represents a man with whom Chaucer is well acquainted. Furthermore, what the eagle tells the poet "was goodly seyd to me, / So nas hyt never wont to be" (ll. 565-66). This has every earmark of a joke about some man with whom Chaucer was quite familiar, but who is playfully pictured as habitually reprimanding the poet. Evidently the unknown is Chaucer's superior. In consideration of the fact that (as has been shown in a previous chapter) John of Gaunt's heraldic symbol was an eagle, that John of Gaunt apparently figures as an eagle in *Troilus and Criseyde* and in the *Parliament of Fowls*, that John of Gaunt was exercising a powerful influence on the government at the time Chaucer was first sent to Italy, and that John of Gaunt and Chaucer were on friendly (perhaps intimate) terms—the eagle probably represents John of Gaunt.

3] If the eagle does represent Gaunt, that nobleman would doubtless have been flattered to be considered a symbol of philosophy or intellect, as some scholars have interpreted the bird. Perhaps Gaunt had a habit of holding forth, somewhat as the eagle did, on natural philosophy; and Chaucer has here good-naturedly caricatured him. Perhaps this caricature accounts for Chaucer's malediction, at the beginning of the poem (ll. 91-108), on those who would take offense at it.

* More than one critic has said that, in these lines, Chaucer is referring humorously to his wife. But this is a romantic (or unromantic) interpretation that, so far as I can see, is quite without evidence or merit. The voice was a *man's*.

4] If the eagle represents Gaunt, there must be an even deeper significance in certain parts of the poem. As I have said in a previous chapter, Chaucer is obsessed by the thought of faithful women deserted by faithless lovers; and I have suggested that the possibility (and the eventual reality) of Gaunt's deserting Katharine Swynford in order to go off to claim the throne of Spain may have been the chief reason for Chaucer's continual concern with this situation. In the tale of Dido and other deserted women in Book I, Chaucer may be once more suggesting that men who desert their mistresses are not admirable. One passage in the poem seems to point straight at Gaunt:

> Allas! is every man thus trewe,
> That every yer wolde have a newe,
> Yf hit so longe tyme dure,
> Or elles three, peraventure?
> As thus: of oon he wolde have fame
> In magnyfyinge of hys name;
> Another for frendshippe, seyth he;
> And yet ther shal the thridde be
> That shal be take for delyt,
> Loo, or for synguler profit. (301-10)

The first of these women could be Constance of Spain; the second might be almost anyone (but note the possible irony of "seyth he"); and the third would almost certainly be Katharine Swynford. Such a passage, pointing at Gaunt, would be reason enough for Chaucer's introductory warning that people not take offense at the poem.

If this poem was written between 1386 and 1389 (when Gaunt was actually away from England, and was hoping to be able to remain away permanently), the bitter story of Dido's desertion by Aeneas would have been highly appropriate as a climactic and ironic conclusion of a poem which begins with Gaunt's (the eagle's) interest in love stories. And the poet's very special aversion toward Theseus ("The devel be hys soules bane!" l. 408), who deserted Ariadne, "lefte hir slepynge in an ile" (l. 416), and "gan to shippe goo" (l. 420), would be understandable. Moreover, the following lines would be especially applicable:

> But wel-away! the harm, the routhe,
> That hath betyd for such untrouthe,
> As men may ofte in bokes rede,
> And al day sen hyt yet in dede. (383-86)

The last line hints at a continuing situation.

But Gaunt did not remain away from England and Katharine; he returned home in 1389, presumably resumed relations with Katharine, and certainly married her when he was free to do so. Accordingly, Chaucer's bitter and ironic poem about women deserted by faithless men was no longer fitting. Perhaps it was at this time that he decided to subject his poem to major revision. He transferred the Dido story from the end to the beginning; he inserted the introductory warning (ll. 91-108) that readers should not take offense at the poem; he inserted the lines (ll. 427-32) excusing Aeneas; and he planned to revise the rest of the poem to conform to his new scheme—but he never got around to it (he even left it in mid-air with a half-finished sentence).

I suspect that it is not coincidental that Chaucer wrote four poems (*House of Fame, Anelida and Arcite, Legend of Good Women,* and the "Squire's Tale") that deal scathingly with faithless men—and that *every one of these poems as we have it today is incomplete.* Did Chaucer write them while Gaunt was preparing to desert (or after he had deserted) Katharine—and then destroy their endings when Gaunt returned to Katharine? Did he plan to write new endings for them when he found time—and never found time?

The House of Rumor is something quite separate from the House of Fame; and what has been said of the latter possibly representing Italy and her literary tradition does not apply to the former.

But the eagle figures in the story of both houses. He tells Chaucer concerning the House of Rumor:

> But certeyn, oon thyng I the telle,
> That but I bringe the therinne,
> Ne shalt thou never kunne gynne
> To come into hyt, out of doute.   (2002-5)

The eagle then adds that "Joves, of his grace," and "thrugh hys myghty merite,... yaf expres commaundement, / To which I am obedient" (ll. 2007, 2019, 2021-22), that Chaucer should be inducted into the House of Rumor. If Jove is the king, and the eagle is John of Gaunt, the House of Rumor must be some place, or situation, into which Chaucer is admitted through royal favor and by princely intercession. This is a place of perpetual whisperings and janglings

> Of werres, of pes, of mariages,
> Of reste, of labour, of viages,

> Of abood, of deeth, of lyf,
> Of love, of hate, accord, of stryf,
> Of loos, of lore, and of wynnynges,
> Of hele, of seknesse, of bildynges,
> Of faire wyndes, and of tempestes,
> Of qwalm of folk, and eke of bestes;
> Of dyvers transmutacions
> Of estats, and eke of regions;
> Of trust, of drede, of jelousye,
> Of wit, of wynnynge, of folye;
> Of plente, and of gret famyne,
> Of chepe, of derthe, and of ruyne;
> Of good or mys governement,
> Of fyr, and of dyvers accident. (1961-76)

It is a place where

> every wight that I saugh there
> Rouned [whispered] everych in others ere
> A newe tydynge prively. (2043-45)

It is a place where every "tydynge" is repeated over and over from mouth to mouth by everyone who hears it—and

> Were the tydynge soth or fals,
> Yit wolde he telle hyt natheless,
> And evermo with more encres
> Than it was erst. (2072-75)

The place where all this happens sounds exactly like a royal court, or palace, filled with busy gossip and rumor-mongering. The entire account may be a fanciful version of Gaunt's helping Chaucer find a place at court in the 1360's, or even at the king's palaces at Eltham and at Sheen in the 1380's—or perhaps inducting Chaucer into the "prees" (see the poem "Truth") of public life that sent him to Italy on at least two occasions.

The meaning

The preceding discussion has attempted to clarify or explain the larger mysteries of the *House of Fame*—including the problem of its unity, the function of the story of Dido, the abrupt ending, the general identity or function of the "man of gret auctorite," and the possible real-life identities of Jupiter, the eagle, the House of Fame, and the House of Rumor. But other problems remain.

Possibly the long account of the suppliants who approach the goddess Fame, together with her arbitrary decrees concerning them, is to be regarded as only another of those drawn-out moralistic digressions of which medieval writers were so fond. And Chaucer's own assertion (ll. 1876-82) that he desires no fame after his death may be taken as either a mere conventional renunciation, or as a Northern mind's sincere reaction to the Italian obsession with fame.

But there may be more here than meets the casual glance. Three or four facts about the poem deserve special notice.

First, Chaucer observes that when the rumors escape from the birdcage House of Rumor, they fly "streght to Fame" (l. 2111), who "yaf hem eke duracioun" (ll. 2112-13). That is (Chaucer is saying), it is of such stuff as these grotesque and gossipy rumors of court or palace that the old "love-tydvnges" of romance have been composed. All the old stories that have achieved fame—the works of Homer, Virgil, Statius, Lucan, Claudian, Ovid, and the other arbitrarily chosen servitors of Fame—are but magnified and distorted rumor, curious but hardly worthy of reverence. This cynical attitude toward the famous old tales is reflected in the cynical treatment of Fame's irrational decrees. Chaucer is saying quite plainly that these famous old tales (some of which he himself had retold in his poems, and in this very poem) are nothing but glorified gossip. He is disillusioned with those romances that Fame has seen fit to immortalize, and he turns away.

There is a second matter to be noted. Chaucer says that he came to the House of Fame "Somme newe tydynges for to lere" (l. 1886), but that what he found there were "no suche tydynges" (ll. 1884-95). He has learned no *new* stories from these writers whom Fame has honored, and placed forever about her palace, and he is not happy about it.

This renunciation of old masters is understandable if we recall a third fact about the poem—namely, its date. Very probably, it was written in the late 1380's (perhaps between 1386 and 1389, when Gaunt was in Spain), and some revision of it may date from the 1390's.[18] This was just the time when, as we know, Chaucer was turning away from imitation of, or dependence upon, ancient romancers, and developing his own original stories and creating original characters. Some of his dissatisfactions with old literary models may be reflected in the acknowledged wearisomeness of the romances that compose the "Monk's Tale," the burlesque of romance in the "Tale of Sir Thopas," and the unfinished series of derivative legends about "good" women. "Chaucer's growing power of artistry," says Manly, "his vast observation of life, and his newly devised method of imaginative reconstruction of the scenes, characters, and events of his"[19] *Canterbury Tales* showed him breaking loose from ancient models. Certain it is that all his genuinely realistic works, in which there is little or no dependence on the famous romancers of antiquity, are to be dated from about 1386, or later. These works include the "General Prologue" of the *Canterbury Tales,* the Prologue of the "Wife of Bath's Tale," and the tales of the Miller, Reeve, Friar, Summoner, Pardoner, Shipman, Nun's Priest, and Canon's Yeoman.

In short (even in a poem that demonstrates, almost ironically, that he *can* use his old masters), Chaucer may have signaled the major turning point of his career. Lines 1873 to 1917 in the *House of Fame* may herald a type of poetry altogether distinct from that which Chaucer wrote earlier. Looking back, from a vantage point of fifteen or twenty years' additional life and experience, to his first visit to Italy, the fountainhead of literary fame, Chaucer now wants none of the kind of fame meted out there. He perceives there no *"newe* tydynges," no *"newe* thinges" (ll. 1886, 1887), but only old gossip and rumor arbitrarily perpetuated. He turns away from it, "Out of the castel, soth to seye" (l. 1917), disappointed and disillusioned. Henceforth, he resolves, he will be independent:

> I wot myself best how y stonde;
> For what I drye, or what I thynke,
> I wil myselven al hyt drynke,
> Certeyn, for the more part,
> As fer forth as I kan myn art.   (1878-82)

(Perhaps he meant to give special emphasis to "myn" in the last line here quoted?) These lines may be a Declaration of Literary Independence as significant as Wordsworth's Preface to the *Lyrical Ballads*. They may mark the beginning of modern English literature. Scholars have long troubled themselves about the "Medieval-Modern Conflict" in Chaucer; perhaps it is right here that the conflict is decided, and English literature takes a new direction— away from preoccupation with *old* books, *old* masters, *old* "auctoritee," and toward "*newe* tydynges," "*newe* thynges": the real world of actual people. Perhaps this very poem, which seems to many readers only another dull example of medieval abstractionizing, is one of the most largely meaningful poems Chaucer ever wrote.

Why he decided to turn from his medievalistic early tales to more "modern" themes and methods is anybody's guess. Perhaps he merely matured (as Manly suggests) as a person, a thinker, and an artist; or perhaps, like other great artists, he was almost unconsciously sensitive to the groundswell of literary change that was moving quietly beneath him; or perhaps he grew personally disillusioned with the romantic ideals and the unrealistic romancing of the Middle Ages—with the puffed-up glory of kings, the "extravagantly brilliant décor" of royal government, the foolish artificialities of the poetry that had long been fashionable at court. Perhaps the growing corruption of England, and the fading of English power and honor everywhere, made him turn away disgusted from the glittering unrealities of his romantic masters. Perhaps, indeed, it was the seemingly final withdrawal of John of Gaunt from his mistress, in 1386, that brought Chaucer's ideals of courtly and romantic love crashing about him. In the *Book of the Duchess*, the second and third parts of the *Parliament of Fowls*, the *Complaint of Mars, Troilus and Criseyde*, and some of the *Canterbury Tales* written before the mid-1380's, Chaucer had been the willing spokesman and defender of these romantic and courtly ideals. Ever since John had first courted Blanche, and then since he had courted Katharine, Chaucer had before him what seemed to be living evidence of the reality of those ideals. But then, when Gaunt deserted Katharine and went to Spain, the living evidence collapsed, and Chaucer entered the disillusioned period in which he produced *Anelida and Arcite*, the tragic tale of the falcon in the "Squire's Tale," the dismal series of poems about "good" women deserted by their lovers, and the bitter story of Dido's tragedy that was intended to be the harsh climax, the "knotte," of the *House of Fame*.

Chaucer had discovered that romance and courtliness cannot forever endure in the human heart; they are only capricious rumor, palace gossip, the buzzing talk of the market place or the court, arbitrarily magnified and immortalized by Fame. This is the reason that the poem was to end (if the hypothesis that the story of Dido originally came last is correct) with the poet emerging from the

Temple of Love on to a wide, barren desert. It will be recalled that, in the *Parliament of Fowls*, the poet emerged from the Temple of Love on to "an hil of floures" (l. 302). The contrast is obvious. What Chaucer is trying to say in the *House of Fame* is that romantic love is "fantome and illusion" (l. 493), and that the famous romances of antiquity are mere rumor arbitrarily perpetuated by Fame. Henceforth, the poet resolves, he will reject the famous old romances, of this sort, and seek after "newe thynges."

Chapter VII. The daisy and "Good Alceste"

If the *House of Fame* is a poem of profound intellectual complexity, the Prologue of the *Legend of Good Women* is a poem of nebulous and elusive suggestion. It is a continuous fugitive from logic, an adventurer outside the bounds of rationality. More than with any other poem discussed in this book, the critic who would understand the Prologue must depend on imaginative intuition to help him comprehend the general direction in which the poem flows, and then hope that a closer study of details will confirm his intuitions. If the Prologue can be approached in any other manner, I have not discovered it.

The poem begins with a tribute to books, goes on to say how passionately the poet worships the daisy, and then tells how the poet sleeps and dreams. In his dream he sees the God of Love, approaching hand in hand with Queen Alcestis. The god is clothed in silk, green-embroidered; Alcestis is clothed in a green gown and wears a white crown with a golden circlet so that she resembles a daisy. These two are followed by a train of innumerable ladies. The god forthwith accuses the poet of showing heresy against Love's laws in poems he has written. Alcestis intervenes and pleads in the poet's behalf. He is forgiven but is required as penance to write, year after year, a series of tales of women who have been faithful in love.

Three questions that scholars have often raised concerning this Prologue are these: (*1*) Is the daisy, whom the poet worships, an allegory of anybody or anything, and if so, of whom or of what? (*2*) Is Alcestis an allegorical representation of some real person, and if so, of whom? (*3*) Is the God of Love an allegorical representation of some real person, and if so, of whom?

As usual with Chaucerian scholarship, the answers to these three crucial questions have been almost as numerous as the scholars attempting to answer them.

The daisy

Ten Brink says, "It is clear that the Alcestis of the Prologue represents Richard's Queen Anne."[1] Skeat concurs;[2] so does Root;[3] and so do a good many other scholars. J. B. Bilderbeck argues that

if Alcestis is Anne, then the God of Love is Richard II;[4] Skeat concurs; and Brusendorff thinks it "not unlikely" that the God of Love
represents Richard.[5] Lowes, however, denies that the two figures
represent the English royal couple;[6] and Kittredge,[7] in 1909, bluntly
showed the illogicality of regarding either the daisy or Alcestis as
representing Anne. Miss Galway[8] has maintained that Alcestis
represents Joan, the Black Prince's widow, and that the God of Love
is her son Richard. But other writers have shown that the evidence on which Miss Galway based her identification does not really
bear out her conclusions;[9] and Miss Galway herself has modified
some of her original views.[10]

Most of the recent scholarship has veered away from precise
historical identification of the figures in the poem. Brewer expresses
a common idea: "There is no need to suppose any allegorical significance."[11] Other scholars have taken positions somewhere between
that of the historical allegorists and the absolute non-allegorists.
Speirs, for example, finds that "The lady in green is the daisy—or the
daisy is she—and she is Alcestis; and she, who is both daisy and
Alcestis, and perhaps the Queen of England, is herself a symbol; a
symbol of the courtly ideal of womanhood."[12] Tatlock seems to be
of much the same mind as Speirs. "What would it mean," asks Tatlock, "to say that Alcestis is the daisy and that both are Queen Anne?
The identification is of course undefinable. It is impossible to say
more than that the poet is passing on to the Queen the beauty,
sweetness, and goodness of the daisy, and of the Greek lady. Any
reader or auditor would understand the Prologue in no other way
than this, as high and unmistakable tribute to Queen Anne."[13]
Jefferson takes a truly middle-of-the-road position. He thinks that
Chaucer first worships the daisy as Anne; then the poem moves into
a neutral zone where Anne and Alcestis merge into each other; and
finally (in the last one hundred and fifty lines of the Prologue)
Alcestis is not Anne. As for the daisy, Chaucer's "prolonged adoration of the daisy through almost two hundred lines is really irrelevant in the sense that it contributes nothing essential to the introduction of the Legend of Good Women."[14]

In trying to throw new light on these matters, we should try first,
perhaps, to determine whether the daisy that Chaucer worships in
the first part of the poem really *is* one and the same with Alcestis.
Chaucer says that Alcestis was crowned in white "For al the world,
right *as* a dayesye" (F 218; G 150); and this crown above the green

"Made hire *lyk* a daysie" (F 224; G 156). The God of Love, while standing beside Alcestis, sees Chaucer kneeling by the daisy and asks how he dares come so near that flower (F 316)—with no suggestion that the flower and Alcestis are the same. Then the god, Alcestis, and the women with them sit in a circle about the daisy as it grows in the meadow—a gesture manifestly impossible if the daisy were Alcestis herself. The women then sing "to this flour / That bereth our alder pris in figurynge" (F 297-98), which means, I take it, that "this flower figures forth, or reflects, or represents, what we all value." None of these passages implies that the daisy and Alcestis are identical. They imply instead that the virtues of Alcestis are reflected in the daisy, and the virtues of the daisy reflected in Alcestis.

On the other hand, at least one passage in the poem *seems* to imply that Alcestis is the daisy. The God of Love asks Chaucer:

F 510 "Hastow nat in book, lyth in thy cheste,
511   The grete goodnesse of the quene Alceste,
512   That turned was into a dayesye;
513   She that for hire housbonde chees to dye,
514   And eke to goon to helle, rather than he... ?"
517   And I answered ageyn, and sayde, "Yis,
518   Now knowe I hire. And is this good Alceste,
519   The dayesie, and myn owne hertes reste? ...
523   Wel hath she quyt me myn affeccioun,
524   That I have to hire flour, the dayesye.
525   No wonder ys thogh Jove hire stellyfye,
526   As telleth Agaton, for hire goodnesse! ...
530   In remembraunce of hire and in honour
531   Cibella maade the daysye and the flour
532   Ycrowned al with whit, as men may see.

It looks as if Chaucer were saying here (l. 512) that Alcestis was actually turned into a daisy. Yet Chaucer immediately speaks of "hire flour" (l. 524) as if she and the daisy were separate things. Furthermore, though Alcestis "turned was into a dayesye," Jove has made a star of her (l. 525); and though Alcestis was both turned into a daisy (it seems) and made a star, Cibella created the daisy (l. 531). All this is so ambiguous and, apparently, so self-contradictory that it almost discourages attempts to find logic in it. Lines 518-19 are equally puzzling. Here Alcestis, the daisy, and "myn owne hertes reste" seem to be in apposition with one another, as if they were all the same. If this is the case, and even though the matter is put as a question and not as a statement of fact, the lines do seem to equate Alcestis and the daisy. But before the reader leaps to the conclusion that when Chaucer speaks of the daisy he invariably means Alcestis, and that when he speaks of Alcestis he invariably means the daisy, I should like to ask the reader to proceed a little farther in this chapter. The identification of Alcestis with the daisy may not be so cut-and-dried as it would appear from lines 512 and 518-19.

In any event, if these lines do equate Alcestis and the daisy, they are the only lines in the poem that do suggest such a thing. Moreover, as I have already said, ll. F 218, F 224, F 297-98, and F 316 suggest that Alcestis is *not* the daisy. If we choose to accept this latter interpretation (as I think we should), the question still remains: What is the daisy?

The answer to this question involves another: What is Chaucer trying to do in the Prologue? Lowes thinks that the Prologue is only another link in a chain of artificial *marguerite* (daisy) poems extending back through Machaut, Deschamps, and Froissart;[15] Kittredge suggests the same thing, with the additional hint that Chaucer may have sent the Prologue to Deschamps as a graceful gesture in answer to a complimentary communication of the French poet.[16] Marsh sees the Prologue as the first appearance in English poetry of the Flower *versus* Leaf controversy[17]—"a sentimental debate which was amusing the leisure of high society in England."[18]

This view of the lightness of the Prologue may be correct; and the poem may have no more purpose than fashionable dilly-dallying with the subject of love. On the other hand, its solemn beginning on the subject of an afterlife, its tribute to books and learning, its passionately expressed reverence for the daisy, its emphatic disclaimer of concern with the Flower-Leaf controversy (F 188-96; G 71-80), its creation of the tragic figure of Alcestis as the inspirer of a series of tragic tales, and Chaucer's own complex mind that includes ulterior meanings (as we have seen) in even such seeming fantasies as the *Parliament of Fowls*, the *House of Fame*, the *Complaint of Mars*, and *Troilus and Criseyde*—these considerations alone would make us suspect that the Prologue of the *Legend of Good Women* is not merely a light and meaningless fantasy on the artificialities of courtly love.

All this brings us back to the original question: If the Prologue is too serious to be *merely* a conventional *marguerite* poem, and if its author tells us flatly that it is not *merely* a traditional Flower-and-

Leaf poem, and if it *does* contain a deeper meaning than appears on the surface—what is the daisy?

The most noticeable thing about that section of the poem showing Chaucer's devotion to the daisy is the poet's concern, just here, with bookish matters. He leads up to his daisy by telling of the wisdom to be found in books (F 17-28; G 17-28). He goes on to say that he seldom gives over his reading unless it be to pay reverence to the daisy (F 29-39; G 29-39); he wishes he "had Englyssh, ryme or prose, / Suffisant this flour to preyse aryght" (F 66-67; see also G 59-60); he pays tribute to others who in their "fresshe songes" have honored the daisy and served it just as Chaucer himself tries to serve it (F 73-83; G 61-70); and he ends the passage on the daisy by announcing his intention "in English to declare / Of many a story" (G 86-87; see also F 101-2). In other words, the entire daisy passage is linked throughout with matters literary.

This hint suggests an interpretation that, surprisingly, has not been heretofore recorded. The daisy itself may be a symbol of literature or of literary creation. It has every appearance of being "the passion poesy" which dominated Chaucer's heart—in particular, that type of poetry which he wrote in his early years, and which he is about to write in the *Legend of Good Women*—that is, poetry about love. Evidence for this interpretation seems to me most convincing. As a matter of fact, if one reads the entire daisy passage (F 40-124, 180-87; G 40-106) with this interpretation in mind, it is at once illuminated and clarified in every detail.

The poet so delights in books, study, and devotion (F 30-39; G 30-39) that he rarely leaves them. But on holidays and in the month of May, that "tyme of love and jolite,"[19] he goes out to see the daisy "ayein the sonne sprede" (F 48; G 48). He is overjoyed to be with it; he pays it all reverence; he sees it as

> of alle floures flour
> Fulfilled of al vertu and honour. (F 53-54)

Chaucer knew that love can die (this very poem is mostly a record of the faithless loves of men); he knew that life is short; he knew that Fortune has her way with men. But this one flower, this daisy, this passion poesy, is "evere ylike fayr and fressh of hewe, / As wel in wynter as in somer newe" (G 57-58). This is the poet's "joy forever":

That blisful sighte softneth al my sorwe,
So glad am I, whan that I have presence
Of it, to doon it alle reverence . . .
And I love it, and ever ylike newe,
And evere shal, til that myn herte dye. . . .
She is the clernesse and the verray lyght
That in this derke world me wynt and ledeth.   (F 50 ff.)

Even while expressing this passionate devotion, Chaucer drops innumerable hints that the real object of this devotion is poesy. He says that he is only repeating what others in their "fresshe songes sayd" (F 79; G 67), and that he is only "glenyng here and there" (F 75; G 63) after the old poets. All this he does "in service of the flour / Whom that I serve as I have wit and myght" (F 82-83). She is the "maistresse of my wit" (F 88). And

My word, my werk ys knyt so in youre bond
That, as an harpe obeieth to the hond
And maketh it soune after his fyngerynge,
Ryght so mowe ye out of myn herte bringe
Swich vois, ryght as yow lyst, to laughe or pleyne.
Be ye my gide and lady sovereyne!
As to myn erthly god to yow I calle,
Both in this werk and in my sorwes alle.   (F 89-96)

Without spelling it out in so many words, the poet could hardly have said more clearly that he is calling the spirit of poesy to help him in the work he has undertaken.

My besy gost, that thursteth alwey newe
To seen this flour so yong, so fressh of hewe,
Constreyned me with so gledy desir
That in myn herte I feele yet the fir.   (F 103-06)

But though the daisy itself can be an eternal joy to him, it flourishes only in "the brightnesse / Of the sonne" (F 64-65). "So hateth she derknesse" (F 63), and "So sore it is afered of the nyght" (G 53) that "whan the soone gynneth for to weste, / Thanne closeth it, and draweth it to reste" (G 51-52; see also F 61-63). That is, the flower of poesy flourishes only in the sunlight of encouragement and approval, of peace and joy, of innocence and youth.

It has been suggested by several scholars that the daisy represents "the incarnation of love."[20] This conception is partly right—since the kind of poesy Chaucer seems to have symbolized in the daisy is love poetry, or perhaps the poetic quality of love. This is especially true of the F version; the much later (and more religion-slanted[21]) G version shows Chaucer carefully correcting any idea that the daisy symbolizes love poetry alone. In the F version the God of Love asks Chaucer, " 'What dostow her / So nygh myn oune floure?' " (F 315-16); but in the later G version Love asks, " 'What dost thow her / In my presence?' " (G 241-42). Two lines later, in the F version, Love again reprimands Chaucer for approaching so near "my flour" (F 318); but in the G version Love reprimands the poet for coming merely "in my syght" (G 244).

In this very passage, in which Love objects to the kind of poetry Chaucer has written, the god says:

"What dostow her
So nygh myn oune floure, so boldely?
Yt were better worthy, trewely,
A worm to neghen ner my flour than thow." (F 315-18)

Relating Chaucer's poetry to his worship of the daisy, as the god does here, could not more plainly suggest the real nature of the daisy.

Love's last word to the poet, in telling him to write of faithful ladies, is this:

"Make the metres of hem as the lest—...
And serve alwey the fresshe dayesye." (F 562, 565)

That is, "Write in any manner that you wish—but serve always the true spirit of poesy."

In this poem introducing a series of poems that are admittedly gleaned from other poets (F 75-79; G 61-67), we have, in the long passage about the daisy, what is almost certainly the first major tribute to poetry ever written by a major English poet.

Alcestis

The point has already been made that we have good reason to believe that Alcestis is not to be invariably identified with the daisy. No doubt she is symbolical of faithful wifehood—just as was her mythological prototype. But is that all? Does she stand for something, or somebody, else?

Many writers have said that she represents Queen Anne. But (as Kittredge pointed out long ago) Chaucer's reference to her as having died and gone to hell (F 514; G 502) was hardly calculated to please a "queen who was but nineteen or twenty years old, full of the joy of life, and the center of a brilliant court."[22]   Again, if Alcestis represents the queen, it would be a "queer whimsy" for Chaucer to have Alcestis tell him that, when this very poem is finished, he should "yive it the quene" (F 496).   Furthermore, the God of Love commanded Chaucer to write, among his Legends of Good Women, the story of Alcestis—a "clumsy fiction" that would be "fraught with embarrassments and perplexities of every kind" if Alcestis were Anne.   Kittredge's reasoning is so cogent that I think we may discard, once and for all, the Alcestis-equals-Anne hypothesis.

Miss Galway's hypothesis that Alcestis equals Princess Joan is based (it seems on close examination) on no positive evidence.   Besides, the Princess Joan outlived her husband nine years; she did not die in his place, as Alcestis died in her husband's place.   This fact alone would make Joan an extremely unlikely candidate as the model for Alcestis.*

If we do seek to identify Alcestis with any actual person (and such an effort is probably justifiable), we must search for a good wife who was dead at the time the poem was written, who died before her husband, who was of high rank, who was of interest to Chaucer, who was of interest to court circles likely to read (or hear) Chaucer's Prologue, and who, possibly, might have had some interest in Chaucer himself—since she knew a good deal about him, and spoke in his behalf.   (It might be tentatively added that, in view of the role played by John of Gaunt and some of his connections in other poems by Chaucer, we might also look for a woman, the original of Alcestis, who would have some connection with Gaunt.)   The first woman one thinks of as meeting these requirements is, of course, the Duchess Blanche of Lancaster.

Though I do not think the evidence for this identification is absolutely conclusive, I do think more can be said for it, and less against it, than is the case with any other identification yet proposed.

* Miss Galway and others have taken the lecture on the duties of kingship that Alcestis gives the God of Love (F 373-411; G 353-97) to be the sort of dressing-down that the Princess Joan, or Queen Anne, might have given Richard.   But it is the same sort of lecture that Chaucer himself uttered in "Lak of Stedfastnesse" without benefit of princess or queen.   Actually, the lecture in the Prologue is mostly a plea for the king not to mistreat his great lords who "ben half-goddes."   It is just the sort of thing that Chaucer might have been expected to write between 1384 and 1389, when the king was feuding with the greatest lords in the realm—John of Gaunt, Thomas Duke of Gloucester, and Henry Bolingbroke.

In the first place, we should remember that Alcestis' dying for her husband implied something more than merely a life for a life. Alcestis' death implied that (as the *Oxford Classical Dictionary*, p. 30, puts it) "the rest of her life was transferred to her husband." Thus, Blanche's early death might be poetically interpreted as a guarantee of long life for Gaunt. The appropriateness of this fancy was probably augmented by a coincidence which Miss Anderson describes: "The war with France had been re-opened in 1369, and John of Gaunt had been sent to Calais in July with a small army. On September 12 the English and French armies lay facing each other, the English, who were outnumbered, expecting an attack, when, to their surprise, the great fires seen in the French camp proved to be a sign of the French departure. On that very day— September 12—Blanche died."[23] Superstition or poetic imagination might well have seen the coincidence as a mysterious exchange of Blanche's life for additional years to be enjoyed by Gaunt. Accordingly, Blanche could have been regarded as another Alcestis— giving her life to increase the life-span of her husband.

Next, there is a passage in *Troilus and Criseyde* that has a highly significant bearing on the present argument. Cassandra is telling Troilus that Criseyde is faithless. Troilus replies angrily:

> "As wel thow myghtest lien on Alceste,
> That was of creatures, but men lye,
> That evere weren, kyndest and the beste!
> For whan hire housbonde was in jupertye
> To dye hymself, but if she wolde dye,
> She ches for hym to dye and gon to helle,
> And starf anon, as us the bokes telle." (V, 1527-33)

If Criseyde represents Katharine Swynford (as she most probably does), the reference to Alcestis can hardly be anything but a reference to Blanche—to whose perfect goodness all contemporary historical records, as well as poems of Chaucer and Froissart, bear witness.

Almost at the end of the *Troilus* Chaucer, writing of the faithlessness of Criseyde, says:

> And gladlier I wol write, yif yow leste,
> Penelopees trouthe and good Alceste. (V, 1777-78)

If Criseyde represents Katharine, the references here must be, first, to Queen Constance (who needed, and seems to have exhibited,

Penelope's patience—and whose sufferings may be vaguely adumbrated in the "Man of Law's Tale"), and then to the dead Blanche. These lines have their echo in the Prologue now under examination. The God of Love asks Chaucer:

> Why noldest thow han writen of Alceste,
> And laten Criseide ben aslepe and reste? (G 530-31)

In short, it appears that Blanche is twice referred to as Alcestis in the *Troilus*, along with a half-promise that the poet will write about her—and that this half-promise is deliberately recalled in the Prologue of the *Legend of Good Women*. The pieces fit together remarkably well.

Some possible heraldic hints in the Prologue deserve at least a passing glance. Much is made of the colors green and white that Alcestis wears. Now Richard II's standard was "divided lengthwise into white and green, and bore the royal motto in gold. The border was also white and green."[24] This circumstance might suggest that, after all, Alcestis represents Richard's Queen Anne—were it not for the obvious contradictory elements noted by Kittredge and already referred to.

Green and white were the colors that the Black Prince's Welshmen wore into battle,[25] and that have long been associated with Wales. This circumstance might suggest that Miss Galway was right, and that Alcestis does represent Joan, Princess of Wales. The difficulty here lies in the fact that Joan could not possibly have been imagined as giving her life for her husband, since she outlived him by nine years.

Marsh probably has the truth about these colors. He has pointed out that the green and white were long associated with the Flower-and-Leaf cult. The colors played a major role in the continental festivities celebrating the cult, in the costumes that the participants in the festivities wore, and in poems about the cult.[26] The celebrants, however, did not wear both colors at once—as Alcestis does. Some of the celebrants wore white, and some wore green; they did not wear parti-colored costumes. It would seem, therefore, that Chaucer, in garbing Alcestis in both white and green, was trying to suggest that she encompassed the virtues of both the Flower and the Leaf.

It is just possible that certain other details of color may have some bearing on the identification of Alcestis with Blanche of

Lancaster. Her "white coroune" is emphasized much more than her green gown. In less than ninety lines (ll. 216-303) Chaucer mentions the white crown no less than six times, and several more times thereafter. He is evidently calling particular attention to it. In fourteenth-century England kings and queens wore gold crowns; the only nobles allowed to wear crowns of any kind were dukes and duchesses—and their crowns were *silver*.[27] Thus, Alcestis, though called a queen, is really crowned like a duchess. Chaucer's repeated emphasis on her white crown may be, therefore, a deliberate device to inform his hearers that he is *not* writing about Queen Anne. Furthermore, there may be some echo, in the whiteness of the crown, of the "good faire White" of the *Book of the Duchess*.

Another curious heraldic possibility should be mentioned. No commentator has ever explained the following lines:

> In remembraunce of hire and in honour
> Cibella maade the daysye and the flour
> Ycrowned al with whit, as men may see;
> And Mars yaf to hire corowne reed, pardee,
> In stede of rubyes, set among the white. (F 530-34)

Since there is no known connection, in myth or literature, between Cibella (Cybele) and the daisy, we may wonder whether Chaucer is here punning on the name of Blanche's mother Isabella, who gave Blanche her name ("Ycrowned al with whit")—though this interpretation would imply identification of the daisy with the woman. Isabella was a Beaumont; and the Beaumont crest was a "chapeau" with a wide turned-up brim of white ermine. When the great warrior Henry of Lancaster married Isabella, he brought her the ducal crown and the red rose as a badge. Isabella and Henry's daughter Blanche thus inherited both white and red for her crown. This bit of heraldic fancy is not offered as anything like proof that Alcestis is Blanche. But it does accord with that hypothesis, and explains lines hitherto mysterious.

More convincing evidence can be found in the poem. The God of Love asks Chaucer:

> "Hastow nat in book, lyth in thy cheste,
> The grete goodnesse of the quene Alceste,
> That turned was into a dayesye?" (F 510-12)

Now there is no book or myth known in which Alcestis is turned into a daisy. But if the daisy represents poesy, then Blanche of

Lancaster was indeed turned into a daisy, and Chaucer must have had in his chest the very book which effected the transformation—his own *Book of the Duchess*. (It is to be noted that he kept the book in his "cheste," not "at his beddes heed" where he would have kept ordinary books.)

A few lines farther on, Chaucer's question that seems so mysterious takes on a new meaning in the light of this interpretation. " 'And is this good Alceste, / The dayesie, and myn owene hertes reste?' " (F 518-19). The question might be translated: "And is this Blanche, the spirit of poesy, and the ideal which I worship?" Evidently he is already acquainted with her (his immediately subsequent remarks show that he knows all about her); and his adoration of her may hark back to the years that he knew her in the 1360's.

Two lines later the poet says of Alcestis

> That both aftir hir deth and in hir lyf
> Hir grete bounte doubleth hire renoun.   (F 521-22; G 509-10)

Though Robinson glosses the word "bounte" as "goodness, kindness; virtue, excellence," the word had also (as early as 1300, according to the *N. E. D.*) its present meaning of *liberality, generosity, munificence*. In both senses, the word fits Blanche more than it does the mythological Alcestis. Blanche was not only kind and virtuous, but also munificent in bringing her husband the immense Lancaster estates, and leaving them to him "aftir hir deth."

A few lines farther on, the God of Love tells the poet that Alcestis "taught al the craft of fyn lovynge, / And namely of wyfhod the lyvynge" (F 544-45). She, like Blanche in the *Book of the Duchess*, is both the perfect lover and the perfect wife. Everything said about Alcestis fits what we know about Blanche, and what Chaucer said about Blanche in his earlier poem.

Chaucer says that the poet "Agaton" has told about Jove's "stellyfying" Alcestis (F 525-26; G 513-14). If the Greek poet Agatho told such a tale, no one ever heard of it. Chaucer chose the name at random (it is generally believed) from lists of writers in Dante or Boccaccio, and the choice has no significance. But the "stellyfying" is another matter. Possibly there is a pun involving "dayesye," the literal meaning of which is, of course, "day's eye"—that is, the sun. Thus the question asked by the poet, "And is this goode Alceste, / The dayesye, and myn owene hertes reste?" (G 506-07; F 518-19)

could mean, "And is this Blanche, who is the spirit of poetry, the
light of my world, and my heart's peace?" Read so, the lines would
echo some earlier lines about Blanche in the *Book of the Duchess*:

> For I dare swere, withoute doute,
> That as the someres sonne bryght
> Ys fairer, clerer, and hath more lyght
> Than any other planete in heven,
> The moone, or the sterres seven,
> For al the world so hadde she
> Surmounted hem alle of beautee.   (820-26)

One final detail may be worth noting. Though the Alcestis
of legend was Queen of Thessaly, Chaucer makes her Queen of
Thrace (F 432; G 422), which is traditionally a rough northern
region, just as Lancashire was a rough northern region.

In general, the identification of Alcestis with Blanche of Lancaster is suggested because no other prominent figure of Chaucer's
time, and one in whom Chaucer would be likely to have an interest,
fits the conditions of Alcestis' imagined existence and personality so
well as does Blanche. Furthermore, a multitude of details in the
poem are consistent with the hypothesis that Alcestis is Blanche—
and no details (except Alcestis' title of "Queen") are inconsistent
with that hypothesis.

In addition to being Blanche, Alcestis clearly symbolizes, of
course, the faithful love of woman and the virtue of perfect wifehood. This love is associated with poesy (partly because Chaucer
was writing the Prologue to a series of poems on love and lovers,
and partly because he had already celebrated Blanche in a famous
poem), which in turn is symbolized by the daisy. The daisy was
chosen because the *marguerite* poems of France had long since
established a tradition of love and poetry for Chaucer to follow.
Blanche was chosen because John of Gaunt and his now mature
and influential son Henry Bolingbroke would have been interested
in a poem about her—and because, having written the *Troilus* about
Katharine Swynford, Chaucer might have felt (even if public
opinion had not influenced him) that writing about Gaunt's legitimate wives would now be in order and appropriate. In the *Troilus*
he had hinted, as I have said, about telling the stories of "Penelopeës
trouthe and good Alceste" (V, 1778). The Prologue of the *Legend
of Good Women* looks very much like a poem that redeems the
latter part of this half-promise.

The God of Love

The last remaining important mystery about this poem centers about the God of Love. Does he represent any real person? And if so, whom? In answering these questions, we should note that Love never does call Alcestis "*my* queen"; and only once (F 302) in Robinson's edition is she designated as "his queen." But in some of the manuscripts even this phrase appears as "this queen"; and the G version has "this queen" (G 228). In other words, it seems that Chaucer did not regard the God of Love and Alcestis as a wedded couple—and that therefore, even though Alcestis may represent Blanche, the God of Love does not represent Gaunt. It should be said, however, that it would have been very unlikely for Chaucer to refer to Alcestis as "his queen" even if the God of Love is to be identified with Gaunt—for Gaunt already had a queen, Constance of Spain, when this poem was written. Consequently, Gaunt as the original of the God of Love cannot be entirely ruled out.

Perhaps the God of Love is nothing more than the God of Love. At any rate, he says, toward the end of the Prologue, that he must "goon hom...To Paradys" (F 563-64). Nevertheless, several details suggest that he may be doing double duty—as God of Love and as one of the Lancaster family. In the F version his robe is ornamented with "rede rose-leves" (F 228)—a Lancastrian badge. In the G version the phrase becomes "A garlond on his hed of rose-leves, / Stiked al with lylyle floures" (G 160-61). The lilies have made several commentators think that the royal fleur-de-lys is meant, and that therefore Chaucer must have had Richard II in mind here. Actually, the entire royal family had a right to show the fleur-de-lys on a coat of arms, and a blue field sown with fleur-de-lys was a prominent part of Gaunt's shield; indeed, the fleur-de-lys figured in the shields of a good many noblemen who were not royally connected. The F version has Love "corowned with a sonne" (F 230)—a sunburst being one of the badges of Richard II; but in the later G version this is changed to the garland of rose-petals and lilies already mentioned. Moreover, the sunburst was sometimes used with the Lancastrian red rose. Alcestis says in so many words that the God of Love is a king (F 431; G 421), and implies in several other places that he is a king (F 376, 382; G 356, 366, 368). Richard II could be meant here; but John of Gaunt could be meant just as well, for he too was a king—the nominal

King of Spain. All this leaves us in a quandary. There seems to be evidence that links the God of Love with the Lancasters—but not with Gaunt exclusively.

One passage, however, does possibly suggest Gaunt. Speaking to the God of Love in defense of Chaucer, Alcestis says:

> In preysinge of your name
> He made the book that hight the Hous of Fame,
> And eke the Deeth of Blaunche the Duchesse,
> And the Parlement of Foules, as I gesse,
> And al the love of Palamon and Arcite. (F 416-20)

As I have tried to show in this book, all the poems mentioned here, except the last, do serve to praise John of Gaunt; even the "Palamon and Arcite" may have some hidden reference to Gaunt's career, and at least the beginning of it (as explained in Chapter IX of this book) is reminiscent of an episode in Gaunt's life.

It must be admitted, however, that all this is vague and merely tantalizing, not convincing. Probably Chaucer intended the God of Love to *remind* his reader (or auditors) of Gaunt—not actually to identify the God with Gaunt.

Allegories (and in particular Chaucer's allegories) are nearly always like that. They are not history; they do not even pretend to reproduce reality in every detail. Just as the reader thinks he has grasped them as a fact, they dissolve away into fancy; at the very moment when he perceives one well-defined symbol in the purest clarity, he perceives ghosts of other symbols moving between him and the pure symbol. In this Prologue the daisy is undoubtedly a symbol of poesy—but of love poesy especially—and, by extension, of love—and of a wife's faithful love, of Alcestis' love, which was Blanche's love, which was "turned into" a daisy that was a poem. The images flow into one another, and merge, yet do not merge, and remain themselves even when they become a part of something else. The God of Love is the God of Love—and a certain royal magnificence—and, perhaps, the magnificence of John of Gaunt, King of Spain. But we must not press this parallelism to the sticking point. John of Gaunt has appeared over and over in Chaucer's poems as a symbol of Love; but anything like an absolute identification of the God of Love as John of Gaunt does not seem to be justified by the evidence. Besides, as Professor Bronson has said, "The God of Love...can only be debased by the imposition of human features, to the detriment of the work of art as a whole."[28]

Chapter VIII. Chaucer's best joke — the "Tale of Sir Thopas"

nfortunately for Chaucer, Victorian critics got hold of him a century ago and established an "image" of him that is still current—and still Victorian. Of course, it is a little difficult for prudish souls to shrug off the "Miller's Tale" and the "Summoner's Tale"; nevertheless, criticism has had a habit of slighting such tales, and several others like them in Chaucer, or of referring to them only casually as "unworthy." This attitude, lingering on into the twentieth century, is the reason, very probably, that criticism has generally failed to discern the very best joke in the Chaucer canon.

In the course of the *Canterbury Tales*, the blunt and bullying Harry Bailey calls on the pilgrim Chaucer to tell a story. Harry's manner is arrogant, and he makes crude jokes at the expense of the mild-mannered pilgrim: "You are a doll fit for a woman to hug— little and pretty, with a face like a fairy's. Come now, let's have a merry tale, and don't waste time about it."

> "This were a popet in an arm t'embrace
> For any womman; smal and fair of face
> He semeth, elvyssh by his contenaunce....
> Sey now somwhat, . . .
> Telle us a tale of myrthe, and that anon."   (B 1891-96)

Chaucer answers agreeably that he will tell "a rym I lerned longe agoon" (B 1899). "Good!" says Harry Bailey. Then he turns to the other pilgrims and remarks with his usual clumsy wit: "Judging by his appearance, we are going to hear some dainty little thing."

> "Ye, that is good," quod he; "now shul we heere
> Som deyntee thyng, me thynketh, by his cheere."   (B 1900-01)

Chaucer remains polite, and proceeds to tell the "Tale of Sir Thopas"—on the face of it a silly romance about knighterrantry. He has jogged through thirty-odd stanzas of it when Harry Bailey erupts with a great oath: "Namoore of this, for Goddes dignitee!" (B 2109). Within fourteen lines he swears thrice in the name of God; twice he denounces the tale as filthy (*drasty*); once he calls it lewd (*lewed*, with an implication of both stupid and lewd); he curses it as "nat woorth a toord"; he consigns it to the devil; and he emphatically forbids the teller to go on with it (B 2109-22). What accounts for all this anger? There is a mystery hidden in this poem.

About Chaucer's intention in writing "Sir Thopas" says Baum, "scholars and critics have shown little doubt": it is a "deliberate burlesque" of a typical medieval romance.[1] Some other scholars (accepting the arguments of Miss Winstanley[2] and of Manly[3]) believe that, "in addition to the literary satire, or even in place of it, social satire at the expense of Flemish knighthood" is the major theme of the tale.[4] That it is burlesque romance is certain, and that it is social satire is possible. But is it nothing else? Why should mere burlesque romance or social satire excite the Host to such fury?

He is not a dreamy, romantic soul who might have resented Chaucer's ridiculing the romances. Nor is he so sensitive a literary critic as to have grown violent merely because the tale lacks literary merit. Nor (in case Winstanley and Manly are right) is he the kind of man to harbor intense sympathy for the Flemish. We must look elsewhere for an explanation of his livid wrath. Does he see something in the tale that we have been missing?

The name of Sir Thopas furnishes a clue. As Ross has shown,[5] the topaz (thopas) was generally regarded in Chaucer's time as a protection against sensuality and unchasteness. Therefore a knight named Thopas would hardly be a model of sexual virility. As a matter of fact, women, not men, usually bore the name in medieval romances. "Chaucer's use of the name, then, would appear to be a part of his general desire to make his hero 'deliberately effeminate.' "[6] Finally, an application of medieval rules of physiognomy to Thopas' features shows that "Chaucer conceived of his knight as a very effeminate creature."[7] All this would suggest that the poem contains some sort of joke involving Sir Thopas' sexual peculiarities.

Another clue pointing in the same direction is the way in which Chaucer (as Robinson's note has it) "rings the changes on the word" *prik* throughout the poem. The word appears no less than eight times in eighty-three lines. This device of repetition for the sake of emphasis has already been noted as a peculiar trick of Chaucer's with the boar in *Troilus and Criseyde* (Book V) and the white crown in the Prologue of the *Legend of Good Women*. If Chaucer repeated the word *prik* over and over in this poem, he did so because he wanted us to notice the word. The ribald meanings of the

word are well known. According to the *N. E. D.*, the noun *prick*
was used to refer to the penis in the late sixteenth century.* How
much earlier it was used thus I do not know; but Chaucer certainly
used the word as a verb with sexual implications in the "Reeve's
Tale," where the clerk John, lying with the miller's wife, "priketh
harde and depe as he were mad" (A 4231). And he may have used
it as a noun with ribald double meaning in the "Man of Law's Tale":
"There is no man koude brynge hire to that prikke" (B 1029). The
point is that Chaucer's eight-fold repetition of the word may have
been intended to alert the reader to sexual undertones in the "Tale
of Sir Thopas."

Be that as it may, we need go no farther than the plain words
of the poem itself to perceive that Sir Thopas is what an undergrad-
uate would call a "pansy," or perhaps a "queer." He has white skin,
red lips, rosy cheeks, long golden locks (B 1915-21). He is "sweete
as is the brembul flour" (B 1936). He wanders through forests
where deer and hares are the wildest creatures, and where birds sing
and sweet herbs savor the air (B 1944-61). He refuses to love any
woman (B 1981-82); he runs away from a fight (B 1981-82, 1997-
2022); he wants to hear romances of popes and cardinals—heroes as
unmilitary and as celibate as himself. He prepares for battle by con-
suming sweet wine, gingerbread, licorice, and sugar (B 2041-46).

Such a figure would naturally invite ribald jokes about homosexuality. Even in the fourteenth century, such jokes were probably
unacceptable in mixed company. Therefore, Chaucer had to veil,
in ambiguous diction, any such jokes that he wished to make—and
he was a master in the use of double meanings.[8] Nor can we believe
that the fourteenth century was too "wholesome" to be much aware
of homosexuality. It was universal gossip that Edward II had
practiced it (the manner in which he was murdered being a gross
and awful caricature of pederasty); and Richard II was accused of
it.†

Thus alerted to the possibility of obscene implications in the
poem, the reader may discern phallic, or autoerotic, or homosexual,
innuendoes throughout the poem—occurring most often near the
climactic end of stanzas. Sir Thopas bears "in his hand a launcegay
[a short, slender lance]" (B 1942). The lines "And I yow telle in

* Cf. *Romeo and Juliet,* II, iv, 119: "The bawdy hand of the dial is now upon
the prick of noon."

† Cf. Shakespeare's *Richard II,* III, i, where Bolingbroke condemns Bushy and
Green to death because of their illicit sexual relations with the king.

good certayn, / He hadde a semely nose" (B 1918-19) may have an
obscene double meaning, as reference to the nose sometimes does in
Shakespeare;* and they may refer to the folk wisdom (of uncertain
antiquity) that judges the size of the male member by the size of the
nose.[9] The giant Olifaunt[10] is armed with a *staf-slynge* (B 2019)—
a stick attached to the pouch of a sling, the phallic resemblance being
obvious. Thopas threatens to use his *launcegay* to pierce the giant's
mawe (B 2011-14) (with homosexual implications?); his spear has
a "heed ful sharpe ygrounde" (B 2073); and his "swerdes shethe"
is of ivory (B 2066). He is given to "wrastlyng... / Ther any ram
shal stonde" (B 1930-31). Skeat glosses the word *ram* here as "the
usual prize at a wrestling match"; and *stonde* as "to be placed in
sight of the competitors." But that a knight so highborn as Thopas
should wrestle for a ram in the village lists, like a low miller, seems
extremely odd. The entire expression doubtless carries an obscene
meaning that never once occurred to the Reverend Walter W. Skeat.
According to the *N. E. D.*, a fourteenth-century meaning of "to
wrestle" was "to twist or writhe about"; *ram*, with its connotations
of maleness, a projecting beam from a ship's prow, and its plunging
action, must long have had phallic associations;† and *stonde* means
"stand erect."

If we were better informed about the popular connotations of
certain other medieval words and references, we might see even
more sub-decent innuendoes in this poem. For example, the thrice-
mentioned "contree of Fairye" (B 1992, 1994, 2004) may have sexual
implications that moderns only dimly appreciate. And the word
steede, used six times in the poem, may have phallic connotations by
being related to the word *stud*, meaning both a "stallion" and an
"upright prop" or "projecting knob." Sir Thopas "bistrod" his steed
(B 2093); his steed ambled "Ful softely and rounde" (B 2076); Sir
Thopas, after "prikyng on the softe gras" (B 1969) lay down "To
make his steede som solas" (B 1972); the steed "in his prikynge / So
swatte that men myghte him wrynge" (B 1965-66); and the giant
threatens to slay Thopas' steed, not Thopas himself (B 2002).

* Cf. the bantering between Iras and Charmian, *Antony and Cleopatra*, I, ii,
56-59; Lafeu's remark to Parolles, "Thou were best to set thy lower part where they
nose is," in *All's Well*, II, iii, 267; the double-meaning "nose-painting" of the
Porter's speech in *Macbeth*, III, iii, 28; etc.

† Cf. modern Standard English *ram-rod*, meaning "penis"; and Shakespeare's
"Ram thou thy fruitful tidings in mine ears, / That long time have been barren,"
Antony and Cleopatra, II, v, 24-25.

Other words and phrases of possible obscene implications might be listed. But those already cited are enough to show the general nature of this tale, and also to explain why the excessively masculine Host halts the tale with a show of violent anger. He reacts like a typical "he-man" to a tale of an effeminate, autoerotic, and probably homosexual creature. Significantly, he reacts so violently only one other time in the *Canterbury Tales*—against the Pardoner, whose eunuchoid nature resembles that of Sir Thopas. Evidently, this is a type that the Host cannot endure.*

But the best part of the joke is the way in which the pilgrim Chaucer gets even with the Host for those early slighting remarks about a "popet," a "fair face," and a tale about some "deyntee thing." Chaucer needles that self-consciously masterful man by forcing him to listen to a double-meaning tale about another "popet." Whether or not the Host realized what was happening to him, the outrage (and the amusement of the more sophisticated pilgrims) would be the same. Actually, the unsubtle Host does not catch on till he has heard thirty-two stanzas of the salacious drivel that the pilgrim Chaucer is uttering. When he does finally see through the innuendos of the tale, he explodes with a magnificence unequaled elsewhere in English poetry. Both his intelligence and his manliness have been insulted by a "popet."

Perhaps we should not expect Chaucer to have included personal allegory in a tale like this, and perhaps he did not. The thing could have been dangerous. Furthermore, if he did introduce personal allegory in such a poem, he would doubtless have taken pains to cover his tracks so well that only the initiated could follow him—and readers at this late date are not among the initiated. On the other hand, a little guessing on our part can do no harm, and may turn up something very interesting.

The fair complexion, golden locks, and general good looks of Sir Thopas suggest both John of Gaunt and Richard II. John of Gaunt seems like a particularly good candidate because both he and Sir Thopas were born in Flanders. But to offset this possibility are the facts that even Gaunt's worst detractors never accused him of homo-

---

* It is a well-known psychological principle that aggressive masculinity is often an overcompensation for latent homosexual impulses subconsciously feared. For example, policemen (I am told by a psychologist friend) have among them a larger proportion of men with homosexual tendencies than does the general population. In having the Host react so violently to the Pardoner and to Sir Thopas, Chaucer showed his usual extraordinary understanding of human nature.

sexuality or effeminacy, and that Chaucer would hardly have ridiculed here a man whom he praised so often and so fulsomely elsewhere, and who seems to have been his lifelong friend. Thus, if Thopas really does represent any actual person, the mention of Flanders may have been a deliberate device to throw uninitiated readers off the scent, and to clear Chaucer's own skirts in case of question.

Thopas could represent Richard II—who, like Thopas, was "Yborn ... in fer contree" (B 1908), that is, in Bordeaux. His father, the Black Prince, was, like Thopas' father, "lord ... of that contree" (B 1912) where Richard was born—as Gaunt's father was *not* lord of Ghent, where Gaunt was born. One of Richard's favorite badges was a sprig of broom (*planta genista*) with pods attached; and Thopas is compared to "the brembul flour / That bereth the rede hepe [hip]" (B 1936-37). And the word "royal" is thrice (B 2038, 2043, 2092) associated with Sir Thopas. Admittedly, these details constitute no real evidence that Thopas represents Richard; nevertheless, the details are consistent with that hypothesis.

About midway in the poem (B 1997-2006) Thopas encounters a "*geaunt*" (mentioned several times thereafter) who swears by "Terma*gaunt*"—the possibility of a pun being obvious. If we assume that Chaucer first lighted on "geaunt" and "Termagaunt" as keys to the identity of this character, his selection of the name "Olifaunt" for the giant would be a mere accidental choice of a rhyming name, and would have no significance beyond indicating something about the giant's size.

The giant is notable for three things: he has a "fel staf-slynge" (B 2019); he is the protector of the "queene of Fayerye" (B 2004-6); and he has three heads (B 2032). I have noted already that the "staf-slynge" may have phallic implications—which would be consistent with Gaunt's reputation as a lover, and with Chaucer's constant depiction of him as a lover. "Fayerye" is then, very probably, the Land of Love, which the giant calls "myn haunt" (B 2001); and, from Chaucer's point of view, the "queene of Fayerye" would be none other than Katharine Swynford. The three heads might then be a reference to Gaunt's three wives.

But the giant drives Thopas back from Fairyland, or the Land of Love—the implication being that Gaunt could best Richard in feats of love. But there may be still another implication. Four times in twelve lines (B 1978-89) Chaucer says that Thopas will have none but an "elf-queene" to wife. *Elf* here doubtless implies *small*. Now if Thopas really represents Richard II, the reference to the elf-queen may be a satirical commentary on Richard's insistence (a bit shocking even in a century of child-marriages) on wedding Isabella of France (September, 1396) when that princess was only seven years old, and Richard nearly thirty. This interpretation would give an ironic significance to Thopas' assertion that "no *womman*" is worthy to be his wife (B 1981-82); that is, only a child is worthy of being the wife of such an effeminate person.

The conflict with the "geaunt," in which Thopas is forced to retreat, may refer to Gaunt's marriage to Katharine Swynford a few months before Richard married Isabella. This marriage of Gaunt's was opposed by virtually everyone in the king's court. What we may have here, therefore, may be a particularly outrageous account of a disagreement (that never came to actual blows) between a homosexual king, who was willing to marry a child with whom intercourse would have been impossible, and the thrice-virile Gaunt who insisted on marrying the Queen of Love, and did marry her despite the opposition of the king.

If this allegorical interpretation is really correct, we can be fairly certain that Chaucer did not show the poem to Richard. Perhaps he showed it to Gaunt, Bolingbroke, and others of the Gaunt entourage, and they all laughed over it together. After 1396 (which would be an early limit for the poem) no love was being lost between Richard and the Lancasters—and Chaucer's sympathies would certainly have been with his old friends rather than with the criminally weak and foolish king whom the old poet had counseled so earnestly in "Lak of Stedfastnesse."

In any event, whether or not the historical allegory I have outlined is actually present in the poem, the "Tale of Sir Thopas" is plainly an exercise (like the *1601* of America's greatest humorist) in deliberate ribaldry by England's greatest humorist. Furthermore, as a mere account of the interplay between the pilgrim Chaucer and the Host, it constitutes a high point in the dramatic humor of the *Canterbury Tales*.

Chapter IX. "Many Sondry Werkes"

I am sorry that the following chapter is necessarily disjointed and scrappy. But since the point of this book is that Chaucer's interest in actual persons (especially Gaunt and his circle) found expression in his poetry, I could not, in justice either to my own argument or to the reader, bring myself to leave the subject without another glance at the *Canterbury Tales* and some of the minor poems not previously examined in this book.

Manly, in *Some New Light on Chaucer* (1926), believed that he had found real-life originals for numerous characters in Chaucer's work—among them the Host, the Reeve, the Miller of the "Reeve's Tale," the Man of Law, the Franklin, the Shipman, the Merchant, and the Prioress. In what follows, I shall not refer to Manly's identifications unless I have something of additional interest to add.

The Knight] A. S. Cook regarded Chaucer's Knight as a composite of Gaunt's father-in-law, Henry of Lancaster, and Gaunt's son Henry Bolingbroke.[1] If this conjecture is correct, Chaucer's picture of the Knight is one more instance in which the poet's affiliation with Gaunt influenced his poetry.

The Prioress] Manly originally identified the Prioress as a certain nun living in the convent of St. Leonard's in Chaucer's time.[2] Later on, Manly partly withdrew this identification because the nun in question was not actually the prioress of the convent.[3] It would seem, however, that this discrepancy in rank would make very little difference in the identification. It only indicates the way in which Chaucer (like many another writer—*vide* Dickens, Maugham, Conrad, Joyce, Wolfe, and scores of others), while starting from real-life prototypes, altered actual facts to suit his artistic purposes. He did the same sort of thing in all the other poems so far discussed in this book. What is of rather special interest, however, is the fact that an aunt of Gaunt's (sister of Gaunt's mother) was the chief resident personage at St. Leonard's during Chaucer's career, and that this royal aunt left a small legacy to the nun who (Manly thought) sat for the portrait of the Prioress. It is still another indirect connection between Chaucer's poetry and John of Gaunt's circle.

The Sergeant of the Law and the Franklin] Manly believes that these two pilgrims were modeled on well-known public personages in Lincolnshire[4]—where the Swynfords had their estates, where Gaunt granted Katharine Swynford certain additional manors, where Gaunt was earl, and where Gaunt was, for decades, the dominant personage in the county. In other words, here again Chaucer's interest lies within the shadow of John of Gaunt.

The Guildsmen] Kuhl has pointed out that the guildsmen, with the exception of the Carpenter, were all associated with the mercers' trade—and that it was the mercers who were Gaunt's supporters in his quarrels with the victuallers' guilds of London.[5] No victuallers appear among these prosperous and distinguished tradesmen.

The Reeve] Manly suggests that Chaucer may have learned about the "rascally Reeve" of Baldeswelle, in Norfolk, from personal association with Sir William Beauchamp—who was charged with caring for the interests of a young lord on whose estates the Reeve was employed.[6] This Sir William Beauchamp has already been mentioned. He was a member of Gaunt's retinue, a friend of Gaunt's, and a witness for Chaucer in the Cecilia Chaumpaigne affair. Furthermore, the young lord whom the Reeve cheated was, according to Manly, the third Earl of Pembroke—to whom Gaunt's daughter Elizabeth had been betrothed (in effect, married) until she decided to elope with John Holland early in 1386.[7] In other words (if Manly is right) Chaucer's interest in the Reeve was closely, if indirectly, associated with that knot of fourteenth-century personalities of whom Gaunt was the central figure.

The churchmen] Protests against the worldliness and the corruption of churchmen were common in fourteenth-century England, and came to a head in the reform movement led by Wyclif. The Black Prince's widow, many knights of the king's court, and Gaunt himself supported Wyclif in the latter's attempts to recall the church to worldly purity. As late as May, 1390, Richard II, Gaunt, and a group of other persons prominent in the government sent a letter to the pope inveighing against the "thorns and nettles," the "false shepherds and hirelings," of the church who were guilty of scandals, oppressions, and unholy greed.[8] Chaucer's attitude toward these worldlings who dishonored the church they professed to serve was exactly that of John of Gaunt.

On the other hand, Gaunt refused to follow Wyclif when the latter attacked the basic principles and beliefs of the church. Gaunt's position was that the church itself was not false, but that the church's servants needed to re-emphasize the essential elements of Christ's teaching. This was evidently the position shared by Chaucer. His Parson is his ideal Christian—not a man in rebellion against the church, but a man who practiced perfectly what the church taught. Whether or not Chaucer's portraits of churchmen (good or evil) are based on actual persons, we shall probably never know. But these portraits are precisely the sort that John of Gaunt and the people surrounding him would have heartily approved.

The Knight's Tale] Though the Theseus of classic myth was a king, Chaucer, in the "Knight's Tale," makes him a duke. The change may have been made as a means of subtly associating Theseus' wisdom and courage with John of Gaunt, Duke of Lancaster. The association seems all the more credible when we find Theseus returning from abroad with his new-wedded queen and the queen's sister. The situation irresistibly suggests the return of Gaunt to England, in 1371, with his new-wedded Queen of Spain, and her sister Isabella. Of course, the parallelism breaks down almost immediately; for the Queen of Spain's sister was married to Gaunt's brother Edmund. Nevertheless, Chaucer has given his tale, from its very first lines, a kind of "hook" with which to catch the interest of his hearers. It is the same principle that an after-dinner speaker resorts to when he attaches the name of some well-known person to the anecdote he is about to tell.

A similar "hook" may be used in ll. 1462-63, where Palamon escapes from his prison on May 3. If these lines were added (or were altered from some earlier version) after May 3, 1389, they would instantly bring to mind that very day. It was on that date that Richard II asserted himself and re-assumed the power that the Duke of Gloucester had seized from him nearly three years before. The same date, May 3, appears again in the "Nun's Priest's Tale" (B 4277 ff.) as the day on which Chauntecleer escaped the fox;* and the same date is used again in *Troilus and Criseyde* (II, 55), when Pandarus first tells Criseyde of Troilus' love. Apparently, Chaucer considered the day to be one of good omen. It was on May 3, 1389, that Richard II began to set the wheels in motion for Gaunt's return to England.

Cook has argued that the original of Emetreus (described in ll. 2155-86) was Henry Bolingbroke, Earl of Derby, son and heir of John of Gaunt.[9] This identification has been disputed; and indeed one must not expect point-by-point resemblances when Chaucer converts real life into fiction. The poet was only trying to increase the immediacy of his appeal by including timely references that his hearers would recognize. To Cook's argument I can add only one item. Emetreus bears on his hand "An egle tame, as any lilye whyt" (l. 2178). The white eagle appeared also in a famous passage in *Troilus and Criseyde*, and is almost certainly to be regarded as a badge of the Lancaster family (see Chapter IV).

What Chaucer seems to have done in this poem is to retell an old story, but to include timely references that would titillate his hearers in the Lancastrian court.

The Miller's Tale] I should be the first to admit that what follows is highly speculative in nature. Nevertheless, the chief character in the "Miller's Tale," "hende Nicholas," curiously suggests Chaucer himself. Like Chaucer, this Nicholas was learned in astronomy and astrology; like Chaucer, he owned an astrolabe (an instrument about which Chaucer later wrote a scientific treatise); like Chaucer, who, as we have seen, was evidently expert in mathematics, Nicholas owned a complicated abacus for doing mathematical problems; like Chaucer, he owned "bookes grete and smale"; like Chaucer, very probably, as we have seen, Nicholas was a musician and singer. Chaucer himself casually explains how Nicholas could have been so poor and yet live so well as he did. Nicholas, Chaucer says, lived partly on his own income, and partly on *what his friends provided* (l. 3220).

All this brings up the question of Chaucer's education. There is considerable evidence that he attended the Inner Temple as a student of the law. This evidence consists of hearsay records, Chaucer's more than perfunctory knowledge of the law and of legal

* But here Chaucer says plainly that the day was Friday (B 4532), whereas May 3, 1389, fell on a Monday.

terms, and his inclusio nof a manciple (provision-purchaser for a college of the Temple) in his cast of Canterbury characters. A more improbable personage than a manciple for a poet to light upon is hardly imaginable—unless the poet had been familiar with a manciple in times past. If, however, Chaucer was in the employ of the Countess Elizabeth of Ulster when he was about seventeen (1357), and remained with her until he was twenty-one (1361), it is not likely that he studied at the Temple till Elizabeth and Lionel departed for Ireland in 1361.

But now the matter of expense enters the picture. Education at the Temple was so excessively expensive (over $5,000 a year) that only persons of the very highest economic class sent their children there. One doubts that Chaucer's father could or would have sent his son to this place primarily designed for the sons of noblemen and the very rich. A man who let his son go into poorly paid employment, possibly semi-menial, before the boy was seventeen, would not be likely to spend large sums to send him to the Temple.

There is also a long tradition that Chaucer attended Oxford. Expenses here for an ordinary student were only about $500 a year, and John Chaucer might have been able to spend that much money on his son. The evidence that Chaucer was at Oxford is all indirect. One of his best friends, Ralph Strode, to whom he dedicated *Troilus and Criseyde*, was a tutor at Oxford in the 1360's, just when (as we shall see) Chaucer was probably at Oxford, if he was there at all. Chaucer's *Treatise on the Astrolabe* is adapted to the latitude of Oxford, and Chaucer mentions in it two Oxford professors, contemporary with himself, from whom he received astronomical information. The inclusion of the Clerk of Oxford among the Canterbury pilgrims may indicate a relationship to Oxford as much as the Manciple indicates a relationship to the Temple. Chaucer's religious and social views correspond pretty well to those of the religious reform movement centered at Oxford. And both the "Miller's Tale" and the "Reeve's Tale" deal with student life (the former at Oxford, the latter near Cambridge), even though the original tales on which these two are based include no references to students.

Possibly, then, Chaucer was a student at both Oxford and the Temple. He could have been a student at Oxford as a boy, before he entered the employ of the Countess Elizabeth; on the other hand, it is unlikely that a father who had sent him to the university would withdraw him at an early age to take employment at a poorly paid job in the Countess' household. Therefore, it is possible that Chaucer attended both Oxford and the Temple *after* 1361. If we assume that this really occurred, a good many otherwise odd details begin falling into logical place.

For a century or so a conflict between civil law and canon law had been stirring in England—with earlier decisions going mostly to the canon lawyers. But by the time of Edward I a class of professional civil attorneys had risen under the encouragement of kings and noblemen who were growing weary of seeing cases, under the domination of ecclesiastical attorneys, generally being decided in favor of the church. It was not uncommon for the king, or the great noblemen, of the fourteenth century to sponsor the education of "clerks" who would become useful to their patrons in matters of law interpretation, historical precedent, public accounting, and so on. Gaunt is known to have maintained several students at Oxford later on in his life, and he probably began the practice in the earlier period (the 1360's) for which we have no good records.

Possibly Chaucer's lost years, 1361-66, saw him at Oxford first, and later on at the Temple. His Oxford expenses would have been paid partly by his father, and partly by Gaunt.* Gaunt's motive in educating him would have been not only to assist a likeable and brilliant young man, but also to prepare this brilliant young man for service to Gaunt later on. Providing that Chaucer should be established eventually in the king's court was characteristic of Gaunt, who placed many of his men there.

To be sure, all this smacks a bit of romantic speculation. But when we consider all the peculiar facts—that Chaucer's father was not a rich nobleman, and yet Chaucer probably studied at the Temple; that evidence for Chaucer's attendance at Oxford is rather insistent; that "hende Nicholas" looks remarkably like Chaucer; that Nicholas was partly dependent on the financial help of friends; that Gaunt helped several young men through Oxford, and was especially interested in the place; that Chaucer (according to his own reckoning in the *Book of the Duchess*) was associated with the Lancasters from 1361; that Chaucer's whereabouts between 1361 and 1366 are unknown; that Gaunt himself (if I have interpreted

---

* Later on in life Gaunt gave ample evidence of his interest in Oxford. He drew Wyclif from Oxford, and visited him there. He visited Oxford on several other occasions; he helped support several students at Oxford; and he sent both his son Henry Beaufort and his grandson Henry (Henry V) to Oxford (Armitage-Smith, p. 414).

the *House of Fame* correctly in a previous chapter) inducted Chaucer into the king's court—if we consider all these details, the interpretation offered here seems not unreasonable. If the interpretation is really correct, it presents another example of the way in which Chaucer used his own experience, and in particular his experience in relation to John of Gaunt, as a starting-place for his poetry.

The Man of Law's Tale]   In the midst of the "Man of Law's Tale" the teller cries out for sympathy toward his heroine Constance:

> O queenes, lyvynge in prosperitee,
> Duchesses, and ye ladyes everichone,
> Haveth som routhe on hire adversitee!   (B, 652-54)

Since there were no queens, duchesses, or even ladies (in the plural) among the Canterbury pilgrims, it is obvious that we have here another uncorrected lapse of Chaucer's. The tale must have been originally read to a group of court ladies among whom were queens and duchesses. But since the only two queens living in England at the same time during Chaucer's career were Richard's Queen of England and Gaunt's Queen of Spain, Chaucer must have read this poem to a gathering where the Queen of Spain, Constance, was present.

The story of Chaucer's fictional Constance does not accurately match that of the real Constance of Spain—nor should we expect it to. That was not Chaucer's method. Nevertheless, the real Constance, like the fictional one, had weathered a multitude of losses and many perils, and had barely escaped with her life, before she was taken under the protection of Gaunt. Persons hearing the story of the fictional Constance, and having the real Constance among them, could not have helped thinking of the real Constance, and sympathizing with her past misfortunes. Of more importance to Chaucer, perhaps, is the virtual certainty that this little trick of connecting the fictional with the real made his hearers more appreciative of the story he was telling. Once again he uses the narrative-writer's familiar hook—that is, the insertion into an old story of timely references to excite the special interest of his hearers.

The Wife of Bath's Tale]   The Wife's tale is not merely a joke on woman's desire for "sovereynetee" over her husband; it is even more a serious lecture on true "gentilesse." As we have seen, Chaucer was almost obsessively concerned with the fate of women betrayed by men; and, as we have seen also, this obsession may have been associated with Chaucer's fear that Gaunt would desert Katharine Swynford—as indeed he did desert her from 1386 to 1389, when he was in Spain.

In the Wife's tale the young knight is reminded that a man of true "gentilesse" does not cast away a bride merely because she is old, lowborn, and poor. The man who does such a thing, "He nys nat gentil, be he duc or erl" (D 1157). The last three words here quoted could hardly be directed more pointedly at Gaunt.

The Clerk's Tale] The story of patient Griselda is still another example of Chaucer's concern for woman mistreated and betrayed. Throughout the story Chaucer condemns the husband who persecutes his wife (a poor girl, like Katharine Swynford, who has been honored by the love of a great nobleman), and praises the steadfast love of Griselda, and of all women:

> Though clerkes preise wommen but a lite,
> Ther kan no man in humblesse hym acquite
> As womman kan, ne kan been half so trewe
> As wommen been.   (E 935-38)

The Squire's Tale] Though Chaucer speaks, in the "Squire's Tale," of "The knotte why that every tale is toold" (F 401), this particular tale is one of the most uncertainly constructed of all the *Canterbury Tales*. It rambles; it contains stories within stories; it appears to have been destined to have half a dozen "knottes" (see F 654 ff.); and it is left unfinished.

The story commences with an account of Cambuscan's birthday feast; and Part One ends as follows:

> But thus I lete in lust and jolitee
> This Cambyuskan his lordes festeiynge,
> Til wel ny the day bigan to sprynge.   (F 344-46)

Though Chaucer says here that he is going to leave ("I lete") the company feasting till dawn, he does no such thing. In Part Two he takes them on into bed, sleep, and dreams, all described briefly as an introduction to Canace's sleep, dreams, and rising. And at the end of Part Two, he writes, "And ther I lefte I wol ayeyn bigynne" (F 670). In other words, Part Two looks like a conscious digression from the main story; indeed, Part Three, begins, with dawn rising, just where Part One ends.

In Part Two Canace rises early in the morning and walks out into the open. She hears a female falcon shrieking; the falcon falls to earth in a swoon; Canace revives her; and the falcon tells about having given her love to a faithless male and having been deserted by him. This is a peculiarly bitter, name-calling story that exists today only as a fragment. Naturally, it brings to mind Chaucer's long obsession with the subject of women betrayed by their lovers—an obsession which I have tried to explain as owing to Chaucer's fear that Gaunt would desert Katharine Swynford, and leave Katharine, Katharine's sister Philippa Chaucer, and Katharine's sister's husband Geoffrey Chaucer, without a patron and protector in surroundings generally hostile to Gaunt, and therefore hostile to his erstwhile friends.

Early in her complaint the female falcon speaks of her lover's "crouned malice" (F 526)—which Robinson glosses as "consummate malice," but which could well be a pun on Gaunt's royalty (see also the "corones tweyne" of *Troilus*, II, 1735). Moreover, just as Criseyde and Pandarus insist on the honorableness of Troilus' obligations to his mistress, so the female falcon grants her love in language that sounds remarkably like that of *Troilus and Criseyde*:

> [I] Graunted hym love, on this condicioun,
> That everemoore myn honour and renoun
> Were saved, bothe privee and apert. (F 529-31)

Her lover, after "many a year," is forced by Fortune, and "For his honour," to leave "that place which that I was inne." The similarity between this situation and Gaunt's departure for Spain in 1386 is obvious. The lover swears devotion to his mistress, and she, making a virtue of necessity, allows him to depart. But he "repeirynge to his kynde," suddenly gives all his love to a certain kite, and forgets the falcon whom he has left at home. All this is plainly reminiscent of Gaunt's deserting Katharine, going away to Spain, and devoting himself, at last, to his Queen Constance—or perhaps to some new mistress. But what almost clinches the whole matter is the language of the female falcon in describing her farewell to her lover:

As I best myghte, I hidde fro hym my sorwe,
And took hym by the hond, Seint John to borwe,
And seyde hym thus:...   (F 595-97)

The phrase "Seint John to borwe" is used (it seems) in the "Complaint of Mars" to identify John of Gaunt; and the name of Saint John, or clear reference to the historical saint, is used, very probably, to identify Gaunt not only in the *Book of the Duchess* but also in the *Parliament of Fowls* and *Troilus and Criseyde* (see previous chapters in this book).

What I should like to believe is that this bitter Part Two of the "Squire's Tale" was written out of Chaucer's anger and despair while Gaunt was in Spain, 1386-89. But when Gaunt returned, and renewed his old relationship with Katharine, Chaucer thought better of him, and decided either to abandon this harsh poem altogether, or to destroy its ending. That is the reason why we have the "Squire's Tale" as a mere fragment.

The Franklin's Tale] Perhaps no direct relationship between the Gaunt circle and the "Franklin's Tale" can be demonstrated. But if it is true (as has been tentatively suggested by several students of Chaucer) that the poet did have a kind of "courtly love" for Blanche of Lancaster—the kind of love that a worshiper has for a goddess, or a servant for a queen—this tale may indicate something of Gaunt's attitude (poetically exaggerated, no doubt) toward his wife's humble lover. Trusting his wife and trusting Chaucer, Gaunt may have been aware of the "desire of the moth for the star," and may have accepted it as a fairly normal situation—just as did the husband in the "Franklin's Tale."

The Physician's Tale] One of the most interesting items in the Physician's otherwise colorless tale is the digression in which he lectures governesses on the manner in which they should train "lordes doghtres" (C 72-92). It has generally been assumed that Chaucer is here addressing, somewhat ill-naturedly, Katharine Swynford, who is said to have been a governess of Gaunt's daughters before she became the great man's mistress. In view of the fact, however, that Katharine *was* the great man's mistress, it seems hardly likely that Chaucer would have referred to her in the reproachful language that he uses here. His tender treatment of Criseyde, in *Troilus and Criseyde*, is more in character. If the passage contains an implied reference to any specific person, that person might be Philippa Chaucer—who served in Gaunt's household longer than Katharine did, and who may possibly have been the mother of a "lordes doghtre"—that is, Gaunt's own daughter. In either case, if a personal reference is intended, we have here one more example of Chaucer's poetry being influenced by his personal associations.

Chaucer's Tale of Melibeus] Professor Hotson sees the "Tale of Melibeus," with its emphasis on peace and moderation, as an allegory intended to dissuade John of Gaunt from undertaking the dangerous Spanish adventure that he finally did undertake in 1386. "In a last effort to leave nothing untried which might keep Lancaster in England and so avert the impending strife, the few friends who saw straight may well have turned to Chaucer, the greatest English writer and close friend of the Duke, for aid; or Chaucer may have acted on his own initiative."[10] Hotson continues: "But, besides a powerful body of moral argument, Chaucer must have found in the original Latin *Melibeus*, a document almost incredibly well fitted in innumerable details to the present case of John of Gaunt.... He had but to translate the thing as it stood, changing no essential, and the Duke could not fail to see, as in a mirror, himself as *Melibeus* and his own better sense (or perhaps that of Kathryn Swynford) as the allegorical *dame Prudence*."[11]

This remark about Katharine Swynford is very curious; Hotson does not mention her elsewhere in his discussion. Did he have some sort of intuition that Katharine was connected with the story? In any event, Lawrence[12] and Stillwell[13] disagree with Hotson. The tale, says Stillwell, "cannot be said to have had an exclusive bearing upon any one political situation in Chaucer's time. The tale must have had many meanings for fourteenth-century England."[14] But, though the story meant various things to his contemporaries—what did it mean to Chaucer himself? At the risk of committing the "intentional fallacy," I shall say that I think the answer to this question is important. Under the peculiar personal circumstances of Chaucer's career, Chaucer probably did mean the tale (partly at any rate) as an admonition to Gaunt not to go off on a warring expedition to Spain. It would have been almost impossible for Chaucer (evidently obsessed with the fear that Gaunt would desert England and Katharine) not to have read that meaning into the tale he translated.

The Monk's Tale] Three of the Monk's "tragedies" concern three fourteenth-century characters: King Peter of Cyprus, who visited England in 1363; Pedro the Cruel, of Spain, father of Gaunt's wife Constance; and the tyrant Bernabò, of Milan, whose daughter married Chaucer's first master, Prince Lionel, and whom Chaucer himself visited, probably in Gaunt's behalf. The reflection of personal relationships is obvious.

Anelida and Arcite] The beginning of *Anelida and Arcite* is much like that of the "Knight's Tale": Theseus (called a *duke* in both poems) returns to Athens with his new-wedded queen and her sister. I suggested that, in the "Knight's Tale," this beginning was reminiscent of Gaunt's coming home from Spain, in 1371, with a new-wedded queen and her sister—and that Chaucer may have used the episode to add an extra dimension of interest to his tale. The same suggestions would apply here. The poem as a whole has long been a tantalizing mystery. The narrative plot is essentially the same as that of the "Squire's Tale," Part Two, in which a trusting damsel gives her love to one who betrays her for another mistress. It is a well-worn theme in Chaucer; and reasons for his interest in it I have already suggested.

In the "Squire's Tale," Part Two, the false lover leaves his mistress, goes abroad, and *then* finds another mistress; in *Anelida and Arcite* the lover takes another mistress, whose slave he becomes, and who sends him flitting on fool's errands thither and yon. Whether Gaunt took another mistress, besides Katharine, in the 1380's is not known; but whether he did or did not, the situation in which a faithful woman is deserted by her lover remains the same, and remains applicable to the Gaunt-Katharine situation in the 1380's. Like the "Squire's Tale," *Anelida and Arcite* has come down to us in an incomplete state. Perhaps the return of Gaunt to Katharine after his three years' Spanish adventure influenced Chaucer not to finish these two ill-tempered poems, or, if he did finish them, to destroy their endings.

Legend of Good Women] Since Prologue F of the Legend contains a kind of dedication to Queen Anne, it must have been written sometime between her marriage to Richard, June 14, 1382, and her death, June 7, 1394. "Within these limits," as Robinson says, "no exact date has been established."[15] But there is about the Prologue a kind of golden serenity, a happy fancifulness, that would lead us to believe that it was written in those halcyon years after the return of Gaunt from Spain in 1389. There is no evidence, however, as to when the legends themselves were written. Doubtless they were composed at odd times over a number of years; nor is the order in which they appear in the manuscripts, and are printed today, necessarily the order in which they were written.

The first two (Cleopatra and Thisbe) tell of men, as well as women, who were faithful lovers; two more (Lucrece and Philomela) tell of brutal, murderous lovers; and the rest (Dido, Hypsipyle, Medea, Ariadne, Phyllis, and Hypermnestra) tell of faithful women who were abandoned by their lovers. Of these last, Dido, Hypsipyle, Ariadne, and Phyllis were abandoned by lovers who sailed away from them to go to lands beyond the sea. It is certain that if Chaucer had read aloud the legends of these last four women, at least some of his hearers in the royal court would have thought instantly of Gaunt's deserting Katharine. Perhaps these were never read aloud; perhaps they were written during the period when Gaunt was in Spain, and they remained safe in Chaucer's chest till after his death. In his "Retractions" he speaks of having written "the book of the xxv. Ladies"; and in the Prologue of the *Legend,* Alcestis commands him to write a book about faithful women, "And when this book ys maad, yive it the quene" (F 496). Perhaps Chaucer did write a book about twenty-five faithful women (the Man of Law names many more than those that we actually have), and gave the book to the queen, after whose death the book disappeared; and perhaps what we have left of the original *Legend* is (with the exceptions of the legends of Cleopatra and Thisbe) only a group of unpleasant discards that Chaucer never made public, and that were discovered among his belongings after his death.

But all this is hardly more than interesting, or idle, conjecture. The one solid fact is that Chaucer wrote a series of legends about women who were deserted by their lovers, and that he almost certainly wrote them at a time when he must have been gravely disturbed by Gaunt's prospective, or actual, desertion of a mistress who was closely related to Chaucer.

Short poems] Some of the most unmistakable examples of the manner in which Chaucer's experiences with individual persons affected his poetry are to be found among his very short poems. He wrote poems to Adam (his scribe), to Philip Vache ("Truth"), to his friends Scogan and Bukton, to King Richard ("Lak of Stedfastnesse"), and to King Henry ("Complaint to His Purse"). In addition, the poem "Fortune" addresses three princes, who are doubtless Richard's uncles John of Gaunt, Edmund of Langley, and Thomas of Woodstock; and in the same poem he refers thrice to his "beste frend," who is generally believed to be John of Gaunt.

As will be seen in a moment, the "Complaint of Venus" does not quite belong among those poems whose center of gravity is Gaunt and his circle. The poem is, of course, sadly misnamed. As has long been known, it is really three poems—translations of three ballades by the French poet Otes de Graunson, with an entirely original "Envoy" by Chaucer. Oddly enough, though two of Graunson's ballades are clearly written to or about a lady, Chaucer's versions are about a man loved by a woman. The reason for the change seems to be revealed in the "Envoy," which is addressed in extremely reverent language to a "Princesse." In view of the fact that the man described in the poems is obviously the noblest of the noble, that the lover of a princess would doubtless be a prince, and that much of the phraseology of the first lyric resembles that in which Chaucer praises the figure whom I have identified as the Black Prince in the *Parliament of Fowls* and *Troilus and Criseyde*, we might be justified in guessing that the "Princesse" of the "Envoy" is princess Joan, wife of the Black Prince. If this guess is correct, it would seem that Chaucer must have written the three poems (or translated them) at the request of Princess Joan, or for her benefit, as an expression of her love for the Black Prince. Chaucer's apology, in the "Envoy," for not having made a better translation would sustain this interpretation.

Though Chaucer says in this poem that age has made him less facile in rhyming than he could wish (l. 75), he may be merely implying that, as a mature man, he cannot write love verses so fluently as he once did. He was thirty-six when the Black Prince died—which is hardly aged even by medieval standards. But if he wrote the poems for Princess Joan within a year or so of her death, in 1385, he might have considered himself, at forty-five, elderly by medieval standards. Possibly a date close to 1385 is acceptable. It was about this time (as I have tried to show in examining the *House of Fame*) that Chaucer seemed to be growing weary of writing romantic love poems based on the work of French or Italian masters. Moreover, it was about this time that Joan and her brother-in-law John of Gaunt seemed to be most friendly. They had been drawn together in their support of Wyclif, and the Princess was especially eager to have good relations between Gaunt and her wayward son Richard II. As a matter of fact, the Princess permitted herself to be surrounded in her last years (as I have pointed out in a previous chapter) with old friends and retainers of Gaunt. Though it would not be correct to say that she was a part of the Gaunt circle, she moved close to that circle in the 1380's—so close that Chaucer's immediate personal interest in her must have been quickened.

But whoever the Princess may be, and whenever Chaucer translated the three ballades of Graunson—the "Complaint of Venus" is one more element in the "new view of Chaucer" that I have tried to present in this book. This is a view of a poet whose work reflects, more often than not, his interest in the affairs of those people with whom he was intimately associated during most of his life.

Chapter X. Summary and discussion

Before examining some of the larger literary implications of matters discussed in the previous chapters, we might briefly summarize those chapters:

Chapter I] Certain singularities of contemporary scholarship have tended to obscure the view of Chaucer that is offered here. These include preoccupation with factual and philological commentary, disregard of the poet's manifest intentions when he wrote, tacit assumption that Chaucer's aesthetic standards were the same as those of modern criticism, disregard of Chaucer's working methods, a disinclination to bother with personal (or historical) allegories in Chaucer's poems, confusion about Chaucer's birth year, and a long-standing squeamishness about linking Chaucer too closely with John of Gaunt.

Chapter II] All evidence indicates that Chaucer was closely, perhaps intimately, associated with John of Gaunt—both in Chaucer's official capacities and in his personal relationships.

Chapter III] The *Complaint of Mars* seems to be a record of an episode in the lives of Gaunt and his mistress Katharine Swynford at the time of the Good Parliament, April, 1376. The poem is an attempt to ameliorate public disapproval of Gaunt's infatuation with Katharine.

Chapter IV] *Troilus and Criseyde* is an allegorical retelling of at least certain aspects of the love affair between Gaunt and Katharine Swynford, and Chaucer's (conjectural) part in furthering the affair. The poem continually stresses the point that Gaunt is honor-bound to Katharine. It is suggested that Chaucer insisted on this latter point because, at the time the poem was written, Gaunt was contemplating deserting Katharine and sailing off on his expedition to try to seize the throne of Spain. This possible desertion was enough to alarm Chaucer, not only on Katharine's account, but also on account of Katharine's sister (who happened to be Chaucer's wife), and perhaps Chaucer himself (whose chief friend and protector in England was Gaunt). (The Appendix of the present book consists of a running commentary on the poem to show how the interpretation here offered is substantiated throughout.)

Chapter V] The *Parliament of Fowls* is divided into three distinct parts that were apparently written at three different times. The last part, written very early in Chaucer's career, depicts the courtship of Blanche of Lancaster by Gaunt and (by courtesy) two of his brothers; the first part, written in the last year of Chaucer's life, tells of events after Gaunt's death; and the middle part, dating from about 1380, is written in the spirit of Gaunt's middle years.

Chapter VI] The tale of Dido in the *House of Fame* may have been originally meant to be the last part of the poem. The House of Fame itself is an allegorical representation not only of the past as a treasury of story and history, but also, and more specifically, of Italy. The House of Rumor represents "the world" in general, or public life, or perhaps, more specifically again, the official career into which Chaucer was inducted by the eagle of the poem. This eagle seems to be an allegorical representation of John of Gaunt. The poem as a whole is a statement of Chaucer's discontent with old romances, and his resolve to write more independently about "newe thinges."

Chapter VII] In the Prologue of the *Legend of Good Women*, the daisy stands for poesy; and Alcestis is a fanciful reincarnation of Blanche of Lancaster, who was herself the epitome of faithful wifehood and of the spirit of poesy that found expression in Chaucer's *Book of the Duchess*.

Chapter VIII] Sir Thopas (in the "Tale of Sir Thopas") is probably a homosexual. Chaucer depicts his nature so slyly that the Host does not immediately catch on—but when he does, he immediately bursts forth in a rage at Chaucer for having told such a story (and for having fooled Harry Bailey). Possibly Sir Thopas represents the homosexual Richard II, and the giant who swears "by Termagaunt" represents John of Gaunt, whose third marriage (to Katharine Swynford) Richard opposed.

Chapter IX] Many of the *Canterbury Tales* and of the minor poems bear evidence of Chaucer's interest in Gaunt and his circle.

Jean Paul Sartre introduces a book on literature by asking: *"What is writing? Why does one write? For whom?"*[1]

He answers his first question thus: "For the poet, language is a structure of the external world.... he considers words as a trap to catch a fleeing reality.... all language is for him the mirror of the world."[2] These generalizations are peculiarly applicable to Chaucer. In the elemental sense of the word, Chaucer is a *worldly* poet. The principal subject of most of his work is the world and the people in it. Every reader of the *Book of the Duchess* knows how the world of actual persons has been brought imaginatively into that poem; and ever since Manly's *Some New Light on Chaucer* appeared (1926) most readers have believed that several characters in the *Canterbury Tales* are fictional representations of actual persons whom Chaucer must have known personally, or known about. In the preceding chapters of this book I have done hardly more than widen the road that Manly laid out. I have tried to show that many other works of Chaucer, besides the *Book of the Duchess* and those portions of the *Canterbury Tales* discussed in *Some New Light*, are structured about the "external world," the "fleeing reality," of persons whom Chaucer knew, and with whom his own life was more or less intimately associated.

Sartre answers his next question ("Why does one write?") by saying that one writes in order to be read. "The operation of writing implies that of reading as its dialectical correlative."[3] With Chaucer, the "reading" was often "hearing"; and many of his poems bear internal evidence of their public performance. Whoever first said that "Oratory is to be heard, poetry overheard," could not have been thinking of Chaucer, for here is a poet who talks to himself but rarely, and writes nearly always with the conscious intention of being heard or read. He is one of the most *public* of poets. That is, he seems to have been almost always acutely aware that writing, as well as reading, "is a pact of generosity between author and reader,"[4] with each of them (author and reader) giving of himself to the other. Legouis' remark that Chaucer's "sole aim was poetry for its own sake"[5] is simply not true. One of Chaucer's main aims in most of his poetry was to be heard, or read, by his own particular public. This does not mean that he prostituted his art in order to please his public. An actor or a musician does not prostitute his art by trying to please his audience; Scott brought no discredit to himself when he gave up writing long narrative poems because he found he could please his readers better with prose fiction; and Shaw brought no discredit to himself when he turned from unsuccessful fiction-writing to his more popular play-writing. Even the crusty Ben Jonson said, having literary critics in mind, "Our wishes ... are not to please the cookes table, but the guests."[6] As a matter of fact, Chaucer was probably so well adjusted to the society in which he moved that it is hard to conceive of any real conflict in his heart between what he wanted to say and what his public was willing to accept. But whether or not the private Chaucer was seriously at odds with the public Chaucer, there can be no doubt that most of his poems were written for public consumption. They "contain within themselves the image of the reader for whom they are intended."[7] This is a view of Chaucer that much contemporary criticism has forgotten, but that this book tries to bring back into focus.

"For whom does one write?"—this is Sartre's last question. For whom did Chaucer write? Manly answers the question precisely: "Chaucer wrote his stories not for the world in general and not for patrons, in hope of preferment, but as a source of interest and amusement to his friends."[8] And who were his friends? His "beste frend" was almost certainly John of Gaunt, and many of his other friends were those whom John of Gaunt's shadow touched at one time or another. He wrote his poetry (or a very large portion of it) "as a source of interest and amusement" to this particular group of people—which included, at various times, Gaunt himself, King Richard, Queen Anne, Princess Joan, Blanche of Lancaster, Queen Constance, Edmund of Langley, Henry Bolingbroke, Katharine Swynford, and the many less celebrated men and women of Gaunt's court, retinue, and association.

That Chaucer wrote about the world he lived in, and not merely "poetry for its own sake"—that most of his poetry was written deliberately for his own particular public—and that this public was, for the most part, John of Gaunt and the people surrounding him: this is the "new view" of Chaucer offered in the preceding chapters. Calling it *new* is obviously a misnomer; nothing is new under the sun. Its newness consists mostly in its attempt to show that much of Chaucer's poetry (besides the *Book of the Duchess* and a few passages in the *Canterbury Tales*) depicts imaginatively certain specific persons of the fourteenth century, and that it was written "as a source of interest and amusement" to a limited audience who would recognize the real-life originals of the characters depicted in the poems.

It will be asked, of course, whether the conclusions arrived at here are sound beyond all doubt or question. The answer is that virtually nothing (not even existence itself) is absolutely provable. Experience with the multiple varieties of the "Baconian heresy" shows how difficult it is to persuade many literary historians to believe what seems to many other literary historians perfectly obvious. What I think the preceding chapters have accomplished is the presentation of a massive series of plausibilities so fully and so intricately concatenated that they cannot be accidental.

Another question that may well be asked is whether it is at all likely that any poet would have written so many poems relevant to one person and his circle as Chaucer wrote in relation to Gaunt and his circle. The answer is: Yes, many poets have done so. Shakespeare wrote more poems relevant to some unknown young man (possibly "Mr. W. H."); and Tennyson (if the separate lyrics of *In Memoriam* may be counted as single poems) wrote more poems relevant to Hallam than Chaucer wrote relevant to Gaunt. If we count poems to one's mistress as being "relevant to one person," Dante wrote more poems relevant to Beatrice, Petrarch to Laura, and Sidney and Spenser to their loves than Chaucer wrote about Gaunt. If, however, we count the number of lines of verse devoted to one person, Chaucer comes out ahead. The *Book of the Duchess*, the poems to which separate chapters have been devoted in this book, and the minor poems mentioned in the preceding chapter, together with the "Squire's Tale" and passages in the *Canterbury Tales* that refer to Gaunt or to persons about him—these total between 15,000 and 20,000 lines, or about half the poetry that Chaucer wrote. None of the other poets mentioned above can match this total.

Though it is possible that no other Western poet has written more lines about one living person, at least two of Chaucer's contemporaries were not far behind him. His old master Guillaume de Machaut wrote at least three long poems (*Le Jugement dou Roy de Navarre, Le Confort d'Ami*, and *Le Lay de Plour*), totaling more than 8,000 lines, that are relevant to his friend Charles the Bad, King of Navarre; he wrote nearly 3,000 lines (*La Fontein Amoreuse*) relevant to John, Duke of Berry; he wrote over 2,000 lines (*Le Jugement dou Roy de Behaingne*) about his longtime friend

King John of Bohemia; and he wrote over 9,000 lines (*Le Prise d'Alexandrie*) about King Peter of Cyprus. Boccaccio wrote six long romances (*Ficolo, Filostrato, Teseida, Fiametta, Amorosa Visione*), some in verse, some in prose, and some in both verse and prose, that are somehow relevant to his mistress Maria d'Aquino. Chaucer, then, was not the only poet of his time, or of later times, who wrote at length about some contemporary figure who meant much to him.

One final comment must be made. It is not a denigration of Chaucer's art to show that a great deal of his poetry consists of imaginative reconstructions of the relationships among actual persons whom he knew. Joyce's *Ulysses* is no less a great work of art for being the imaginative reconstruction of actual relationships of actual persons; neither is Lawrence's *Sons and Lovers*; neither is Maugham's *Of Human Bondage*; and neither are numberless characters and episodes in the stories and novels of Fielding, Dickens, George Eliot, Thackeray, Conrad, Proust, Virginia Woolf, Dreiser, Thomas Wolfe, and dozens of others. If it is true (as Dover Wilson and others have maintained) that certain characters in the dramas of Shakespeare and Marlowe represent contemporary political figures— that fact has no effect whatever on the greatness of the dramas of Shakespeare and Marlowe; it is only an interesting and revealing piece of information that shows Shakespeare and Marlowe in another light, and helps us view their plays in still another dimension. Any number of Wordsworth's poems (e.g., "Michael," "Matthew," "Resolution and Independence") are imaginative reconstructions of actual events or persons; the same is true of many of the poems of Crabbe, Cowper, Burns, Scott, Byron, and any number of others.

The material upon which a poet's imagination works must come from somewhere—dreams and nightmares (Poe and Baudelaire), classical myth (Swinburne), history (Scott), personal experience (Wordsworth and Byron), religion (Hopkins), voluminous reading (Coleridge), the objective world of manners and people about the poet (Burns), and so on. If Chaucer found much of his material in the Gaunt circle (which is still so romantically fascinating that it was the subject of a best-selling novel only a few years since), who can blame him? The fact that he was able to find material for poetry in the world about him, and to sublimate this material into a fanciful, intellectually complex, technically masterful poetry that bears the strong imprint of his own personality and possesses at the same time both the splendor of romance and the substance of actuality, as well as an appeal to readers that has been increasing for nearly six centuries—this is a tribute to his greatness, not a denigration of his genius. After all this book was not meant to be a critical study of Chaucer; its purpose has been to present him as a poet even more responsive than has been generally believed to the world of people with whom he was immediately involved.

Appendix: Notes on *Troilus and Criseyde*

Evidence for the hypothesis outlined in Chapter IV of this book is scattered thick throughout *Troilus and Criseyde*. The evidence exists not only in passages that are original with Chaucer, but also in his alterations of, additions to, and omissions from the *Filostrato*. The following notes indicate something of the abundance of the evidence. No single note is intended as absolute proof that the suggested hypothesis is sound; rather, what seems to be an overwhelming weight of circumstantial evidence (with virtually no evidence to the contrary) does make the hypothesis look valid.

Passages previously discussed are not re-examined here unless they reveal something additional to what has been said already. Moreover, since passages more or less directly translated from Boccaccio cannot fairly be adduced as evidence either for or against the hypothesis (unless they run directly counter to the hypothesis), nearly all the following notes deal with passages entirely original with Chaucer. Direct translations from Boccaccio (including the one stanza in the poem that seems to be at variance with the hypothesis offered here) are marked with an asterisk.

It will be observed that most of the passages cited in the following notes are clearly meant to have one of the following effects on the persons to whom Chaucer originally read the poem:

1] To shame those scandalmongers who would condemn the lovers in the poem—an objective that would hardly have occurred to Chaucer if the lovers had been mere fictional characters.

2] To praise Troilus as a military hero—an objective that is not present in Boccaccio, and that may be explained on the supposition that Chaucer was trying to flatter a real person, or to defend him from slander.

3] To show that the love affair ennobled Troilus—an objective not understandable unless Chaucer was trying either to encourage illicit love among the general public, or to remind a real lover how much he owed to his mistress, or to defend a real lover from unsympathetic gibes about his weakness.

4] To extenuate as much as possible the disloyalty of Criseyde—an objective that is inconsistent with the conception of Criseyde as only a faithless lover in a fictional romance.

5] To elevate the love affair out of the realm of mere physical infatuation—an objective that is not in Boccaccio, and that Chaucer must have aimed at only because certain people considered, or pretended to consider, the love affair in the worst possible light.

6] To emphasize again and again the profound and honorable obligation that Troilus assumed in winning Criseyde's love—an objective that would be hard to account for unless Chaucer were trying thus to remind some actual lover of his permanent obligations to an actual mistress.

Notes

I, 5. Here is one of the many indications that the poet is reading aloud to a company of people. The famous *Troilus* frontispiece (see article cited in n. 10, Chapter IV) suggests that the poem was read aloud to the court of Richard II at one time or another. If the poem was first read at court about 1383-86, its many passages intended to put the best possible interpretation on the love affair are understandable in the light of then-current history. Gaunt was just then becoming the target for vicious hostility on the part of some of Richard II's favorites; and since the chroniclers of the time never tire of harping on Gaunt's illicit love affair with Katharine, it is likely that his enemies at court made much of the same affair. Chaucer's poem is a polite and brilliant answer to these court critics. Other passages indicating that at least the first three books were read to a company are I, 450; II, 30, 43-46, 1751; III, 45-46, 495-99, 1330-37, 1681-82.

I, 38-39. Cf. *Complaint of Mars*, 206-7, 272-98—where a very similar plea is made for understanding and sympathy for the lovers (John and Katharine?) rather than condemnation by "tunges horowe."

I, 51. Chaucer says that he has as much compassion for the lovers "As though I were hire owne brother dere." Is this a reminder that he actually was a kind of legal brother of Katharine and of Gaunt?

I, 97-98. Criseyde, Chaucer says here, was "allone / Of any frend to whom she dorste hir mone." Later on in the story she proves to have three nieces and a sister (II, 814, 1563); and Chaucer himself (after Boccaccio) says that she was "both of yonge and olde / Ful wel biloved" (I, 130-31). Probably, therefore, the word "frend" here is meant to imply a powerful protector who would take her part in the legal and financial difficulties to which well-to-do widows and orphans were customarily subjected in fourteenth-century England. Chaucer is suggesting that Criseyde had no such protector—an extenuating circumstance if she represents Katharine seeking help from Gaunt very soon after she was widowed.

I, 156. Boccaccio has the love affair of Troilo and Cressida commencing indefinitely in spring. Chaucer has the affair commencing in April. The change may be due to Chaucer's preference for the specific over the general. But since it was doubtless well known that the Gaunt-Katharine affair was consummated in May (see n. 23, Chapter IV), Chaucer may have wished to defend Katharine by postponing the beginning of the affair to the latest possible date.

I, 206-10, 218-31. Just as in the *Complaint of Mars* (220, 278) the lover (Gaunt?) protests that one must love in spite of himself, Chaucer here shows Troilus (Gaunt?) as a powerless victim of Cupid. This is plainly an apology; the lover is blameless because love is his fate, and is irresistible. Cf. I, 330-53, 520; II, 680-86; V, 587.

I, 214. Is the exclamation "kaught is proud and kaught is debonaire" a pun on the word *Kate*?

I, 232-66. This famous passage (already referred to in Chapter IV) reproves those "wise, proude, and worthi folkes" who think love can be resisted. Rather, says the poet, the strongest, worthiest, and greatest men are those who love most. Furthermore, love, instead of debasing a man, makes him kinder and more worthy. The whole passage is obviously a plea for the forgiveness and tolerance of Troilus' love—exactly what Chaucer would say to counteract the criticisms of those many enemies of Gaunt who chided him for loving Katharine. Perhaps also it is a reminder to Gaunt that he is under obligations to Katharine. The passage is quite out of keeping with anything in Boccaccio, and must have been inserted by Chaucer for very specific reasons. Cf. I, 1076-85; III, 23, 1654-55, 1776-78.

I, 330-53. Here Troilus makes believe that he still scorns love and the weakness of lovers. The lines intensify the effect of those just noted—namely, that Troilus (Gaunt?) did not fall in love because of light whim or lawless lust, but because, in spite of his low opinion of lovers, he could not resist love. Cf. I, 206-10.

* I, 499-501. There is a curious, perhaps unconscious, use of a grammatical tense here that can be explained under the hypothesis that Chaucer is writing about the Gaunt-Katharine affair. Boccaccio says that Troilo feared that Cressida might be in love with another (I, st. 49). Chaucer writes:

> for ay his drede
> Was this, that she som wight hadde loved so,
> That nevere of hym she wolde han taken hede.

Chaucer puts any possible love of Katharine's for another man in the past tense; there is no suggestion that Troilus thinks she loves another man *now*. He fears only that she still loves her dead husband so much that she will not love Troilus. This deliberate effort to play down even the possibility that Criseyde had another lover at the time she commenced the affair with Troilus is consistent with Chaucer's effort throughout the poem to make the love affair seem noble and exclusive. It is exactly what Chaucer would have done if the two lovers represent Gaunt and Katharine.

I, 548. Boccaccio writes, at this point, that Pandaro was "of high lineage"; Chaucer omits this phrase in introducing his Pandarus. It would have been inappropriate if Pandarus represents Chaucer himself.

I, 554-60. Perhaps Pandarus is jesting ironically at Gaunt's well-known piety. This jest at once differentiates Pandarus from Boccaccio's Pandaro—who is introduced as a serious and deeply concerned friend of Troilo.

I, 566-67. This outright praise of Troilus does not appear in Boccaccio. It is another indication that Chaucer is trying to build up the best possible case for Troilus (Gaunt?) as a superior person.

* I, 614-15. In Boccaccio, Troilo, on being questioned as to his sudden illness, refuses to assign any cause for it (II, st. 3). Later on, after he has finally revealed that love is the cause of his pain, he says that he has concealed it only because the object of his love is Pandaro's relative (II, st. 15). But in Chaucer, Troilus *first* admits that he is in love, and then, even before he reveals the identity of his beloved, adds that he has not dared to tell anyone that he is in love, "For harmes myghten folwen mo than two, / If it were wist." In other words, it is the mere fact that he is in love (not that he is in love with Pandarus' niece) that would be dangerous news if spread abroad. This alteration of Boccaccio makes Chaucer's poem fit perfectly John of Gaunt's situation: the mere fact that he, who had just married the Queen of Spain, was in love with another woman would cause "harmes ... mo than two."

I, 631-72, 715-21. Nearly all these lines are original with Chaucer. They enlarge upon Pandarus' own love, and its unsuccess. This brings up a problem. Is Chaucer, who continually protests that he "knowes nat love in dede" (*Parliament of Fowls*, 8), a person incapable of love—or is he one who can love but has loved unhappily? Perhaps a case could be made for either view. If we should accept the romantic notion that Chaucer was sincere in his hint (in the *Book of the Duchess*) that he had loved Blanche—with that hopeless courtly love typical of the time, a kind of "desire of the moth for the star"—and that he had been forced by Blanche's husband to marry Philippa Roet, there would be an extraordinary poignancy in these lines that Pandarus addresses to Troilus, and that are altogether original with Chaucer:

If God wol, thow art nat agast of me,
Lest I wolde of thi lady the bygyle!
Thow woost thyself whom that I love, parde,
As best I kan, gon sithen longe while.
And since thow woost I do it for no wyle,
And seyst I am he that thow trustest moost,
Telle me somwhat, syn al my wo thow woost.   (I, 715-21)

I, 894-96. Another suggestion that Troilus' love is a good, not evil, thing. That this is not an accidental remark is shown by Chaucer's omission here of two stanzas from the *Filostrato*. In II, st. 23, Boccaccio has Pandaro tell Troilo: "Only one thing will give you trouble, which is that my cousin is more virtuous than other women"; and in II, st. 25, Pandaro adds: "I see well that affairs such as this do not become a worthy lady." Clearly Boccaccio regards the love affair as something of a debasement of Cressida. But by omitting the two stanzas, and simultaneously insisting both that Criseyde's good name is not to be damaged (I, 902-3), and that "good it is / To loven wel," Chaucer lifts Boccaccio's somewhat sordid story to a much higher plane.

I, 976-79. Boccaccio says, with scurrilous implications, that every woman is warmly amorous (II, st. 27). Chaucer changes this to make both men and women amorous, and calls their love "celestial." Clearly, he is trying to remove blame from Criseyde.

I, 985-87. Once again Boccaccio's implied moral censure is converted by Chaucer into hearty approval of love that elevates Criseyde as well as Troilus. She should "loven and cherice" a worthy knight, says Chaucer. "And but she do, I hold it for a vice."

I, 1076-85. Here Chaucer tells how profoundly Troilus' character was improved as a result of his love. Cf. I, 232-66. Cf. also *Complaint of Mars*, 36-40, where love has exactly the same ennobling effect, in almost the same words, on Mars.

II, 8-11. Referring to Chaucer's invocation to the muse Clio, Root notes: "Clio is the Muse of history. Chaucer means that his story is sober matter of record. He needs no art of invention; it is enough if he can 'ryme wel' the story as he finds it." But then Root adds: "As a matter of fact, Book II departs very widely from Boccaccio." We may infer from this that Chaucer is telling sober history—but history as he found it in life, not in Boccaccio's poem.

II, 43-44. Chaucer reminds the company that (if it is thinking of John of Gaunt's marriage vows) it should not be too self-righteous—for hardly anybody has "in love seid lik, and don, in al."

II, 106-7. Pandarus, like Chaucer, knows the story of the seige of Thebes—from which Chaucer (the original of Pandarus?) fashioned his *Palamon and Arcite*—probably just before he wrote the *Troilus*.

II, 191-203. This praise of Troilus' military prowess is without counterpart in any of Chaucer's sources. Did Chaucer insert it here because Gaunt was considered the chief military man of his day?

II, 204-5. The description of Gaunt in the *Book of the Duchess*, 529-35, corresponds exactly to this description of Troilus.

II, 218-19. Chaucer is aware, as already suggested, that a widow with small children in the fourteenth century was sore beset in matters of property and debts. This awareness is again apparent in the appeal, later in the poem, of Creseyde to Deiphebus—an episode altogether original with Chaucer. Probably the poet was here trying to suggest to his audience that Katharine was troubled, needed a "frend" in high place to protect her, and was accordingly the more excusable for turning to Gaunt. Cf. II, 1418-19, 1469.

II, 292-308. Here is insistence once again on the strict honorableness of Troilus' love, and of Pandarus' intentions in interceding with Criseyde. Gaunt is being reminded that, according to the laws of honor which he values so highly, he cannot shuffle off Katharine as if she were a mere passing mistress. It is a theme that occurs again and again in the poem. Cf. II, 351-57, 468, 472, 480, 738, 762, 1133; III, 159-65, 944; IV, 567, 570.

II, 315. At approximately this place Chaucer omits several of Boccaccio's stanzas (II, st. 37-42, 54), most of them devoted to extolling Troilo as being *above all others* in manly virtue. As was noted previously, if Troilus represents Gaunt in Chaucer's poem, it would have been perilous for Chaucer to have praised Troilus above his older brother Hector (the Black Prince).

Chaucer omits another stanza (II, st. 45) in which Cressida asks, "Who has the right to have the full pleasure of me unless he should become my husband?" This would have been an embarrassing question if Chaucer's Criseyde does represent Katharine. It was probably a question that a good many people were already asking about her.

In this same connection, Cressida, of Boccaccio's poem, says: "Since my husband was taken from me, my wishes have been far from love, and I still have a heavy heart for his sad death, and shall have as long as I live, keeping in memory his departure" (II, st. 49). Chaucer omits this entirely. If his Criseyde had been only a fictional character, he might have had her raise this additional obstacle to loving Troilus. But if she represents Katharine, Chaucer could hardly picture her (after she had long been Gaunt's mistress) as being true to another man's memory. The omission is most significant.

In the next stanza (II, st. 50) Boccaccio has Cressida suggest that Troilo's love is the kind of fancy that passes away in a few days. Chaucer omits this stanza; it would contradict the conception of profound and honorable love, on the part of Troilus, that the poem tries hard to convey. Making the love profound was, perhaps, an artistic device to create a more intense tragic effect in the end; but making it honorable is something else again. The most obvious explanation for this insistence on honor I have already mentioned: it is to remind Gaunt of his obligations to Katharine.

In II, st. 52, Boccaccio has Pandaro tell Cressida that Troilo is one whom he would commend to his sister, his daughter, or his wife (if he had one). Chaucer omits this stanza. If Pandarus really represents Chaucer, and Criseyde represents Katharine—and if Gaunt had really been the lover of Chaucer's wife—Chaucer's including this stanza from Boccaccio would have been almost the most indecorous thing he could do.

II, 330. Pandarus shows a consistent deference toward Troilus because of the latter's high station in life. This deference, which is not present in Boccaccio, is understandable if Troilus represents the greatest man (after the king) in England.

II, 624-37. Gratuitous praise of Troilus as a military man; without parallel in Boccaccio.

II, 666-79. This is an open and deliberate attempt (without parallel in any of Chaucer's sources) to disprove what must have been cause for considerable gossip in court circles—namely, that Katharine began to love Gaunt in too "sodeyn wise" after her husband's death.

II, 680-86. Again the insistence that fate ordained the love of Troilus and Criseyde, and they, powerless to resist their fate, were accordingly blameless. Cf. the note on I, 206-10, and also the passage from the *Complaint of Mars* cited there.

II, 684-85. Troilus is said to be a favorite of Venus, even from his birth. The same idea, that Gaunt has always been Love's servant, is expressed in the *Book of the Duchess*, 764 ff.

* II, 750-56. Though this stanza is freely translated from the *Filostrato* (II, st. 69), it omits Cressida's phrase "I have no children." Katharine had two children at the time her affair with Gaunt commenced. Furthermore, the rather severe disparise of husbands in Chaucer's stanza is without parallel in Boccaccio—either in II, st. 69, or II, st. 73. At this point Boccaccio has a stanza (II, st. 74) in which Cressida tells herself that "the joy of love, when it is kept secret, surpasses that of a husband held always in one's arms." This shows an almost wanton spirit that would have discredited Katharine and cast doubts on her faithfulness to her late husband. Chaucer omits it.

II, 793. Chaucer calls attention once again to the frequent "tresoun that to wommen hath ben do." Cf. the note on II, 292-308; and V, 1779-85. As was said previously, Chaucer's insistent reiteration of the theme of woman deserted by her lover is most remarkable. Very probably it was associated with Gaunt's impending desertion of Katharine.

II, 827-82. Antigone's song bears an obvious resemblance, in diction, mood, and idea, to the "Complaint of Venus"—which is addressed in

formal respect and reverence to a "Princesse." In the "Complaint of
Venus" the characterization of the knightly lover is so fulsome, and yet
plainly so sincere, that the reader thinks immediately that there was no
man in Chaucer's lifetime to whom the words could apply so precisely
as to the Black Prince. Furthermore, this characterization is couched
in much the same words as the characterization of a figure in the
Parliament of Fowls whom I have identified as the Black Prince; and
it is much like the characterization of Hector (who, I think, stands for the
Black Prince) throughout the *Troilus* itself. At the end of the song,
here in the *Troilus*, Criseyde asks Antigone, "Who made this song?"
And Antigone answers:

> "Madame, iwys, the goodlieste mayde
> Of gret estat in al the town of Troye,
> And let hire lif in moste honour and joye."

The first two of these lines point unmistakably to Joan Princess of Wales,
"Fair Maid of Kent." Likewise, the line of the song in which the
woman says, "Al dredde I first to love hym to bigynne" could describe
Joan's first trepidation in loving the most famous warrior and, next the
king, the greatest man in all England when she married him. Another
line of hers, "Now good thrift have he, whereso that he be!" suggests that
her lover was dead—as was the Prince when the *Troilus* was written.
In sum, this concatenation of similarities and applicable references that
fit together so justly does not look accidental: rather, it tends to authenti-
cate the interpretation of the *Troilus* suggested in this book. If the song
does apply to the Prince, we have here another example of Chaucer's
careful provision that nobody shall think that he is setting up Gaunt as
a superior to the late Prince of Wales. One final point must be added.
The line "And let hire lif in moste honour and joye" is in the past tense;
evidently the lady who made the song is now dead. Since Princess Joan
died in early August, 1385, this portion of the *Troilus* (or a revision of
this particular line) must have been written after that time.

* II, 1002-3. Boccaccio has Pandaro tell Troilo, "I know that in everything you can see six times better than I." Chaucer, much more complimentary, as would have befitted the situation if Pandarus represented
Chaucer, and Toilus Gaunt, has Pandarus say, "I woot wel that thow
wiser art than I / A thousand fold."

At this point Boccaccio includes several stanzas (II, st. 115-17) in which
Cressida tells herself that she is not planning to deny herself the delight
of Troilo's love. Chaucer omits these stanzas. They would have made
his Criseyde too forward, too quick to love—and it is from precisely this
accusation of loving too quickly that Chaucer is trying to defend his
heroine.

II, 1274. Chaucer, in his own person as author, expresses his hope that God will send other women such loves as Criseyde's. This is another instance of his attempt to take every shadow of opprobrium from the affair. The same approbation of illicit love is expressed in the *Complaint of Mars,* and is explicitly recommended in ll. 15-21 of that poem. Cf. I, 985-87; III, 1223-25.

II, 1291. In refusing to speak to Troilus, Criseyde (in Robinson's text) feels "shame" because "it were ek to soone." But a variant word, which Root prefers, is "speche" instead of "shame." In other words, Root's version would make the line consistent with the feeling Chaucer expresses in II, 1274.

II, 1735. Here is the reference to the "corones tweye"—a line that has been hitherto unexplained. But if Troilus stands for Gaunt, the phrase is not obscure. Momentarily forgetting that he is writing about a fictional character, Chaucer refers to Gaunt's two crowns: his ducal crown in England and his kingly crown in Spain.

III, 87. Cf. *Book of the Duchess,* 531. The same phrase describes both Troilus and John of Gaunt.

* III, 239, 264, 330. Pandarus calls Troilus "brother." Boccaccio's Pandaro, in parallel passages, repeatedly calls Troilus "my friend" (II, st. 5-10). Only once before has Pandarus referred to Troilus as "brother." But now that Troilus and Criseyde (Gaunt and Katharine?) are on the verge of consummating their love, Chaucer begins using the word regularly, as he does throughout the rest of the poem.

III, 239-329. Six of the thirteen stanzas included here are original with Chaucer, and the seven imitated from Boccaccio are far more intense and earnest than Boccaccio's stanzas. All the stanzas remind Troilus that he has given his word of honor not to treat Criseyde as a common bawd, that he is honor bound to love her, and that Pandarus would never have furthered the affair had he not trusted implicitly in the honor of Troilus. At the time this was written, Gaunt and Katharine had been lovers more than ten years, but Gaunt was contemplating deserting Katharine. Under these circumstances, Chaucer would have been at pains to do just what he is doing here—that is, remind Gaunt, who was ever sensitive to the claims of honor, that he must not cast Katharine aside.

* III, 407-13. This stanza, very literally translated from Boccaccio, shows Troilus (in order to prove the sincerity of his love for Criseyde) offering a sister of his to Pandarus. *It is the only part of this entire poem* that seems to me to be, possibly, inconsistent with the interpretation offered here. John of Gaunt would never have offered a sister of his to Chaucer—unless, indeed, he was referring to Philippa Chaucer, who had, now that Katharine was won, become a kind of sister to Gaunt. If the

stanza had been quite original with Chaucer, it would have been more disturbing.

III, 451-55. These lines emphasize (as Boccaccio does not) the fear and caution with which the lovers meet. The fear and caution would be unmotivated if the lovers were mere fictional characters. But in the early months of Katharine's widowhood, and of Gaunt's marriage to the Queen of Spain, extreme circumspection would have been much more necessary than it was later on.

III, 470-82. This passage (without parallel in Boccaccio) shows how Troilus fulfils Criseyde's need for a "frend" that was mentioned early in the poem (I, 98), of someone to take control "of hire estat and of hire governaunce" (II, 219). Troilus became "to hire a wal / Of stiel, and sheld from every displesaunce" (III, 479-80). In the same way, the widow Katharine Swynford found a protector in Gaunt.

III, 488. Pandarus bore letters between the lovers "whan Troilus was absent." Where could Troilus have gone in a besieged city? Is Chaucer here remembering a real-life situation between Gaunt and Katharine, and forgetting the allegorical situation? Pandarus acts as a courier between them, as Chaucer acted as a courier for Prince Lionel. Cf. III, 569-70.

III, 569-70. Again, Troilus is said to be "out of towne," even though Troy is besieged. We have here a picture of a busy man, like Gaunt, attending to business outside a peaceful city, like London. Cf. III, 488.

III, 924. "She did al for goode." Another attempt to remove any blame from Criseyde (Katharine?).

III, 1200. Chaucer has Criseyde tremble "as an aspes leef"; Boccaccio's Cressida shows no such hesitancy. Chaucer is trying hard to prevent anyone from regarding his heroine as bold and pushing.

III, 1210-11. These are the famous lines in which Criseyde, having at last yielded to Troilus in Pandarus' house, says to her lover:

> "Ne hadde I er now, my swete herte deere,
> Ben yold, ywis, I were now nought heere!"

The lines are generally regarded as an example of Criseyde's (and Chaucer's) psychological subtlety. They are that; but if Criseyde represents Katharine, Chaucer would have had her say just this. Her words are a flattering assurance that she really loved Gaunt before consummating the affair with him.

III, 1223-25. These lines are Chaucer's own devout approbation of the illicit affair, and his advice to every woman to do as Criseyde did. It is just what Chaucer would have said of the Gaunt-Katharine affair. Cf. II, 1274.

* III, 1317-23. Boccaccio's version of this stanza is as follows: "O sweet night, much desired, what were you to the two blissful lovers!

If the great knowledge that the poets have had were given to me, (that night) could not be described by me. Let him who has been before now so much blessed by love as these, think about it, and he will partly understand their delight" (III, st. 33). Chaucer's translation not only is more personal, but also is more in the nature of a judgment:

> O blisful nyght, of hem so longe isought,
> How blithe unto hem bothe two thou weere!
> Why nad I swich oon with my soule ybought,
> Ye, or the leeste joie that was theere?
> Awey, thou foule daunger and thow feere,
> And lat hem in this hevene blisse dwelle,
> That is so heigh that al ne kan I telle!

Such overwhelming approval (in stark contrast to the moralizing element that enters the last portions of the poem) is understandable if the two lovers represent Gaunt and Katharine. The poet is clearly trying to build up good will for the affair, and to remove from his hearers' minds any tendency toward moral judgment. The third and fourth lines are especially interesting in relation to Chaucer's own profession of fruitless love.

III, 1332-35. A similar plea to other lovers for sympathetic understanding is made by Mars (Gaunt?) in the *Complaint of Mars*, 272-89.

III, 1387-93. Once again there is blame of those "wrecches" who despise the love of Troilus and Criseyde, and assertion that these people, and not the lovers, are foolish and vicious. This repeated and extraordinary insistence on defending the lovers, absolving them from all blame, and showing them all the better for love is incomprehensible if they are only fictional characters.

III, 1490. Boccaccio has Troilo tell Cressida that she is "more dear to him than the Trojan kingdom" (III, st. 47); but Chaucer has his Troilus tell Criseyde that being her lover is more pleasing to him "than thise worldes tweye." This may be an echo of the mysterious "corones tweye" of II, 1735.

III, 1607-8. Chaucer inserts a passage, not in Boccaccio, in which Troilus declares that he is Criseyde's, "and shal, tyl that I deye, / And that I thus am hires, dar I seye." The lines would be another reminder to Gaunt that he is permanently committed, by his own word of honor, to Katharine.

III, 1654-55. Another reference to the ennobling quality of this love. It is a reminder to critics of the Gaunt-Katharine affair that the great man was not debased by the love, and a reminder to Gaunt himself that he received good in return for the love he gave Katharine. Cf. note on I, 232-66.

III, 1786-1806. Chaucer expands and intensifies Boccaccio's praise of

Troilo. Except in the single matter of making Troilus inferior to Hector, Chaucer's poem is far more flattering to Troilus than is Boccaccio's to Troilo.

III, 1807-20. Here are the last two stanzas of Book III:

> Thow lady bryght, the doughter to Dyone,
> Thy blynde and wynged sone ek, daun Cupide,
> Yee sustren nyne ek, that by Elicone
> In hil Pernaso listen for t'abide,
> That ye thus fer han deyned me to gyde.
> I kan namore, but syn that ye wol wende,
> Ye heried ben for ay withouten ende!

> Thorugh yow have I seyd fully in my song
> Th'effect and joie of Troilus servise,
> Al be that ther was som disese among,
> As to myn auctour listeth to devise.
> My thridde bok now ende ich in this wyse,
> And Troilus in lust and in quiete
> Is with Criseyde, his owen herte swete.

No other book in the poem ends with such a formal invocation-farewell; nor does any other book (except the last) end with that unmistakable tone of finality that is so obvious in the second stanza just quoted. Furthermore, Chaucer says in so many words, "I seyd *fully* my song," and "I kan namore"; and he adds that the muses are leaving him: "syn that ye wol wende." Finally, two of the best early manuscripts show the third line from the end as reading, "Me my boke now ende ich in this wyse."

From all this it seems altogether probable that the portion of *Troilus and Criseyde* that Chaucer "published" by reading it to the court of Gaunt or of Richard II might have ended with Book III. Everything in the poem up to this point has been a depiction of a love affair that ended happily. This would have been the perfect place for Chaucer to end the poem if Troilus and Criseyde represent Gaunt and Katharine; if it had been mere fiction, only an English version of Boccaccio, it would have continued (as Boccaccio's poem does) without a break. Cf. notes on IV, 13, 26-28; V, 270, 272.

IV, 13. This invocation is presented as *writing*, not as if it were being *spoken* to a company at court. This would indicate that Chaucer added the invocation after the poem itself was completed—or else that this entire Book IV was not read at court. Possibly Chaucer, averse to portraying Katharine as fickle in love, did not care to "publish" Books IV and V (in which the heroine misbehaves), but did wish to finish his rendering of the *Filostrato*. Therefore, he wrote Books IV and V, but never displayed them at court.

IV, 15-16. Chaucer says that he is now going to tell "how Criseyde Troilus forsook, / Or at the leeste, how that she was unkynde." Since he must have known how Boccaccio's story ended, the suggested alternative to Criseyde's treachery seems odd. Perhaps Chaucer originally intended to soften the story—which is what he would certainly have done if Criseyde represents Katharine, and if he planned to "publish" Parts IV and V at court.

IV, 19-21. This is a vigorous attack on those who would vilify Criseyde. Nothing could seem more curious if this were merely a fictional romance. The lines have meaning only if we assume that Criseyde represents some actual woman whom Chaucer is trying to defend. Cf. IV, 1415-21.

IV, 26-28.   This ilke ferthe book me helpeth fyne,
             So that the losse of lyf and love yfeere
             Of Troilus be fully shewed heere.

These lines contain several items that bear examination. The first of these items is the word "book." The early MSS of the poem have capital letters indicating major breaks or divisions, but these divisions are nowhere labeled "books." Furthermore, fourteenth-century writers do not seem to have used the English word "book" for internal divisions of a longer work (except in reference to books of the Bible). Apparently the word was used only for a complete work, a volume. The *Middle English Dictionary* (ed. Hans Kurath, Ann Arbor, 1958; p. 1019) notes only three examples of the word used in the sense of "a major division of a long treatise or literary work" during the Middle Ages: the "laste bok" of the *House of Fame* (l. 1093), the "thridde bok" of the *Troilus* (III, 1818), and once in a fifteenth-century MS version (much altered from the original thirteenth-century MSS) and the *Ancrene Riwle*. (The *N. E. D.* quotes this last example, dates it 1225, and offers no other example before 1526.) I have already indicated that the two Chaucerian examples are open to question as references to divisions within a larger work; but those two, with the "ferthe book" in the lines quoted above, are the only examples in all of Chaucer's poetry and prose where the word "book" does not clearly designate a complete work.

Under the circumstances, we might be a little suspicious of this "ferthe book." Our suspicions will be sharpened when we know that the entire stanza containing the phrase is omitted from one of the best of the primary MSS, and that the stanza is included with "Book III" in most of the early MSS. Moreover, the lines quoted state that the "ferthe book" will show fully the loss of Troilus' life and love—though "Book IV" does no such thing. The use of "like" referring to a fourth book that has not previously been mentioned seems odd. However, Chaucer has mentioned "my book" nine lines earlier, meaning, obviously, the entire poem. The "ilke" could refer back to this earlier line—in which case "ilke ferthe book" would be meaningless. The implication of all this is that Chaucer's very first version of the *Troilus* did not contain the phrases "thridde bok" and "ferthe book." These phrases were created by the author in some subsequent revision of the poem, or (much more probably) by some copyist of the generation subsequent to 1380-85.

IV, 323. At this point Chaucer omits a stanza of Boccaccio's (IV, st. 37) in which Troilo says that he might conceivably have learned, if forced by long usage, to endure the absence of Cressida. Including this suggestion would hardly have added weight to Chaucer's effort, obvious throughout his poem, to encourage the lover not to desert his mistress. Cf. IV, 407-38, 497.

IV, 407-38. Troilus passionately rejects Pandarus' wild suggestion that he try other loves. Troilus declares that he would have to be "a fend, / To traysen hire that trewe is unto me!" In this passage Chaucer accomplishes two things: he affirms the depth and earnestness of Troilus' love, and reminds him that he has sworn not to desert his mistress. It is significant that the words of IV, 421-27 (in which the suggestion is made that many circumstances may cause diminution of love) were spoken by Troilo in the *Filostrato* (IV, st. 59), but by Pandarus in Chaucer's poem. Chaucer would not allow the mere idea of unfaithfulness to enter his hero's mind; that would have canceled out the poet's constant insistence that Troilus was honor-bound to Criseyde.

IV, 841-47. These lines, in which Criseyde expresses her utter misery at having to separate from Troilus, were spoken by Pandaro in the *Filostrato* (IV, st. 97). Chaucer seems to be trying to emphasize the genuine faithfulness of Criseyde. It is most curious that Chaucer would have made such a continuous effort to excuse Criseyde, the supreme example of disloyalty to that love which Chaucer so extols, if she had been only a fictional character.

IV, 958 ff. Though Troilus' long and famous speech on predestination is concerned here with the tragic aspects of fate, the entire poem, as has been already noted (cf. note on I, 206-10), makes the reader feel "a deep sense of overruling destiny" (Robinson, p. 830). It was ineluctable fate that made Troilus fall in love with Criseyde, it is ineluctable fate that makes him lose her. If the two lovers really represent Gaunt and Katharine, Chaucer is here answering criticism of their love by saying that it was foreordained in all its details. The passage would be out of place and would serve no function in a mere fictional romance; but as an apologia for Gaunt and Katharine, it is altogether appropriate.

IV, 1095. At this point Chaucer omits a stanza of Boccaccio's (IV, st. 111) in which Pandaro tells Troilo that Cressida's grief at having to part with him "surpasses yours twenty to one." Chaucer does try to show that Criseyde truly loves Troilus; but the real emphasis in the poem is on Troilus' love for Criseyde, and his obligation to remain loyal to her. Reasons for this emphasis have already been mentioned.

IV, 1127. This line, "I shal yow tellen soone," is the only suggestion that Chaucer is, perhaps, reading this Book IV to a company. But even this line is ambiguous; it could imply readers of the poem instead of hearers. If Chaucer was trying to romanticize the love affair of Gaunt and Katharine for the benefit of the two lovers themselves and of the courtiers about John King of Spain and Richard King of England, or if he was trying to make the court feel the true depth and sincerity of the affair, or if he was trying to remind Gaunt of his continuing obligation to Katharine—the first three books would have been quite sufficient for public reading. What I am trying to suggest is that, very possibly, Chaucer read the first three books at court, and that he finished the last two books in private—just to get the job completed, however hastily and unoriginally. These last two books, with their portrayal of Criseyde's disloyalty (even though Chaucer tries hard to excuse it) would have done much to counteract the sympathetic attitudes Chaucer had tried to propagate in the first three books.

IV, 1415-21. This stanza, entirely original with Chaucer, is an emphatic statement of Criseyde's genuine loyalty and good intentions. Nothing is clearer than that Chaucer is reluctant to tell of Criseyde's eventual unfaithfulness, and that he does so only because his "auctoritee" requires it. This reluctance would be meaningless if Criseyde were merely a character in romance. Cf. V, 1093-99.

IV, 1667-82. In Boccaccio this passage is spoken by Troilo in compliment to Cressida (IV, st. 164-65). Chaucer's reversal of the speakers has the effect of making the passage particularly flattering to Troilus—which is understandable if Troilus represents some real person of royal rank whom Chaucer is trying to flatter or to please.

V. Unlike the other four books, this last book has no Proem. This is another indication that this book (showing Criseyde's perfidy) was not written to be read at court. Cf. V, 270.

V, 1. Another suggestion that the entire affair is controlled by inescapable destiny.

V, 229-30. In a passage otherwise closely similar to Boccaccio (V, st. 19 ff.), Chaucer inserts a passage recalling the singleness and the sworn perpetuity of Troilus' love. The poet will not allow the lover to forget his vows to his mistress.

V, 270, 272. These lines indicate definitely that Chaucer is writing for *readers*, not listeners. That is to say, this last book, with its unfavorable picture of Criseyde, was not written for court consumption. As has been pointed out by a good many critics, "his heart was not in the writing of this book."

V, 344-50. This stanza, quite original with Chaucer, would be entirely explicable (and excruciating) if Philippa Chaucer had really been Gaunt's mistress—or if Chaucer had really loved Blanche.

V, 527. Chaucer says of Troilus at his palace: "A cause he fond in towne for to go." In Boccaccio there is no indication that Troilo's palace was not in the city. But Gaunt's great palace, the Savoy, was outside London's walls. The line quoted here would apply if Troilus' palace represented the Savoy.

V, 1037-99. This entire passage, original with Chaucer, is filled with efforts to gloss over Criseyde's disloyalty. The poet keeps repeating that he is telling only what "Men seyn—I not!" (V, 1050). He insists that "the storie telleth us" (V, 1037); "I fynde ek in the stories" (V, 1044); "the storie telleth us" (V, 1051). He has Criseyde herself cry out, "Thise bokes wil me shende!" (V, 1060). And he writes the famous stanza beginning:

> Ne me ne list this sely womman chyde
> Forther than the storye wol devyse. (V, 1093-94)

Clearly, the writing of this part of the story is most distasteful to him.

V, 1240-41. Boccaccio pictures (VII, st. 24) the boar of Troilo's dream tearing out Cressida's heart. Chaucer pictures the boar holding her in his arms and kissing her. The emphasis is not on fierce conquest, but on gentle love. This is a point to be remembered in connection with the note on V, 1443 ff.

V, 1274. At this point Chaucer omits seven of Boccaccio's stanzas (VIII, st. 33-39) in which Troilo is described as actually trying to commit suicide, with Pandaro restraining him by force. If Chaucer had been merely trying to show the excess of Troilus' grief, he had here a perfect opportunity to do so. But since attempted suicide was considered a major sin, Chaucer would not have pictured his Troilus going to such lengths—if Troilus represented a real person whom Chaucer was trying to present in the best possible light. This omission is one of the most suggestive in the entire poem. (It should be admitted, however, that, in IV, 1184-1211, Troilus, believing Criseyde dead, prepares to commit suicide. But the action here never becomes dramatic, or reaches the point of an actual attempted suicide. Besides, the passage is translated almost literally from Boccaccio—IV, st. 120-23.)

V, 1281. At about this point Chaucer omits seven more stanzas by Boccaccio (VII, st. 42-47) in which Pandaro advises Troilo to go die fighting the Greeks. This advice would have been appropriate enough if Troilus were a mere fictional lover ready to die because of his unhappy love, and there would have been no reason why Chaucer should have omitted it. But if Troilus represented John of Gaunt, this advice that he go get himself killed in a war would have been distinctly unfriendly, almost treasonable.

V, 1317 ff. In Troilus' letter to Criseyde, Chaucer makes several significant omissions from Boccaccio. In VII, st. 56-59, Boccaccio has Troilo expressing his suspicion that Cressida has another lover; Chaucer omits this (even though Troilus has already dreamed about Criseyde and the boar). This de-emphasizing of Troilus' suspicion is consistent with Chaucer's invariable purpose of extenuating Criseyde's misbehavior as far as the story will allow. Chaucer also omits Boccaccio's VII, st. 61, in which Troilo threatens to take his own life. Cf. note on V, 1274.

Even in this letter of Troilus, Chaucer omits many of the most beautifully poetic stanzas of Boccaccio—and thereafter hurries through the story, skipping lively incidents, fine poetic passages, intriguing characterizations. It is clear that this fifth book is not to his liking—a disapprobation that can be readily understood if we believe that Criseyde represents Katharine.

V, 1443 ff. Chaucer follows Boccaccio in having Troilus dream that Criseyde loves a boar (V, 1238-74). But then, in an extensive addition to Boccaccio—hardly to be expected in this fifth book where Chaucer is hurrying the story along—he has Troilus consult Cassandra, the prophetess, about his dream. Here Chaucer resorts to a device common with him for calling attention to an idea—that is, repetition of a word or phrase (cf. note on V, 1037-99; also the chapters on the Prologue of the *Legend of Good Women* and the "Tale of Sir Thopas"). In twenty-nine lines he repeats the word "boar" seven times, and then twice more in a stanza a little farther on. This emphasis on the boar, not only in the repeated word but also in the entire episode devoted to the boar, is so insistent that one looks for an explanation. I should like to believe that Chaucer is here punning on the name "Swynford" and referring obliquely to the Swynford coat of arms. The Swynford shield bore a wide chevron with a large boar's head at each end and in the center of the chevron. What Chaucer is saying, I take it, is that John of Gaunt is troubled by the thought that Katharine retains a lingering love for the memory of Sir Hugh Swynford—the boar of the dream.

V, 1541-61. Chaucer here inserts three stanzas, derived from Benoit, concerning the death of Hector. In an entirely original passage, he says that Fortune "Gan pulle awey the fetheres brighte of Troie"—perhaps a reference to the deaths, in 1376 and 1377, of the Black Prince and Edward III, and the killing of many great personages in the Peasants' Revolt of 1381, together with the steady decay of English fortunes in France. In other original lines he tells of Hector's death—

> For which me thynketh every manere wight
> That haunteth armes oughte to bewaille
> The deth of hym that was so noble a knyght.

He adds (from Benoit) that Hector "drough a kyng by th'aventaille."
All this seems to me clearly a reference to the death of the Black Prince,
and to the capture of King John of France by the Black Prince in 1356.
I do not know why else Chaucer would have bothered to include this
material in a poem about the love affair of Troilus and Criseyde.

V, 1765-67. Chaucer here pays tribute to Troilus' military feats, and
says he would have written about them except that he chose Troilus'
love for his theme. This would seem to be a kind of apology for not
writing about the achievements of Gaunt that were more glorious than
his love affair with Katharine.

V, 1772-78. Once again, even at the end of the book, an apology for
Criseyde's misbehavior.

V, 1779-85. Boccaccio concludes his poem by warning youths against
loving faithless women. In direct contrast, Chaucer concludes his poem
by warning women against fickle men! This about face seems so utterly
inconsistent with the story of a faithful man and a fickle woman that
Chaucer has just been telling that it demands an explanation. Perhaps
an explanation may be best suggested in a discussion of the poem's entire
"Epilogue."

The Epilogue. Many scholars have written many pages about the
"*Troilus* Epilogue"—even though there is no part of the poem designated
as an "Epilogue" in any of the primary manuscripts, and nobody can
say just where the so-called "Epilogue" begins.

Since ll. 1744-50 (st. 250) constitute an obviously falling close and a
concluding summary, together with a final pious exclamation, we may
consider the "Epilogue" as beginning at l. 1751 (st. 251)—though, of
course, any of five or six other places after l. 1750 has almost equal claim
to being considered the beginning.

As arbitrarily defined here, the "Epilogue" consists of the following
parts:

1. Two stanzas telling that Troilus fought the Greeks bravely during
   the rest of his life, always seeking Diomede. But Fortune willed
   it that they should both die by the hands of others. Except for
   its last line, the first of these stanzas is original with Chaucer;
   like so much else in this poem (and not in Boccaccio's poem), it
   praises the military prowess of Troilus. The last line of the first
   stanza, and all of the second stanza, are translated from Boccaccio.
   (Ll. 1751-64; st. 251-52.)

2. An original stanza, already mentioned, in which Chaucer offers
   a semi-apology for writing about Troilus' love affair instead of
   about his military prowess. It is just what Chaucer might have
   done if Troilus represents Gaunt, who was regarded by his con-

temporaries (and actually was) the chief English military figure of the 1380's. (Ll. 1765-71; st. 253.)

3. An original stanza pleading once again for all ladies to forgive Criseyde. (Ll. 1772-78; st. 254.)

4. The original stanza, mentioned above, in which the poet warns ladies against faithless men. (Ll. 1779-85; st. 255.)

5. Two original stanzas (beginning, "Go, litel bok, go, litel myn tragedye") that sound exactly like a tailpiece for a completed poem. (Ll. 1786-99; st. 256-57.)

6. A stanza (taken from Boccaccio) that returns to the theme of No. 1 above, and tells how Troilus slew many Greeks till he was finally slain by Achilles. (Ll. 1800-06; st. 258.)

7. Three stanzas, mentioned in the chapter on the *Troilus* in the text of this book, in which the soul of Troilus, like that of Saint John in Dante, ascends to the eighth heavenly sphere, and looks down on the earth. (Ll. 1807-27; st. 259-61.)

8. A stanza (from Boccaccio) commenting sententiously on Troilus' death: "Swich fyn hath, lo, this Troilus," etc. But in this stanza Chaucer does not call Criseyde "base," as does Boccaccio. (Ll. 1828-34; st. 262.)

9. Two stanzas (of which the first two lines are from Boccaccio) in which Boccaccio's prayer that young men be careful not to trust women lightly is converted into a pious prayer that young folk turn their love from earthly to heavenly objects. (Ll. 1835-48; st. 263-64.)

10. A stanza which reverts to the syntactical form of st. 262, and deprecates pagan gods. (Ll. 1849-55; st. 265.)

11. A dedication of the poem to Gower, Strode, and Christ. (Ll. 1856-62; st. 266.)

12. A stanza praying for Christ's mercy on us all. (Ll. 1863-69; st. 267.)

Though much scholarly ink has been spent in an attempt to show that the "Epilogue" is *unified* (according to modern aesthetic taste), an unbiased mind can hardly help seeing the "Epilogue" as a potpourri that contains several possible endings (as at l. 1750, or with No. 5 above, or with No. 7, or with No. 11, or with No. 12, or perhaps elsewhere), at least two separate tailpieces (Nos. 5 and 11-12), reversions to topics originally abandoned (No. 6 and probably No. 10), a prayer against love after a poem devoting thousands of lines to love (No. 9), a warning against faithless men after a poem about a faithless woman (No. 4), and several shifts in mood (as at Nos. 4, 6, 7, and 9).

What I am trying to suggest here is that either Chaucer did not perceive or did not object to a lack of unity, coherence, and consistency that seems plain to us—or else (more probably) some literary executor or self-appointed editor joined together, after Chaucer's death, various stanzas and variant endings that Chaucer had written, but never finally made up his mind about, and appended them, or clusters of them, more or less at random, to *Troilus and Criseyde*.

Certain facts seem to point toward the soundness of the view that the "Epilogue" is a haphazard arrangement. First, as I have already said, Book V was probably never formally "published" by being read aloud at court. Thus Chaucer could have kept revising this last book and its ending as long as he lived—just as he kept revising other poems of his (*vide*, especially, the Prologue of the *Legend of Good Women*). But though Book V is not being read aloud, the poet suddenly addresses "yow" women (V, 1783), and tells them something utterly contrary to what he has been writing only a moment previously. The stanza involved (No. 4 above) seems clearly to be an intrusion. It might not be too wild a guess that this stanza is something discarded, or misplaced, from the end of Part V of the "Clerk's Tale"—somewhere about E 931 or E 938.

Without seeming to argue in a circle (since my point here is something else), I should like to mention that, if indeed Troilus represents Gaunt, the three stanzas describing his death and ascension (No. 7 above) would have been in extremely bad taste had Gaunt been still alive at the time they were written. Probably, therefore, these stanzas (and perhaps some other pious stanzas in the remainder of the poem) were written after Gaunt's death. Confirmation of this surmise may be found in the circumstance that what Root regards as the three earliest and best manuscripts of the poem *lack these three stanzas*. Did Chaucer write the stanzas only after the death of Gaunt, in February, 1399?

The poem is dedicated to Gower and "philosophical Strode"—who has been identified as Ralph Strode, once an Oxford scholar, and a neighbor and acquaintance of Chaucer. Strode died, however, in 1387. Since Chaucer would certainly not have dedicated his poem to a dead man, and asked him to correct it, this stanza must have been written before 1387. Here, then, is what seems to be excellent evidence that different portions of the "Epilogue" were written at least twelve years apart. But if we admit this possibility for two portions of the "Epilogue," we shall have to admit the same possibility for the other portions. That is to say, the "Epilogue" may be only a loosely arranged accumulation of stanzas that Chaucer wrote over a period of years as he kept experimenting with variant endings, or bringing the poem up to date. Some "editor" going through Chaucer's belongings after the poet's death may have found these chips from the master's workshop included with the still "unpublished" Book V, and (with commendable respect for every scrap that the great man wrote) may have preserved them by attaching them, without much regard for unity or logic, to the poem with which he found them included. The alternative to this explanation is that Chaucer himself, not being able to make up his mind finally as to what he should do with all the miscellaneous stanzas and variant endings that he had written at different times, kept postponing a decision until too late. Death called him before he had established a final definitive form for the conclusion of the poem.

Notes

Chapter I. Introduction: Obstructions to the view

1. René Wellek and Austin Warren, *Theory of Literature* (New York, 1956), p. 31.
2. W. K. Wimsatt, Jr., and Monroe C. Beardsley, *The Verbal Icon* (Lexington, Kentucky, 1954), pp. 3 ff.
3. John Crowe Ransom, *The New Criticism* (Norfolk, Conn., 1941), p. 307.
4. J. A. W. Bennett, *The Parliament of Foules* (Oxford, 1957), pp. 2-3.
5. Peter Brieger, *English Art, 1216-1307* (Oxford, 1957), p. 273.
6. D. W. Robertson, Jr., *A Preface to Chaucer* (Princeton, 1962), p. 276.
7. Germaine Dempster, "Manly's Conception of the Early History of the *Canterbury Tales*," *PMLA*, LXI (1946), 380-81.
8. Dempster, p. 384.
9. Robert K. Root, *Chaucer's Troilus and Criseyde* (Princeton, 1945), p. lxxvii.
10. Charles A. Owen, Jr., "Chaucer's Method of Composition," *PMLA*, LXXII (1957), 164.
11. *Chaucer's Troilus and Criseyde*, p. xii.
12. J. M. Manly, *Some New Light on Chaucer* (New York, 1926), *passim*.
13. See, for example, James R. Kreuzer, "The Dreamer in the *Book of the Duchess*," *PMLA*, LXVI (1951), 543-47; Bernard H. Bronson, "The *Book of the Duchess* Reopened," *PMLA*, LXVII (1952), 863-81; Donald C. Baker, "The Dreamer in the *Book of the Duchess*," *PMLA*, LXX (1955), 279-82.
14. Hazel Allison Stevenson, "A Possible Relation between Chaucer's Long Lease and the Date of His Birth," *MLN*, L (1935), 318-22.
15. J. M. Manley, ed., *The Canterbury Tales* (New York, 1928), p. 34.
16. George Williams, "Chaucer's Long Lease and the Date of his Birth," *N & Q*, CCV (1960), 168.
17. *Life-Records, Chaucer Society's Publications*, 2nd series, No. 32 (London, 1886), pp. 105-13.
18. *Life-Records*, No. 193.
19. William Longman, *The Life and Times of Edward III* (London, 1869), II, 44.
20. O. F. Emerson, "A New Chaucer Item," *MLN*, XXVI (1911), 19-21.
21. Samuel Moore, "Studies in the Life-Records of Chaucer," *Ang.*, XXXVII (1913), 1-26.
22. G. D. G. Hall, "When Was Chaucer Born?" *TLS*, June 28, 1957, p. 397.
23. O. F. Emerson, "Chaucer's Testimony as to his Age," *MP*, XI (1913), 117-25.
24. Sydney Armitage-Smith, *John of Gaunt* (London, 1904), pp. 460-63.
25. Cf. *Troilus and Criseyde*, IV, 183-86, 197-201, 211 ff.
26. Lieut.-Col. Alfred Burne, "John of Gaunt's Great Chevauchee," *History Today*, IX (1959), 113-21.
27. Joseph H. Dahmus, *The Prosecution of John Wyclif* (New Haven, 1952), pp. 18-19, 135, 149-50.
28. Armitage-Smith, pp. 24, 26, 32, 123 ff., 166 ff., 249, 304, 376, 406 ff., 409 f.

Chapter II. Chaucer and John of Gaunt

1. J. R. Hulbert, *Chaucer's Official Life* (Chicago, 1912), p. 1.
2. G. G. Coulton, *Chaucer and his England* (4th ed.; London, 1927), p. 22.
3. George H. Cowling, *Chaucer* (New York, 1927), p. 13.
4. G. K. Chesterton, *Chaucer* (London, 1932), p. 93.

5. Nevill Coghill, *The Poet Chaucer* (Oxford, 1949), p. 3.
6. Kemp Malone, *Chapters on Chaucer* (Oxford, 1951), p. 22.
7. Marchette Chute, *Geoffrey Chaucer of England* (New York, 1946), p. 60.
8. Hulbert, p. 58.
9. Hulbert, p. 63.
10. Hulbert, p. 64.
11. Hulbert, pp. 5, 42, 62.
12. Hulbert, p. 63.
13. Hulbert, p. 58.
14. Hulbert, pp. 7-11.
15. *John of Gaunt's Register, 1372-1376*, ed. Sydney Armitage-Smith (London, 1911), Item 832. (This work will be referred to in subsequent notes as *Gaunt's Register*, A.)
16. *Gaunt's Register*, A, Item 1075.
17. *John of Gaunt's Register, 1379-1383*, ed. Sydney Armitage-Smith (London, 1937), Item 1084. (This work will be referred to in subsequent notes as *Gaunt's Register*, B.)
18. *Gaunt's Register*, B, p. 8.
19. *Gaunt's Register*, B, Item 282.
20. *Gaunt's Register*, B, Item 463.
21. *Gaunt's Register*, B, Item 814.
22. *Gaunt's Register*, B, p. 8.
23. *Gaunt's Register*, A, Item 298; B, Item 226.
24. *Gaunt's Register*, A, Item 820.
25. *Gaunt's Register*, A, Item 13, etc.
26. Hulbert, pp. 22 ff.
27. Hulbert, pp. 22-23.
28. Hulbert, p. 23.
29. May McKisack, *The Fourteenth Century* (London, 1959), p. 268.
30. Sydney Armitage-Smith, *John of Gaunt* (London, 1904), p. 130.
31. Armitage-Smith, p. 129.
32. *Gaunt's Register*, B, Item 128.
33. *Gaunt's Register*, B, Item 411.
34. *Gaunt's Register*, B, Item 927.
35. Mary Giffin, *Studies in Chaucer and His Audience* (Hull, Quebec, 1956), p. 81.
36. Hulbert, p. 71.
37. M. T. Waugh, "The Lollard Knights," *Scottish Hist. Rev.*, XI (1913), 55-92. Information in subsequent paragraphs concerning Chaucer's associates is derived from Waugh unless another source is noted.
38. *Gaunt's Register*, A, Item 1342.
39. Hulbert, p. 71.
40. *Gaunt's Register*, A, Item 293.
41. *Gaunt's Register*, A, Item 1342.
42. *Gaunt's Register*, A, Item 1429.
43. *Gaunt's Register*, A, Item 1429.
44. Hulbert, p. 60.
45. N. B. Lewis, "The 'Continual Council' in the Early Years of Richard II, 1377-80," *Eng. Hist. Rev.*, XLI (1926), 249-50.
46. Armitage-Smith, p. 282 n.
47. Armitage-Smith, p. 267 n.
48. Armitage-Smith, p. 340.
49. *Life-Records*, No. 176.
50. Margaret Galway, "Geoffrey Chaucer, J. P. and M. P.," *MLR*, XXXVI (1941), 1-36.

51. Margaret Galway, "Philippa Pan·, Philippa Chaucer," *MLR*, LV (1960), 485.
52. "Philippa Pan," pp. 481-87, 483 n. 4.
53. *Life-Records*, Nos. 41, 44.
54. J. W. Hales, in article on "Chaucer" in *DNB*, p. 158.
55. Hulbert, p. 26; *Life-Records*, No. 53.
56. *Gaunt's Register*, A, Item 1056.
57. *Gaunt's Register*, A, Item 608.
58. *Gaunt's Register*, A, Item 1343.
59. *Gaunt's Register*, B, Item 327.
60. *Gaunt's Register*, B, Item 557.
61. *Gaunt's Register*, B, Item 715.
62. *Life-Records*, No. 186.
63. *Additional Life-Records*, No. 10, pp. 340 ff.
64. *Ibid.*
65. Russell Krauss, *Chaucerian Problems: Especially the Petherton Forestership and the Question of Thomas Chaucer*, 182 pp., in *Three Chaucer Studies*, ed. Carleton Brown (Oxford, 1932).
66. J. M. Manly, "Three Recent Chaucer Studies," *RES*, X (1934), 257-73.
67. B. J. Whiting in a review of *Three Chaucer Studies, Speculum*, VIII (1933), 535.
68. George Williams, "The 'Troilus and Criseyde' Frontispiece Again," *MLR*, LVII (1962), 175-76.

Chapter III.   What is the *Complaint of Mars?*

1. A. W. Ward, *Chaucer* (English Men of Letters Series) (London, 1880), p. 89.
2. D. S. Brewer, *Chaucer* (London, 1953), p. 85.
3. Robert K. Root, *The Poetry of Chaucer* (New York, 1906), p. 63.
4. Robert Dudley French, *A Chaucer Handbook* (New York, 1947), p. 91.
5. W. W. Skeat, *The Works of Chaucer* (2nd ed.; Oxford, 1899), 1, 66.
6. Trinity College, Cambridge, MS. R. 3.20, p. 130.
7. Aage Brusendorff, *The Chaucer Tradition* (Copenhagen, 1925), pp. 265 ff.
8. George H. Cowling, *Chaucer* (New York, 1927), pp. 110 ff.
9. *The Works of Geoffrey Chaucer*, ed. F. N. Robinson (2nd ed., Cambridge, Mass.), 1957, p. 857.
10. Robinson, p. 857.
11. J. M. Manly, "On the Date and Interpretation of Chaucer's 'Complaint of Mars,'" *Studies and Notes in Philology and Literature* (Harvard), V (1896), 124.
12. *Chronicon Henrici Knighton,* ed. J. R. Lumby (London, 1895), II, 147-48; *Thomas Walsingham Historia Anglicana,* ed. H. T. Riley (London, 1864), II, 43.
13. Sydney Armitage-Smith, *John of Gaunt* (London, 1904), p. 138.
14. Margaret Galway, "Philippa Pan·, Philippa Chaucer," *MLR*, LV (1960), 485.
15. *Life-Records*, No. 80.
16. Armitage-Smith, p. 118.
17. Armitage-Smith, p. 133.
18. See Paull F. Baum, "Chaucer's Puns," *PMLA*, LXXI (1956), 225-46.
19. Armitage-Smith, p. 249.

Chapter IV.   Who were Troilus, Criseyde, and Pandarus?

1. J. S. P. Tatlock, *The Mind and Art of Chaucer* (Syracuse, N. Y., 1950), p. 41.
2. Tatlock, p. 40.

3. Robert K. Root, *The Poetry of Chaucer* (New York, 1906), p. 105.

4. Gilbert Keith Chesterton, *Chaucer* (London, 1932), p. 144.

5. John Livingston Lowes, *Geoffrey Chaucer* (London, 1934), pp. 152-53.

6. F. N. Robinson, *The Works of Geoffrey Chaucer* (2nd ed.; Boston, 1957), p. 388.

7. Nathaniel Edward Griffin and Arthur Beckwith Myrick, *The Filostrato of Giovanni Boccaccio: A Translation with Parallel Text* (Philadelphia, 1929), pp. 126-29.

8. This MS is well described, and its frontispiece reproduced, in "The 'Troilus' Frontispiece," by Margaret Galway, *MLR*, XLIV (1949), 161-71.

9. Aage Brusendorff, *The Chaucer Tradition* (London, 1925), p. 21.

10. George Williams, "The 'Troilus and Criseyde' Frontispiece Again," *MLR*, LVII (1962), 173-178.

11. *Chronicon Henrici Knighton*, ed. Joseph Rawson Lumby (London, 1895), II, 147-48.

12. Griffin and Myrick, p. 129.

13. Tatlock, pp. 46, 48. See also "Chaucer's Portrait of Criseyde," by Nathaniel Edward Griffin, *JEGP*, XX (1921), 39; and *Geoffrey Chaucer of England*, by Marchette Chute (New York, 1946), p. 179.

14. Arthur Mizener, "Character and Action in the Case of Criseyde," *PMLA*, LIV (1939), 81.

15. See especially C. S. Lewis, "What Chaucer Really Did to *Il Filostrato*," *Essays and Studies*, XVII (1932), 56-75. See also the many studies of the poem as illustrative of theories of courtly love.

16. *Il Filostrato*, Bk. I, st. 11.

17. Griffin and Myrick, pp. 183, 189. Emphasis supplied.

18. *The Catholic Encyclopedia* (New York, 1910), VIII, 493.

19. C. Wilfrid Scott-Giles, *The Romance of Heraldry* (London, 1929), pp. 75-77.

20. In "Prophecia," *The Works of John Gower*, ed. G. C. Macaulay (Oxford, 1902), IV, 344.

21. Gower, IV, p. 416.

22. Francis Sandford, *A Genealogical History of the Kings of England and Monarchs of Great Britain* (London, 1677), p. 343.

23. Sydney Armitage-Smith, *John of Gaunt* (London, 1904), pp. 462-63.

24. Translated from *Chronica de El Rei D. João I* (Lisbon, 1897), V, lxxxix.

25. Armitage-Smith, p. 409.

26. Robert K. Root, *The Poetry of Chaucer* (rev. ed.; Boston, 1922), p. 120.

27. Eugene E. Slaughter, "Chaucer's Pandarus: Virtuous Uncle and Friend," *JEGP*, XLVIII (1949), 186.

28. Nevill Coghill, *The Poet Chaucer* (London, 1949), p. 65.

29. Coghill, p. 76.

30. See Thomas A. Kirby, *Chaucer's "Troilus": A Study in Courtly Love* (University, Louisiana, 1940), pp. 186-87; and J. S. P. Tatlock, "The People in Chaucer's *Troilus*," *PMLA*, LVI (1941), 95, for discussions of Pandarus' age.

31. See especially Tatlock, article cited above.

32. Kirby, p. 187.

33. See *Troilus and Criseyde*, I, 622-72, 711-18; II, 57-63, 98-99; IV, 397-99.

34. See, for example, *Parliament of Fowls* (ll. 8-9), *Legend of Good Women* (Prologue G, l. 480), and *Troilus and Criseyde*, I, 15-18; II, 19-21.

35. John W. Clark, "Dante and the Epilogue of *Troilus*," *JEGP*, L (1951), 2 n. 3.

36. Clark, p. 10.

37. Some of the MSS read *seventh*, and there has been a good deal of recent comment upholding this reading. But Robinson and most other scholars point out that Boccaccio wrote "ottava," and that *eighth* is more consistent with medieval

conceptions of astronomy. A copyist's misreading of *vij* instead of the original *viij* would have been very easy.

38. See chapters in this book dealing with the *Complaint of Mars*, the *Parliament of Fowls*, and the "Squire's Tale," as well as l. 1319 of the *Book of the Duchess*.

39. J. Leslie Hotson, "The Tale of Melibeus and John of Gaunt," *SP*, 18 (1921), 429-52.

Chapter V. The *Parliament of Fowls*—a three-part mystery

1. R. M. Lumiansky, "Chaucer's *Parlement of Foules*: A Philosophical Interpretation," *RES*, XXIV (1948), 81-89.

2. D. S. Brewer, "The Genre of the *Parlement of Foules*," *MLR*, LIII (1958), 321-26.

3. Gardiner Stillwell, "Unity and Comedy in Chaucer's *Parlement of Foules*," *JEGP*, XLIX (1950), 470-95.

4. Charles A. Owen, "The Role of the Narrator in the *Parlement of Foules*," *College English*, XIV (1953), 264-69.

5. Dorothy Bethurum, "The Center of the *Parlement of Foules*," *Essays in Honor of Walter Clyde Curry* (Nashville, 1954), pp. 39-50.

6. Macdonald Emslie, "Codes of Love and Class Distinctions," *Essays in Criticism*, V (1953), 1-17.

7. Charles O. McDonald, "An Interpretation of Chaucer's *Parlement of Foules*," *Speculum*, XXX (1955), 444-57.

8. R. W. Frank, "Structure and Meaning in the *Parlement of Foules*," *PMLA*, LXXI (1956), 530-39.

9. J. A. W. Bennett, *The Parlement of Foules* (Oxford, 1957), 317 pp.

10. George G. Williams, "*The Hous of Fame* and the House of the Musicians," *MLN*, LXXII (1957), 6-9.

11. See n. 2, this chapter.

12. See n. 8, this chapter.

13. Bertrand H. Bronson, "*The Parlement of Foules* Revisited," *ELH*, XV (1948), 249.

14. See n. 6, this chapter.

15. F. N. Robinson, *The Works of Geoffrey Chaucer* (2nd ed.; Boston, 1957), p. 310.

16. *The Canterbury Tales,* ed. Thomas Tyrwhitt (2nd ed.; London, 1798), II, 415.

17. William Godwin, *The Life of Geoffrey Chaucer* (London, 1803), I, 435.

18. See n. 13, this chapter.

19. John Matthews Manly, "What Is the *Parliament of Foules?*" *Studien zur englischen Philologie*, L (1913), 279-90.

20. Sister Mary Ernestine Whitmore, *Medieval Domestic Life and Amusements in the Works of Chaucer* (Washington, D. C., 1937), p. 206.

21. Charles Boutell, *English Heraldry* (London, 1908), p. 99.

22. R. P. Dunn-Pattison, *The Black Prince* (New York, 1910), p. 176.

23. For biographical facts about the four personages who may be represented by the four eagles, I have drawn on the articles about them in *DNB*, Dunn-Pattison's work referred to in the note immediately preceding, Armitage-Smith's biography of Gaunt, and Marjorie Anderson, "Blanche, Duchess of Lancaster," *MP*, XLV (1947), 152-59.

24. Dunn-Pattison, p. 186.

25. Russell Krauss, *Chaucerian Problems: Especially the Petherton Forestership and the Question of Thomas Chaucer*, in *Three Chaucer Studies*, ed. Carleton Brown (New York, 1932), pp. 14-21.

26. Edith Rickert, "Geoffrey Chaucer: A New Interpretation of the *Parlement of Foules*," *MP*, XVIII (1920), pp. 1-29.

27. Samuel Moore, "A Further Note on the Suitors in the *Parlement of Foules*," *MLN*, XXVI (1911), 11 n.

28. H. R. Patch, "Chaucer and the Common People," *JEGP*, XXIX (1930), 376-84; Margaret Schlauch, "Chaucer's Doctrine of Kings and Tyrants," *Speculum*, XX (1945), 133-56.

29. Robert K. Root, *The Poetry of Chaucer* (Boston, 1906), p. 66.

30. *Complaint of Mars*, l. 9.

Chapter VI. The mysterious *House of Fame*

1. Robert K. Root, *The Poetry of Chaucer* (Boston, 1906), pp. 123-34.

2. J. M. Manly, *Kittredge Anniversary Papers* (Boston, 1913), p. 77.

3. George L. Kittredge, *Chaucer and His Poetry* (Cambridge, Mass., 1915), p. 107.

4. Paull F. Baum, "Chaucer's 'The House of Fame,'" *ELH*, VIII (1941), 253, 256.

5. P. G. Ruggiers, "Unity of Chaucer's *House of Fame*," *SP*, L (1953), 16-29.

6. J. S. P. Tatlock, *The Mind and Art of Chaucer* (Syracuse, N. Y., 1950), pp. 57, 64.

7. A. Rameau, "Chaucer's 'House of Fame' in seinem Verhältniss zu Dante's 'Divinia Commedia,'" *Englische Studien*, III (1880), 209-68.

8. W. W. Skeat, *The Works of Geoffrey Chaucer* (2nd ed.; Oxford, 1899), III, vii-viii.

9. See n. 2, this chapter.

10. R. C. Goffin, "Quiting by Tidinges in the *House of Fame*," *Medium Aevum*, XII (1953), 40-44.

11. Edward K. Rand, "Chaucer in Error," *Speculum*, I (1926), 225.

12. Jacob Burckhardt, *The Civilization of the Renaissance in Italy*, p. 155.

13. *The Poetry of Chaucer*, p. 130.

14. See n. 8, this chapter.

15. See n. 4, this chapter.

16. *The Poetry of Chaucer*, p. 124.

17. John M. Steadman, "Chaucer's Eagle: A Contemplative Symbol," *PMLA*, LXXV (1960), 159.

18. See n. 15, this chapter.

19. J. M. Manly, "Chaucer and the Rhetoricians," *Proc. Brit. Acad.*, XII (1926), 95-113.

Chapter VII. The daisy and "Good Alceste"

1. Bernhard ten Brink, *History of English Literature*, trans. W. C. Robinson (London, 1901), II, 112.

2. W. W. Skeat, *The Works of Geoffrey Chaucer* (Oxford, 1899), III, xxiv, 308-9.

3. Robert K. Root, *The Poetry of Chaucer* (Boston, 1906), p. 140.

4. J. B. Bilderbeck, *Chaucer's Legend of Good Women* (London, 1902), pp. 85-87.

5. Aage Brusendorff, *The Chaucer Tradition* (Copenhagen, 1925), p. 448, n. 3.

6. John Livingston Lowes, "The Prologue of the *Legend of Good Women* as

Related to the French *Marguerite* Poems and the *Filostrato*," *PMLA*, XIX (1904), 669 ff.

7. George Lyman Kittredge, "Chaucer's Alceste," *MP*, VI (1909), 435 ff.

8. Margaret Galway, "Chaucer's Sovereign Lady; a Study of the Prologue of the *Legend* and Related Poems," *MLR*, XXXIII (1938), 145-99; "The 'Troilus' Frontispiece," *MLR*, XLIV (1948), 161-77.

9. Bernard F. Huppe, "Chaucer: A Criticism and a Reply," *MLR*, XLIV (1948), 393-400; Walter E. Weese, "Alceste and Joan of Kent," *MLN*, LXIII (1948), 291-92.

10. Margaret Galway, "Chaucer's Hopeless Love," *MLN*, LX (1945), 431-39.

11. D. S. Brewer, *Chaucer* (New York, 1953), p. 121.

12. John Speirs, *Chaucer, the Maker* (London, 1951), p. 89.

13. J. S. P. Tatlock, *The Mind and Art of Chaucer* (Syracuse, N. Y., 1950), p. 73.

14. Bernard L. Jefferson, "Queen Anne and Queen Alceste," *JEGP*, XIII (1914), 439.

15. Lowes, p. 673.

16. George Lyman Kittredge, "Chaucer and Some of His Friends," *MP*, I (1903), p. 6.

17. George L. Marsh, "Sources and Analogues of 'The Flower and the Leaf,'" Part I, *MP*, IV (1906), 121 ff.; Part II, *MP*, IV (1908), 281 ff.

18. "Chaucer and Some of His Friends," p. 1.

19. Geoffrey Chaucer, *The Romaunt of the Rose*, l. 52.

20. D. D. Griffith, "An Interpretation of Chaucer's *Legend of Good Women*," *The Manly Anniversary Studies in Language and Literature* (Chicago, 1932), pp. 32-41.

21. Griffith, *passim*.

22. "Chaucer's Alceste," 435 ff.

23. Marjorie Anderson, "Blanche, Duchess of Lancaster," *MP*, XLV (1948), 157.

24. C. W. Scott-Giles, *The Romance of Heraldry* (London, 1929), p. 113.

25. May McKisack, *The Fourteenth Century* (London, 1959), p. 241.

26. See n. 17, this chapter.

27. C. W. Scott-Giles, *Boutell's Heraldry* (rev. ed.; London, 1959), p. 185.

28. Bertrand H. Bronson, *In Search of Chaucer* (Toronto, 1960), p. 57.

Chapter VIII.   Chaucer's best joke—the "Tale of Sir Thopas"

1. Paull F. Baum, *Chaucer: A Critical Appreciation* (Durham, N. C., 1958), pp. 78, 81.

2. Edith Winstanley (ed.), *The Prioress's Tale; The Tale of Sir Thopas* (Cambridge, 1922), pp. lxv ff.

3. J. M. Manly, "Sir Thopas: A Satire," *Essays and Studies*, XIII (1928), 52-73.

4. F. N. Robinson (ed.), *The Works of Geoffrey Chaucer* (2nd ed.; Boston, 1957), p. 12.

5. Woodburn O. Ross, "A Possible Significance of the Name Thopas," *MLN*, XLV (1930), 172-74.

6. Roland M. Smith, "Two Chaucer Notes," *MLN*, LI (1936), 315.

7. Carroll Camden, Jr., "The Physiognomy of Sir Thopas," *RES*, XI (1935), 326.

8. Cf. Paull F. Baum, "Chaucer's Puns," *PMLA*, LXXI (1956), 225-46.

9. Eric Partridge, *A Dictionary of Slang and Unconventional English* (2nd ed.; New York, 1938); under the heading, "nose is a lady's liking, a long."

10. Robinson's notes point out that Olifaunt was the name of Roland's great horn —a word with obvious phallic connotations.

Chapter IX. "Many Sondry Werkes"

1. A. S. Cook, "The Historical Background of Chaucer's Knight," *Trans. Conn. Acad. of Arts and Sciences*, XX (1916), 161-240.
2. J. M. Manly, *Some New Light on Chaucer* (New York, 1926), pp. 203 ff.
3. J. M. Manly, "The Prioress of Stratford," *TLS*, Nov. 10, 1927, p. 815.
4. *Some New Light*, pp. 131-68.
5. E. P. Kuhl, "Chaucer's Burgesses," *Trans. Wisconsin Acad. of Sciences, Arts, and Letters*, XVIII (1916), 652-75.
6. *Some New Light*, pp. 84 ff.
7. Sydney Armitage-Smith, *John of Gaunt* (London, 1904), p. 310.
8. E. P. Kuhl, "Chaucer and the Church," *MLN*, XL (1925), 321-38.
9. A. S. Cook, p. 168.
10. J. Leslie Hotson, "The Tale of Melibeus and John of Gaunt," *SP*, XVIII (1921), 435.
11. Hotson, p. 437.
12. W. W. Lawrence, "The Tale of Melibeus," *Essays and Studies in Honor of Carleton Brown* (New York, 1940), pp. 100-110.
13. Gardiner Stillwell, "The Political Meaning of Chaucer's *Tale of Melibee*," *Speculum*, XIX (1944), 433-44.
14. Stillwell, p. 433.
15. F. N. Robinson, *The Works of Geoffrey Chaucer* (2nd ed.; Boston, 1957), p. 839.
16. George G. Williams, "*The House of Fame* and the House of the Musicians," *MLN*, LXXII (1957), 6-9.

Chapter X. Summary and discussion

1. Sartre, *What Is Literature?*, trans. Bernard Frechtman (New York, 1949), p. ii.
2. Sartre, pp. 11-14.
3. Sartre, p. 43.
4. Sartre, p. 55.
5. Emile Legouis, *Geoffrey Chaucer*, trans. L. Lailvoix (New York, 1961), p. 44.
6. Prologue of *The Silent Woman*.
7. Sartre, p. 71.
8. J. M. Manly, *Some New Light on Chaucer* (New York, 1926), pp. 120-21.

Index

Literary works by known authors, other than Chaucer, are indexed by the author's name only, not by titles of the works. Other literary works are indexed by title.

Date Due

NOV 12 '78			
PD			
MAY 1 4 1979			
MAY 2 9 1979			